CHURCH GROWTH AND CHRISTIAN MISSION

CHURCH GROWTH AND CHRISTIAN MISSION

Donald Anderson McGavran, *Editor*
Robert Calvin Guy
Melvin L. Hodges
Eugene A. Nida

William Carey Library
533 Hermosa Street • South Pasadena, Calif. 91030

Reprinted in 1976 by arrangement with Harper & Row, Publishers

Library of Congress Catalog Card Number 65-10702
International Standard Book Number 0-87808-728-1

Published by the William Carey Library
533 Hermosa Street
South Pasadena, Calif. 91030
Telephone 213-799-4559

PRINTED IN THE UNITED STATES OF AMERICA

CONTENTS

THE CONTRIBUTORS

ROBERT CALVIN GUY
Professor of Missions
Southwestern Baptist Theological Seminary
Fort Worth, Texas

MELVIN L. HODGES
Assistant Professor of Missions
Assemblies of God Graduate School
Springfield, Missouri

DONALD ANDERSON MCGAVRAN
Dean Emeritus and
Senior Professor of Missions
Fuller Theological Seminary

EUGENE A. NIDA
Secretary for Translations
American Bible Society
New York, New York

I

INTRODUCTION

DONALD ANDERSON McGAVRAN

Christian mission today is thinking more about church growth than it has in many a year, for mission is coming out of a forty-five-year period when it turned from church growth to other important tasks.

With two world wars and the end of European empires, the milieu in which mission was being carried out has changed so greatly that leaders of the Christian enterprise have had radically to redesign mission. Some of them have assumed that the goal of winning men to Christ and multiplying churches was the unchanging purpose of mission and would automatically remain so while they paid primary attention to other aspects of the total task. A few have entertained the idea that Christian mission itself has become something other than the extension of the Christian faith. In both cases, the outcome has been to divert attention from church growth to other things.

The pendulum is now swinging back to church growth. Its return is speeded by the church growth situation in land after land all around the world. The Consultation on Church Growth at Iberville, Montreal, in the summer of 1963 was an indication of the depth of the renewed concern. As leaders from six continents and many branches of the Church gathered to consider the numerical increase of Christians and churches, they came to a remarkable degree of unanimity, framed in the Iberville Statement (see Appendix).

Secular movements such as the Peace Corps, together with the expanding social services of many governments, are forcing Christians to consider what the essence of Christian mission is. What distinguishes mission from the worthwhile work done by the Peace Corps and the educational and medical services of practically all governments?

Back of much Christian thinking today lies the growing conviction that church growth is a central and continuing business of Christian mission. God expects church growth. We are about our Father's business when we study its crucial issues in these days.

The vital issues set forth in this book must be seen, its authors insist, against today's church growth picture. We are writing about the increase of Christians and churches that God desires, an increase possible in today's revolutionary world, at the current state of church expansion, and influenced by contemporary understandings of world need and world mission. This introductory chapter will therefore depict church growth by means of six broad lines or elements, each an essential part of that complex whole in the midst of which God calls on the churches to multiply. Let us look, one by one, at these six vital characteristics of the modern scene.

World Revolution

The first is this: a world in revolution changes the responsiveness of populations. The seething unheavals of our time have shattered old societies in many lands. Sometimes these changes cause men to resist the Gospel. Occasionally a newly risen secular religion has effectively shut out Christian mission. More often than we realize, however, change wakens a population so that it can hear Christ's call. Revolutions make many populations responsive.

Mexico and Brazil provide a clear example of the process. Both barred the Evangelical Church until late in the nineteenth century. Now, because of repeated revolutions, both are open to the biblical message. These revolutionary changes were of various kinds. The political control of Spain and Portugal vanished and the Constitution of the United States was widely studied and copied. Anticlericalism became popular among the educated classes. Public schools arose, free from the control of the Roman Catholic Church. A degree of religious freedom was written into the law and tested in the courts. The absolutism of the Church of Rome was eroded by the development of science and the pressure of world opinion. Early Evangelicals demonstrated both personal goodness and religious effectiveness.

Many other influences—commercial, political, cultural, and religious—operated with varying intensity in various segments of the population to create a new degree of receptivity to the Christian message. With each revolutionary change, hearing and obeying the Gospel became more—or less—possible. Taken together, these changes have created in Mexico and Brazil a climate absolutely unlike that which obtained a hundred years ago—a climate which is, by and large, favorable. The "bad old days" are gone for the foreseeable future.

The most notable single illustration of how world revolution changes the receptivity of populations can be seen in the recent history of China. In 1920, only forty years ago, Confucianism ranked as one of the five great living religions of the world, in both number of adherents and profundity of thought. In the strong Confucian society of China relatively few became Christians over decades of missionary endeavor.

Today, under the hammer blows of Marxism, the ancient Chinese social order has disappeared and the era of Confucianism as a major religion would seem to have passed. The degree of responsiveness to the Christian faith which this development involves is completely—but temporarily—masked by the tyranny that holds China in its grip; but the widespread responsiveness of former Confucians in Taiwan and elsewhere throughout the world is an indication of what will be manifest when the bamboo curtain, in God's good time, is no more.

Through revolution, this has become the century of the common man. In country after country hereditary bonds have been, and will be, broken; the grip of ecclesiastical overlords has been, and will be, loosened; and the power of religionists so often associated with the exploiting classes, as in the Indian caste system, has been and will be diminished or ended. Among the masses a religious vacuum of enormous size will mark history in the years that lie ahead.

Confronting this vacuum are the many branches of the Protestant Church, a Church which seems particularly designed for the common man. It was founded by a carpenter. Its apostles were called by the Jewish élite "ignorant and unlearned men." It affirmed that God had called the weak, the foolish, and the things which are not, to put to shame the wise, the strong, and the things that are. It stresses the worth of the individual person. It pleads for justice to all men. It has given rise to democracy. The only lands convincedly and successfully democratic are those where biblical Christianity has formed the national character. In these lands, in hundreds of thousands of churches, individuals have faced their political and economic decisions as biblical Christians. They were not as fully Christian as one could desire, but they were Christian with conviction, and much more Christian than they were Hindu, Moslem, or Marxist. Is it not reasonable to assume that as the yeastings of revolution break down old authoritarian controls and the common man searches for a religion which gives him significance and endows him with power, days of tremendous response to the biblical faith lie ahead?

For these and other reasons, at once the most significant and the most overlooked fact about the rapid changes the world is presently undergoing is that through them often arises an amazing receptivity to the Gospel. Both numerically and proportionately, there are more winnable men in the world today than there ever have been before. This may seem a large claim but it is amply substantiated by the evidence.

Paradoxically enough, this developing receptivity among non-Christians has been paralleled by a considerable increase of religious relativism among Christians which threatens to obscure it.

Relativist Christians raise their eyebrows at the thought of a "winnable world." They wonder if non-Christians are *lost* in the sense that our grandfathers and St. Paul used the term. They believe that the right relationship to non-Christian faiths is one of joint search for a commonly but imperfectly known God, and find texts in the Bible that "prove" their point—though these are often quoted out of context with a clear disregard for scholarly exegesis! To relativists, the word *evangelism* is embarrassing, proclaiming the Gospel suspect, and *conversion* a term to be avoided. Misled by the poverty of their expectation, they see only a bleak and hostile world before which the Christian missionary must not be too energetic or aggressive.

The relativist Christians among us may not see the receptive world surrounding them, but it is there just the same. Consider the following facts: The first eighty years of missionary labors in Formosa created a Church of 15,000 communicants or a Christian community of 30,000. During the next twenty years—i.e., by 1960—the Protestant community increased 270,000—a ninefold growth in twenty years. Little Costa Rica had its first effective Protestant mission in 1891; by 1920 there were fewer than 200 Spanish-speaking Evangelicals, and in 1944 there were still less than 700. But in the last sixteen years, Spanish-speaking Evangelical communicants have increased to over 6,300—a ninefold increase in fifteen years.

More men are becoming Evangelical Christians today in Africa and Latin America than did during the days of the greatest "mass movements" in India. Even in the face of persecution in Colombia, some Evangelical Churches are experiencing growth such as they have never known before. The increase of the Church in Korea in the ten years since the Korean War, despite the partition of the country and the Communist menace, has been greater than in any two decades in history. The Protestant community alone has grown from less than half a million to nearly a million and a half.*

* S. H. Moffat, *The Christians of Korea* (New York: Friendship Press, 1962), p. 28.

True, some populations are today hard and resistant. Christianity is still banned among the five million largely illiterate inhabitants of Arabia and the small backward population of Afghanistan. Christianity is not banned but is having a hard time in Communist China. Moslem lands have not yet ripened—though in God's good time they will. The Evangelical Church in the small lands of Paraguay and Panama meets with little response. And the Churches of Europe, as an aftermath of two great wars, are currently in the doldrums. Yet after the most careful acknowledgment of resistant countries and peoples, it remains true that many populations in many lands are receptive. More open doors exist than Christian mission is entering. The basic problem of mission is not resistant populations or rejection of the Gospel. The basic problem is to imbue Christians themselves with enough of the Spirit of Christ to send multitudes of them rejoicing into ripe harvest fields.

One night about the year 52 A.D. a man stood before Paul in a vision, beseeching him and saying, "Come over to Macedonia and help us." This man stands in the history of salvation as a symbol of lands prepared to receive the Good News. Today Macedonias lie in every direction. Some are as small as their original prototype—about the size of West Virginia. Others, like Africa south of the Sahara, are huge in both land area and population. In all of them thousands of nationals are Christians and have been laboring to multiply churches. Men in these many lands are now beseeching us, "Come over to Macedonia and help us."

This revolutionary responsiveness is not happening of itself. It is not that some accidental combination of factors is producing a new climate in which churches can grow. God Himself is ripening fields and directing revolutions. As of old the Lord says, "I have seen the affliction of my people who are in Egypt, and have heard their cry because of their taskmasters; I know their sufferings and I have come down to deliver them out of the hand of their oppressors, and to bring them up out of that land to a good and broad land, a land flowing with milk and honey." God, who uses the wrath of men to praise Him, is in the revolutionary process.

Today God commands His Church to work in the most responsive age she has ever known. Never since the Ascension of our blessed Lord have as many people in as many countries been so ready to obey the summons to repent and be baptized.

Widespread Penetration

The second broad element in the world picture is the very widespread penetration of the Church. With minor exceptions, the Church has now been well planted in every land. Not only are there church buildings and congregations of national Christians, but during the last forty years Christianity has to some extent outgrown its Western swaddling clothes. In each country many Churches have become indigenous.

Over a thousand theological seminaries and training schools, manned largely by nationals, train tens of thousands of pastors, evangelists, and workers. Scores of thousands of congregations in Africa, Asia, and Latin America seldom see a missionary, yet they not only remain soundly Christian but proclaim the faith to others and plant new churches.

The existence of the Bible in whole or in part in 1165 languages proves and extends the widespread penetration. It is hard to conceive of these multitudinous tribes and peoples of mankind, and it is a measure of the devotion and energy of the Christian enterprise that most of them now have the Bible in their own mother tongue.

A new world community has come into being, based not on might, wealth, color, or continent, but on a common faith in Jesus Christ and the scriptural teaching that in Him there is neither Jew nor Greek, slave nor free, white nor black, but one great brotherhood of man. The "one world" so often referred to finds concrete expression in the far-flung Christian Church.

Yet the Church in most lands is a tiny minority, 10 per cent in some, 2 in others, and in many, .1 per cent. The widespread penetration is often very thin! Many congregations in Asia, Africa, and Latin America are weak and dependent. All live in a rapidly changing society which confronts them with great dangers as well as vast opportunity. Rejoicing in the wide spread of the Church and the warm, fertile climate of modern times, the entire Church must also prepare for centuries of labor to extend the successful plantings of the past.

Spotty Growth

The third element is the uneven character of church growth. In almost every country there are some greatly expanding Churches and others that grow slowly if at all. Thus in Mexico we find the (till recently) static Churches of the Southern Baptists and the Disciples of Christ, and also a fervent Presbyterian Church in the State of Tabasco which has grown from nothing to a community of 20,000 in the last twenty-five years. A small "people movement" among the Tseltal Indians has brought in 20,000 souls, or about two-fifths of the tribe, in the last few years. The influence of Evangelicals in the United States, exercised through returning migrant laborers and their relatives who have become Evangelicals in Texas, is rendering some sections in Mexico responsive, though others remain resistant.

In almost all lands some missions and Churches experience very great increase, growing from small clusters of Christians to hundreds or even thousands of congregations. Churches of 300,000 Lutherans in Tanganyika, 400,000 Baptists in Burma, 250,000 United Church of Christ in the Philippines, and 1,200,000 Assemblies in Brazil exist and flourish. (These figures are of total community—not communicants.)

Other Churches grow very little. Take, for example, the Presbyterian, Baptist, Moravian, and Methodist Churches in Jamaica. In 1850 these had 54,000 communicant members, who composed one-eighth of the population of the island. A hundred years later, in 1950, these four Churches had only 60,000 communicants, comprising one twenty-seventh of the population. During a full century, assisted by considerable numbers of missionaries and much money from Britain, those younger Churches had added only 6,000 members, while the population grew by 1,200,000 to a new total of 1,600,000.

In 1931, mid-India (six hundred miles long and four hundred wide) discovered that, of its 145 mission stations, 134 had achieved only an 11 per cent membership increase during the previous decade, rising from about 20,000 to 22,000 communicants.

In Peru, 40 missions have been at work for the last fifteen years, with an average growth of 250 members each. This kind of slow discipling marks many Churches and missions even in responsive lands.

Commonly Alleged Reasons

The fourth broad element in the church growth picture is that of commonly alleged reasons for lack of church growth which are, however, erroneous or invalid. It is surprising to what extent they are found among the denominations across the world. Some with little-growing Churches comfort themselves with the thought, "We are doing a solid piece of work and are interested in quality, not quantity." Evidence does not support their claim to Christian solidity. Theirs may be a more exclusive Church—its few members more highly educated at mission expense—but it would be difficult to prove that it worships God more devoutly, tithes more devotedly, or brings more people in penitent discipleship to the Lord.

Others with little-growing Churches are likely to plead that the field is very difficult. In southern Luzon laymen were explaining why their church did not grow. "Roman Catholic pressure here," they said, "is so great that the church cannot grow." That great Filipino Christian, Bishop Evangelista, listened for half an hour and finally rose to say with great emphasis, "The difficulty, my brethren, is not Roman Catholic pressure but lack of Protestant pressure." Sometimes, of course, a "resistant field" is indeed the true reason; but often it is not, as is abundantly proved by the growth in that very field of other branches of the Church of Christ. Nongrowth also frequently means that growth is not being sought, or is being sought in resistant rather than responsive sections of the population, or that the basic concern of the Church involved is not discipling the nations but world friendship enterprises and cultural interchanges.

Again and again students of church growth around the world find some splendid piece of church or mission work being carried on in connection with a little-growing Church. When students ask, "Why not more growth?" church leaders answer, "Because we do not have enough mission work. We need more schools, more hospitals, literacy, and in general broader concern with wider aspects of life." Yet more work of a diffuse general nature seldom results in church growth. While much "work" continues, a younger Church of 200,000 stops growing. Increasing by the excess of births over deaths, it achieves a slight increase of members from decade to decade, but of normal healthy Christian growth there is extremely little. While much "work" continues, a small younger Church of 4,000 communicants remains at that figure for decade after decade in the midst of winnable multitudes.

An increase in vague, kindly church and mission work, far from making for church growth, generally checks whatever growth would otherwise be possible. Lack of growth in the Church is often due to "mission" being swallowed up in "interchurch aid." In many areas "mission" has become in effect "aid in perpetuity to halted younger Churches." Once a younger Church has been established—whether it be of 3,000 or 300,000 members—almost the whole time of many a mission is spent in educating its youth, solving its problems, collaborating with its leaders, getting out of its way when it wants to move into a larger Christian unity, helping train its pastors, and just being there for it to lean on. Some younger Churches discourage evangelism by their assisting missionaries—and do little of it themselves.

THE SWING TO PHILANTHROPY

The fifth broad aspect of the church growth picture is the pervading tendency in the face of human need and American prosperity to reinterpret mission in terms of philanthropy, cultural influence, and political amity. Persistent pressure is felt today by all missionaries—and indeed all Christians—to de-emphasize conversion and church growth in favor of the relief of physical suffering and the provision of loaves and fishes.

The change in emphasis often occurs through thoroughly Christian motives. Huge surpluses in Americans barns and enormous numbers of oppressed and neglected people—bare existence in "Afericasia" (Africa, Latin America, and Asia)—combine to make Christians rightly sensitive to raw physical need. What they are now doing is all too little. Well-fed Christians East and West cannot cheaply claim to be brothers by petty charity in this cold, hungry, and wretched world. Sacrificial giving by the whole membership of our numerous churches is demanded. Such giving is deeply called for. Whenever Christians pour themselves out in costly relief of suffering they do well; they act in a truly Christian manner.

But the change in emphasis is often sub-Christian. To put it simply and bluntly, when a Christian gives a cup of cold water because he is sure water is needed, and de-emphasizes conversion because he thinks Jesus Christ may not be the only gateway to eternal bliss, then his philanthropy is sub-Christian. Or again, for a disciple of Christ to promote amity between nations is good—if he does it knowing all nations live under the judgment of God and that amity is not their first need. But if his main *gospel* is solely that of good will between nations, then his promotion of amity is sub-Christian.

Fully Christian or sub-Christian—both types of philanthropy de-emphasize church growth. Both are doing something else.

Some switch to philanthropy has negative theological roots. When men cease to believe in the uniqueness of Christ, they often defend themselves by ardent compensatory humanitarianism. The conservative branches of the Christian Church like to believe that these theological roots—this lukewarmness of belief, yet reluctance to face the flinty reality of eternity without God—account for the reinterpretation of mission.

The switch to philanthropy, however, has positive theological roots. Orthodox Pilgrim, on his way from the City of Destruction to Mt. Zion, and believing fully in both, sees the wounded man on the road and cannot pass by on the other side. Looking to Jesus, the Author of salvation, Pilgrim must stop and bind up the man's wounds. Thus, in point of fact, conservative branches of the Church switch to philanthropy as much as do liberal branches. Theoretically perhaps conservatives seek church growth more; but often they obtain no more than the liberals.

Thus it comes about that in this enormously responsive world, more ready to be won than ever before, the degree of church growth is less than God expects, partly because His people have too largely substituted service for evangelism. What Christ demands is both service and mission in true proportion, remembering that this must be determined in the light of both the transient body and the eternal soul.

Reliance on Devolution and Mergers

The sixth conspicuous factor in the church growth picture is an undue reliance on devolution and church mergers to disciple the nations.

Whenever anyone speaks or writes on "missions today," he is certain to emphasize that this is the day of the younger Church—not the mission. He will point out that the missionary is not to lead but to follow. This new role is emphasized in all training programs for new missionaries. They must learn to see the point of view of the national Churches and their national colleagues and how to work harmoniously with them. Supporting churches are addressed at length on the new day, when they are to "give to missions"—not "send missionaries." They are told that their money will support nationals—maybe even nationals of another branch of the Church—rather than missionaries.

The great gathering at New Delhi in 1961 demonstrated that this new day has indeed arrived. Churches of Afericasia participated in that most significant meeting and played a meaningful role throughout. The control of the missionary enterprise can, indeed, no longer rest with Western mission boards. It is not yet clear whether the partnership in obedience (between boards and national Churches, missionaries and national churchmen) is a possibility for the next decades; or whether nothing less than complete control by the emergent Churches will be satisfactory.

Similarly, co-operation, church mergers, Christian unity, and ecumenicity have captured the limelight in mission. The opinion is commonly expressed that, as the evangelization of the world has been the lodestar of the past century, the uniting of the Churches will be that of the coming one. Ecumenical enthusiasts freely estimate that the era of missions is now over and that of the world Church has begun.

Such pronouncements can readily be recognized as one-sided, and they are shunned by thoughtful writers and speakers. Yet the fact that they are possible at all indicates reliance on the mystique of union to disciple the nations. Almost any speaker on union will tell of vast confusion caused in mission by the competing claims of many denominations. He will recount devastating stories of great populations kept out of Christian faith because they could not choose which denomination to join. The following chestnut is still funny. At an all-India Christian conference one Indian delegate says to another, "I'm a Canadian Baptist. What are you?" The other replies seriously, "I'm a Scotch Presbyterian." Told and retold, such amusing tales achieve a certain effect.

The unfortunate fact is, however, that so far United Churches have grown no faster than separated Churches. Some have grown less. The most rapidly growing Churches are not those where several have joined forces. United Churches, desirable as they may be in some respects, are not notably dynamic. If other denominations are getting good growth in a given population, United Church denominations get some, too; but I know of no case where a united denomination is getting growth and separate ones are not.

Nevertheless, some influential Christians today do believe that turning over control to nationals and getting rid of Western denominational differences are the two great new forward steps in discipling the nations. They are convinced that these two modern policies will plant more churches than any other Christian activity.

Make no mistake, both devolution and superseding of Western divisions are necessities in the Church today. They should be achieved, for reasons of justice, brotherly feeling, and expediency. If Christians East and West are to co-operate in a real Body of Christ, they must meet as equals, and the power of the great boards must be matched by the power of great Churches.

Co-operation of Churches East and West has, to be sure, some bearing on church growth. More growth will take place if the Christian Churches in Afericasia work in happy relationship with those in the West than if they hate each other. In this day of ardent nationalisms, Churches with national ministries will prosper better than those led by foreigners. Christianity in most Afericasian lands must be purged of its present image as the white man's religion.

To sum up: without devolution and much Christian unity, Churches will function at less than full efficiency; but devolution and Christian unity will not in themselves bring men to Christ. Church growth must be brought back into the center of the picture.

This is the meaning of repeated emphasis of world councils and associations on evangelism. The International Missionary Council becomes the Commission on World Mission and Evangelism of the World Council of Churches. We pray for it God's rich blessing while begging it to study church growth, multiply churches, and measure its effectiveness neither by organizational smoothness nor by slogans, but by actual discipling achieved through faith guided by factual analysis and clear thinking.

The eleven chapters that follow, depicting crucial issues in church growth, will again and again reflect the modern climate, in which discipling the nations—more possible than ever before—has gradually become a minor part of the enterprise. True, some Churches and boards have found ways to give discipling in some fields high priority. But many carry on "missions," yet are neither aware of the relative lack of church growth nor troubled by it.

The modern theological, sociological, methodological, and administrative issues discussed in this book arise out of that picture.

Christian mission is being carried out in this world—not some other. God sends us as ambassadors crying, "Make your peace with God!" into this existential church growth situation. Tremendous numbers of men in responsive societies are not being won, for reasons that are in fact preventable. That some sections of the world are hard and unresponsive should not conceal the following reality: unnecessarily slow growth marks the Church today, at the very moment when responsiveness for the first time characterizes much of mankind. This is our present crisis and the first crucial issue in church growth.

PART ONE

Theological Issues

II

CREATING CLIMATE FOR CHURCH GROWTH

MELVIN L. HODGES

The Theological Base

The beginning of church expansion is in the heart of God. If we begin anywhere else we miss the Source. Church expansion does not begin with better methods or more money. Rather, it is a continuation of redemption, in the heart of God from eternity, revealed in His Son. This ministry was imparted by Christ to His disciples, energized by the Holy Spirit, and has been given to Christians today as both gift and command.

Most Christians would agree with this theology of church growth, although the vocabulary used might vary from theologian to theologian. The central affirmation that God is a loving God, revealed in Jesus Christ the Savior, and that He Himself sends out His Church filled with the Holy Ghost to bear the Gospel to the ends of the earth—this view would meet with general approbation, especially so long as it remained in a book. As part of a systematic statement of Christian truth it sounds reasonable.

The crucial theological issue to which I speak in regard to church growth today does not, however, lie as between the position outlined above and some other. It lies between this theological position as printed in a book and the same truth written in men's hearts. Printed theological positions do not create a human climate, but truth which becomes incarnated in men, in which they rejoice and for which they sweat and bleed, *does* create a climate. When God seizes men and lives in them, He creates an atmosphere in which churches can grow—in which, indeed, they inevitably do grow.

The missionary is the planter of churches and the sower of seed. But he is more. He brings with him and creates around him the atmosphere, the climate, in which the church is to grow. This depends directly on the theology he lives; on his own "godliness." We communicate our faith or lack of faith, and nurture our converts with our own spiritual vitality. If we ourselves are New Testament Christians with New Testament experience and faith, we will create the climate for the growth of a New Testament church.

New Testament Men and the Climate They Created

As we read the New Testament, we are immediately aware of a spiritual climate very different from that which surrounds most churches today. The primary characteristic of the New Testament climate lay in its leaders. The apostles and missionaries were God's men, filled with God's Spirit. They were only a step away, historically, from the Crucifixion and the Resurrection. Each one had individually experienced the coming of the Spirit to his own life. They were rich in experience with God. This richness was not due to the length of time they had enjoyed Christian life and contacts, for they were only three and a half years away from their lives as simple fishermen, and only weeks away from the Resurrection, when this abundant life began. Rather, the richness existed through the intense personal reality of the living Christ, a reality which was naturally communicated to others.

In reading the Gospels and the Acts of the Apostles, I am impressed with the fact that the disciples did not sit down and map out the strategy for their world conquest. Christ did not neglect the training and instruction of His disciples, but He was primarily concerned that they grasp the significance of the Cross, the Resurrection, and the indwelling Spirit. The apostles advanced, driven by that Spirit rather than following carefully planned tactics. Indeed, it would appear that, thus inspired, they spoke words of wisdom which they themselves may not have fully grasped, and acted in wisdom beyond their own comprehension. Who can say that the Apostle Peter had a clear concept of what was involved when he went to the house of Cornelius and thus opened the door of faith to the Gentiles? Moved by God's Spirit, he built better than he knew.

These first apostles spoke and acted from deep personal conviction, not from dogma or theory. Their individual experience of Christ produced a sense of personal responsibility which resulted, normally and naturally, in evangelism and church growth. They had no money, no church buildings, and only the simplest form of what might be called church organization. Nevertheless, they baffled alike the rulers of Jews, Romans, and Greeks, won converts among slaves and the wealthy, established churches, and extended the Kingdom of God from river banks and desert roads to the palaces of kings and emperors. The New Testament Church's approach to its task is a far cry from the belief, held by many modern missionaries, that philanthropy, community building, and good works are the main ends of mission.

It is not by accident that the Great Commission falls between two stupendous events: the Resurrection and the outpouring of the Spirit on the day of Pentecost. At this time the meaning of the Resurrection was dawning on the souls of the apostles. They had seen the risen Christ, touched Him, and talked with Him. As the magnitude of the truth gripped their hearts, He said, "All power is given unto me in heaven and earth. Go therefore, and make disciples of all nations . . . and I am with you always, even to the end of the age."

It took more than the beautiful example of the life of Christ to make missionaries of the disciples. It took more than acknowledging the truth of His sublime teaching. Although they had walked with Him for three years, when they came to Calvary they were left confused, fearful, and defeated. Thomas was so deeply shaken that he refused to believe in the Resurrection without a tangible manifestation of Christ. This was not at first a conquering group, ready to go out and make an impression upon the world.

God Breathed on Their Souls

Then Christ arose and everything changed. God breathed on their souls; new hope was born in their hearts. The Great Commission came—still they must wait in an upper room until the breath of God burst forth into visible flame and tongues of fire. Their fear and reticence were gone as the Holy Spirit touched their lips and in new languages told forth the glories of God to strangers "from every nation" gathered in Jerusalem.

They went forth with one simple message. "Christ is risen and He is Lord and Savior. Receive Him." This message was the divine answer to the needs of all humanity. They went forth inspired by the Holy Spirit, who worked with them with signs following. Converts were won and churches established as naturally as night follows day. It could be no other way.

They were proclaiming Christ, not following a system—even a Christian system. Probably Paul could have produced masterpieces in Christian apologetics and marvelous essays on the social changes inherent in Christianity. But he said to the Corinthians, "I decided to know nothing among you except Jesus Christ and Him crucified," so that their faith might not be grounded in the wisdom of men but in the power of God. He insisted that each convert know God for himself.

God's Men Completely

The apostles lived as possessed men, which indeed they were—possessed of the Spirit of God. Life and earth were of little importance. They did not look for financial or even physical security. They were in jeopardy "every hour." They were imprisoned and beaten. They prayed with tears for their converts day and night.

They were completely and wholly dedicated, sold to Jesus Christ, the Lord of their lives, and to His cause.

They were men of faith. The Kingdom of God as a living spiritual reality was as factual to them as the ground upon which they walked. They believed the Word of the Gospel. They expected results when they preached in the name of Jesus. Was not Jesus alive at the right hand of the throne of God? Had He not promised to be with them even unto the end of the age? In His name therefore, they would command the lame man to stand upon his feet. They considered spiritual facts truer even than natural facts. That is why they could face persecution and the "beasts of Ephesus," or Nero himself. They sang and prayed their way out of gloomy prisons. Paul rose up after being "stoned and left for dead" and continued to preach the message. Their faith was in a living, resurrected Christ, not just in faith itself.

Because these first messengers were committed men, filled with the Holy Spirit, they expected their converts to be equally committed and filled with God's Spirit. They preached the claims of Christ on the individual and expected men to respond as they themselves had responded, to be filled as they had been filled. They expected converts to assume individual responsibility and to propagate the Gospel, not as a duty but spontaneously and inevitably.

Do Not Answer "Yes" too Quickly

If we are to have New Testament church growth today, flourishing in a New Testament climate, we too must be New Testament men. One asks immediately, "Do we want New Testament church growth in a New Testament climate?"

I beg you not to answer Yes too quickly! Would we really feel at home in the New Testament church atmosphere, with miracles taking place around us, our deacons and leaders being martyred and our members run out of town?

New Testament preachers lived in contact with divine power, and multitudes were converted, both men and women. A great company of priests were added to the Church. So mightily grew the

Word of God, and prevailed. I have been on the border of something like this once or twice and must confess to a feeling of nervousness about it. Something like this can very well get out of hand! We do not feel comfortable, usually, with something going on beyond our control. This fact alone reveals how foreign the New Testament climate is to most of us.

The men who formed the New Testament Church were themselves under the control of God's Spirit. He was moving—they were simply carrying out His will. Are we that kind of men? I seriously doubt that we will have the kind of results they had unless we are the kind of men they were. Do not misunderstand me. I do not mean that they were by nature set apart from ordinary mortals. They were as human as any of us; they had their weak points and their failures. But they knew God, through Jesus Christ; by the indwelling Spirit they became a different kind of man. In our endeavor to stimulate church growth we must start by being the kind of men through whom the Holy Spirit can create the life and climate of the New Testament Church.

What kind of men are we? Methods are no better than the men behind them; and men are no better than their contact with God. We can study methods of church growth and write books about indigenous church principles, all of which is well and good; but we will never have anything like New Testament churches and New Testament growth until we get something like New Testament men with New Testament experience. I do not know how this affects you, but it challenges me to the depths of my being. God's methods are men, and we are the men!

This faith in the living, resurrected, present Christ is simple Christianity as God meant it to be. This is the Gospel of redemption in Christ—a Gospel of love and salvation bringing hope to the hopeless, opening the eyes of the blind, and freeing those that are bound. Because it is a gospel a pagan world can receive, it is the Gospel that will establish churches. This must be our own faith and our joyful personal experience. Unless we are willing to meet God here, discussing methods is useless. We need not just new methods—we need to be a different kind of men.

Have no illusions about it, becoming this kind of a man is a lonely and costly road. Early or late you will find your garden of Gethsemane. God give you grace to pray. "Nevertheless, not my will but thine be done." You will follow on through Calvary and to Pentecost. A lonely road, did I say? Not really, for the Son of God walks this road and says, "Lo, I am with you alway, even unto the end of the age." I would rather know that He is with me than have all the world beside.

Do We Want Power-Filled Churches?

We must remember that the churches "at home" are in part at least responsible for the spiritual climate of their churches on the mission field. Missionaries are themselves a product of church climate. Do we think that we can have victorious growth with some other spiritual air than that of the New Testament in our home churches? Do we want New Testament churches? If so, we at home must turn again to the simplicity of the New Testament message. We tend, today, to take in too much; we spread ourselves too thin. Our message loses its fine cutting edge. Although many theological fine points intended to speak to modern life may have their significance for Christianity at its present stage of development in the homeland, I question their appropriateness when we go to an unchristian world dying without the only Savior. When missions become occupied with secondary matters and leave out the essential, we may find that the good has become the enemy of the best and the indispensable.

Do We Want New Testament Missionaries?

May I add a word about specialized missionary ministry? We are living in an age of specialization, but in mission this should never degenerate into careerism. Sometimes the specialized worker is tempted to look for his professional niche on the mission field. Now the missionary may be a Bible school teacher or have any other specialized skill, but above all and beyond it he must be an apostle, an evangelist, and a *planter of churches*. The task before us demands spiritual giants—it demands an apostolic ministry. Too often we have the tendency to cut the task down to our size, instead of growing up to the measure of the task.

There are hundreds of missionaries, perhaps thousands, good people all, who do not understand their missionary task from the New Testament point of view. They have found their specialized niche; they have put down their roots and are content to fulfill their specialized service as teachers, doctors, agriculturists, or parts of an institutional staff. Their Christian service is limited to their speciality, and they are more than glad to leave everything else to others. They are good people, but they are not New Testament missionaries. They need to be shocked out of their complacency. They need to be transformed from being a cog in the machine to a living, dynamic force for church building.

The missionary must be a man of dedication who will consider himself expendable. He must be willing to keep himself mobile and sufficiently flexible so that his program and plans can be guided by the Spirit of God. He must not think of himself or his ministry in terms of building his own career, but in terms of giving himself in order that churches may result.

Of course, when we have men with a New Testament spiritual life both as missionaries and as national workers in the lands of the younger Churches, church expansion and growth will follow. In fact, it is impossible to imagine that men like the early apostles, having passed through their experience and being filled with God's Spirit, could produce anything except New Testament churches with their accompanying rapid expansion. In my other chapters in this symposium I shall discuss church planting and expansion. Here I am concerned solely with the need to create a climate around ourselves and our converts favorable to New Testament growth.

Climate Encourages Church Growth

Let me give two illustrations of how the right climate encourages church growth, out far away from any missionary.

In one field Denomination X had a thriving church in a country area. Its services were well attended, its pastor was supported by the offerings of the people, and it had five or six branch churches in the area. Less than a mile away was a church of Denomination Y. One day Pastor Y dropped in to see Pastor X. "Would you be interested in opening a new church?" he asked. "A group of people has asked me to come and teach them the Bible, and I wondered if you would care to go instead?" Pastor X replied, "I would gladly take advantage of the opportunity, but have already five or six branch churches and am very busy. Why don't you take care of this Macedonian call yourself?" With surprising honesty, Pastor Y answered, "I'm being paid to take care of my church. I am willing to do what I am paid for, but not to take on additional responsibilities without more pay."

While Pastor Y's frankness as to his view of the ministry is unusual, his attitude is more common than it should be. Many a younger Church could well inquire what would happen to its work if subsidizing foreign funds were withdrawn. When this did happen in a certain area, chapels and churches were left without ministers up and down the country, for there were no funds to support them from outside. The pastors and ministers sought employment in commerce and government circles, and many congregations were left unshepherded. That such a thing could happen to any of our missions or Churches points to the need for a New Testament climate.

Let me give the contrasting example of a young man I knew. He spent six months in prison, by an unjust sentence under false accusations, because he had dared to preach the Gospel. When he came out he immediately continued his ministry. Several years later he was the pastor of a prosperous church.

He told me how he was taking care of an outstation some six or eight miles away over the hills. He had to go on foot over a steep mountain trail, which he explained wasn't so bad except when it rained hard after he had gone over and before he could get back. Then, in order to get up the slippery, muddy track, he had to crawl on hands and knees, reaching home at perhaps two o'clock in the morning covered with mud from head to foot. "But," he said, "there's a wonderful group of believers there, and before too long we can organize them into a church."

A few months later I asked him if he was still going to this outstation. He said with a smile, "I don't go there any more. We have organized it into a church, and Brother Fulano from our own congregation has been put in charge of it. There is a lot of enthusiasm. All the people are contributing food for their new pastor and the work is moving along nicely." Neither this man nor the young worker whom he developed in his church received a subsidy from the mission. What they did have was a sense of responsibility and the New Testament spirit of sacrifice.

Prayer Creates Climate

Prayer has a real place in creating spiritual climate. The outpouring of the Holy Spirit on the day of Pentecost was preceded by days of prayer and supplication during which the disciples were prepared for what was to take place. When the day came, they were all in one place with one accord, and the Spirit came upon them with the sound of a mighty rushing wind. Public, united prayer is described repeatedly in the Book of Acts. The early Church took literally the admonition of the prophet Joel to call a solemn assembly and turn to God with all their heart. There is something irreplaceably vital in the spiritual preparation of worker and church when the church seeks God unitedly.

In 1950 when I went to take charge of our workers' training program in El Salvador, the burden of creating spiritual climate was on my heart. We had about sixty men students. I felt more and more strongly that the Bible School should be not only a center for imparting Bible knowledge, but a place where spiritual life would be born and infused into the whole work. Here the spiritual tide was not as high as it should have been. Accordingly, in the middle of the school year we called time out from studies for prayer. Early in the ten days of prayer that followed, we joined together in firm purpose to seek God until He should meet our spiritual need.

We based our faith on the promise of Jesus that "if two of you shall agree on earth as touching anything that they shall ask, it shall be done for them of my Father who is in heaven" (Matt. 18:19). We continued in prayer approximately ten hours a day, and by the second day there was evidence of God's presence with us. Confessions of faults and of needs were made. Sin was acknowledged and repentance was expressed with tears. Teachers and students alike were humbled under the mighty hand of God.

The result was a tremendous spiritual impact on the student body and on all surrounding churches. Since then it has become the practice in this institute to set aside a week for prayer during the school year. Through it God has been pleased to grant us a remarkable multiplication of churches.

Moving into a Church Growth Climate

At one stage of our work in Nicaragua progress was slow and the churches seemed unable to rise to the challenge of evangelization of their areas. The workers lacked the initiative necessary for the type of aggressive ministry needed. They seemed content to leave forward moves to the missionaries. They did not see how they could advance without money. A spirit of discouragement gripped many hearts. Some talked of going back to secular employment. Then the missionaries called a general prayer conference; missionaries and national workers met together for a week of prayer.

It proved to be a time of deep heart-searching for missionaries and nationals alike. Prayer services ran far into the night. Souls were bared before God and confessions of need were made. By the time the week was out, God had visited the workers with an outpouring of the Spirit which resulted in a deep energy for evangelism and a personal responsibility toward their call, with recognition of the fact that they were servants of God rather than of the mission. Workers entered new fields without being paid or sent by the missionary. Revivals came to their churches. Within two years' time the number of our churches doubled, the number of members doubled, and the number of workers and prospective workers more than doubled.

Leaving aside instances which have come under my own observation in missionary work, let me refer to the Korean revival in 1907—an outstanding instance of revival and growth. Some credit for the amazing church growth in Korea should go to the Nevius method of mission with its emphasis on tithing, Bible study, and no foreign-paid local pastors, but when the Spirit's fire fell on Korea, churches began to grow still more abundantly.

The revival began with an intensive prayer campaign on the part of the missionaries, who prayed daily for months. Finally the local church joined them in a prayer campaign. Eventually, the Holy Spirit moved upon the church as a purging, cleansing flame, and revival was on. How, during the following years, this revival resulted in multiplied thousands of conversions and in the spread of the Gospel even to remote areas is known to most of us. The Korean Church entered into a New Testament climate and prospered and grew correspondingly. Dr. Jonathan Goforth in his book *By My Spirit* gives a graphic description of the spiritual movement.

> As I remember, those missionaries at Pingyang were just ordinary, everyday people. I did not notice any outstanding figure among them. They seemed to live and work and act like other missionaries. It was in prayer that they were different. One evening, Dr. MacKay and myself were invited to attend the missionary prayer meeting. Never have I been so conscious of the Divine Presence as I was that evening. Those missionaries seemed to carry us right up to the very Throne of God. One had the feeling that they were indeed communing with God face to face. On the way back to our host's residence, Dr. MacKay was silent for some time. I could see that he was greatly agitated. Finally, with deep emotion, he exclaimed: "What amazing prayer! Your missionaries in Honan are nowhere near that high level."
>
> What impressed me, too, was the practical nature of the movement. I soon saw that this was no wild gust of "religious enthusiasm," dying with the wind upon whose wings it had been borne. There were, of course, the usual outward manifestations which inevitably accompany such phenomenal outpourings of spiritual power. But beyond all that was the simple fact that here were tens of thousands of Korean men and women whose lives had been transformed by the touch of the Divine fire. I saw great churches, seating fifteen hundred people, so

crowded that it was found necessary to hold two services, one for the men and one for the women. Everyone seemed almost pathetically eager to spread the "glad tidings." Even little boys would run up to people on the street and plead with them to accept Christ as their Saviour. One thing that especially struck me was their abounding liberality. The poverty of the Koreans is proverbial. Yet one missionary told me that he was afraid to speak to them about money; they were giving so much already. Everyone seemed to carry a Bible. And permeating it all was the marvelous spirit of prayer.

In a hard and difficult field where the churches are bogged down in indifference and inertia and the program is not moving forward, my recommendation would be that the first emphasis be a spiritual one. We need Christian theology in action. Let us seek a New Testament climate and New Testament power. Let us organize prayer campaigns for revival as the first step for all-out evangelism and expansion in church growth. Missionary work is not simply a human endeavor. We are in partnership with God. This is His work and it must be done His way and in His power. The only guarantee of success we have is His promise to be with us. Let us first be sure He is in charge of this operation and that we are doing things His way. Let us pray as Moses did: "If thy presence go not with me, carry us not up hence." Without His presence we shall accomplish nothing of eternal value. If He is with us, we cannot fail in our task.

III

THEOLOGICAL FOUNDATIONS

ROBERT CALVIN GUY

Wide Interest in Theology

The Palace of Fine Arts in Mexico City occupies a prominent place in the capital, testifying to the high regard national leaders have for culture. The huge murals, reflecting the restlessness of the nation, are unforgettable. They tell of pent-up longing and barely suppressed rebellion. The building is magnificent but has a foundation problem and is slowly sinking. Although it will probably stand for a long time, the basic weakness is disturbing.

The impressive structure of Christian mission has theological foundations. They are being examined in our day by many thoughtful people. A recently published book, *The Theology of Christian Mission,*[1] is an indication of this concern. Here is a comprehensive volume presenting twenty-five eminent theologians writing from many perspectives. Yet the title of Wilhelm Andersen's chapter, "Further Toward a Theology of Mission," suggests that even this impressive array of talent only begins the task.

Theology of mission, which inevitably involves a theology of church growth, is perhaps being better understood in our day than ever before. The ancient divorce between Church and mission,

[1] Gerald H. Anderson, *The Theology of the Christian Mission* (New York: McGraw-Hill Book Co., 1961).

with a small group within the Church assuming responsibility for evangelism, is now seen to be inadequate. Able Christians are saying that the entire community of believers must be involved in the entire will of God for all His world if the Church is to be the Church. In addition, men are relating the responsibility for world evangelization to something more than a formal command, and the vocation of the missionary to something more vital than cold duty. The very nature of God is the foundation for mission; and the living, guiding presence of the Lord Christ Himself accounts for its vitality.

This chapter will deal with Christian theological foundations only in phases vitally related to crucial issues in church growth. I should like to suggest discernible weaknesses in the foundation and point to trends that need to be reversed as well as insights that need to be strengthened. The treatment will be suggestive, not exhaustive, dealing with issues that are major concerns of the mission movement and basic to its future.

Jesus made a solemn statement about foundations for Christian life. A foundation, He said, has two strengths—one from hearing and one from doing. The parable warned men that they must hear His sayings. The importance of listening to His message can hardly be overestimated. But He gave no encouragement to the dilettante hearer who wanted to be entertained by a new idea but was unmoved by the demands made upon him.

Any football fan knows what should have been done in the game before him, but in giving advice to coach or players he is wise to remember that mental comprehension is a very different matter from putting plays into effect. Just so, theology of missions is not useful if restricted to intellectual comprehension only. A theology of missions is always a blueprint for action, a means to an end, never an end itself. It must be put into effect, not merely known. It is the difference between life and death

Right Approach to a Theology of Missions

The Christian theologian violates a basic demand of his material if he approaches his task without the proper humility. It is impossible truly to learn of the lowly Galilean unless the spirit of pride is checked. A theologian basking in the glory of his own mental accomplishments is unlikely to know the hunger that will permit him to be filled with truly Christian knowledge.

Humility is particularly vital to the usefulness of theology that undergirds church growth, for such theology, while full and true, must be meaningful to people whose theological knowledge is limited. If they are consciously or subconsciously despised, it will be impossible to present to them a true picture of the One Who has so much for them because He Himself sat where they sit, was despised and rejected of men, and died the shameful death of the Cross.

In this materialistic age it is often assumed that superior possessions, whether personal, denominational, or national, are guarantees of superior discipleship. Like ancient Israel, today's Western Christian is apt to believe that his prosperity is a direct result of his righteousness and superior wisdom. Yet this is not so. Israel repeatedly departed from God in her most prosperous days, and He then visited judgment on her. In the face of the past, dare we take our own prosperity as evidence of being good Christians?

Theology of Christian mission also requires a true correlation between mental and functional aspects. Even in the Kingdom of God, each person tends to magnify his own field. The thinker easily assumes that thought is the most important aspect of church life. Thinkers and writers are tempted to move crucial questions into the realm of right thought to the neglect of right action. The Gnostic heresy is a contemporary temptation. On the contrary, Jesus said that if any man would *do* His will, "he shall know the doctrine" (John 7:17). Theology for action and theology in action is the standard of the New Testament. Paul, the greatest theologian of the Christian world, created his parts of New Testament canon in the white heat of mission expansion.

Philosophers are inclined to think that they can solve world problems. Plato assumed that the rule of the philosopher could solve all problems by intellectual processes. On the other hand Christ, without ignoring the intellectual foundation, solved men's problems by involving their total responses. To assume that mental patterns can be substituted for the total involvement of mind and will and emotions is a frequent temptation of educated people.

Nor is the Christian mission at home or abroad immune to it. Thus Roland Allen insisted that missionaries do not go to the field to "tell people the truth" but to "minister the spirit." Every Christian witness has discovered to his own despair that he can present the most logical case for Christianity, only to have it rejected. And what theologian has not been embarrassed when comparing his own efforts in evangelism with those of some relatively untrained, but Spirit-filled, messenger whose logic may be inferior but whose fruit is far richer than that of the trained preacher.

Benefit from Existential Insight

In *Philosophy of Religion* Elton Trueblood says:

> The essence of the existentialist message is that man is always personally involved in the situations which he seeks to examine. All of man's study of the world must always include himself because he is part of the picture. Man, therefore, is marked not so much by pure reason as by "concern." All existentialism begins in the recognition that the elimination of the personal equation is impossible and that all important thinking involves personal decision.[2]

This view of life has particular importance for a theology of mission. God in a book is not the same as God in my life. This truth applies to the study of both the Bible and books of theology. The basic question about an adequate theology of mission is, does it help mediate the redeeming presence of Christ to the hearer or reader? Does it get him involved with God personally and redemptively? Without this redemptive involvement the very purposes of God are thwarted, and no amount of theology, however skillfully stated, can make up for that loss. In a real sense, therefore, every true theology is a theology of redemption and of church growth. An "excellent" theology of mission which checks church growth or is indifferent to it is a contradiction in terms.

[2] Elton Trueblood, *Philosophy of Religion* (New York: Harper & Row, 1957), p. 23.

As my colleague Mr. Hodges has so adequately pointed out, New Testament theology must be our guide at this point. It was motivated by concern and compassion. It was theology, not in detachment, but in deepest personal involvement. However we frame Christian theology to fit today's rapid changes, it must be motivated by Christ's compassion and must involve men with God.

The next firm test we rightly seek in a sound theological foundation for the Christian mission is outcome. We apply the pragmatic test to the work of the theologian. Does his theology motivate men to go into all the world and make disciples? And does it so undergird them that they, thus motivated, succeed in this primary purpose? Theology must stand the test of being known by its fruit.

The Wisdom of the Simple and Uncomplicated

However indebted missionaries and ministers may be to the writers of theology, the man on the street is very little influenced by them. Paradoxically, the movement toward shorter, more understandable sermons has been accompanied by longer, more confusing books on theology. If church growth is to be encouraged, theology of mission must be clear and useful, as well as true. It must be understood by common people and lead them to salvation. Theology must drive those who hold it into redemptive activity. True, utility is not the only criterion in the theological world, but it is one valid test.

The council described in Acts 15 recognized the need for plain language. It wisely decided not to complicate the spiritual life of Gentile converts with the precious, time-hallowed, but unnecessary baggage of Jewish observances. Harry Boer, in *Pentecost and Missions,* suggests that this far-reaching and—for devout Jewish Christians—agonizing decision could have been made only under the guidance of the Holy Spirit. Jewish Christian leaders would not have accepted the conversion of Cornelius and other Gentiles except as Peter assured them that God had given the Gentiles the Holy Spirit, just as He had the Jews. It was the Spirit's presence and guidance that separated the necessary from the incidental and left the Church free to multiply among the Gentiles. Obviously, we should pray for the guidance of the Holy Spirit in writing theology for the Churches of Afericasia.

"Cultural overhang" operates in the realm of theology. We Westerners often compose a theology of missions understandable only to the highly trained men among us, and expect it to guide churches composed of common people from the very different cultures of Afericasia. If it is argued that a certain theology contains only essential statements, one may reply that a valid test of every such "essential" statement in a theology of Christian mission would be: Is it simple? Is it clear? If not, either it is not essential or it needs rephrasing.

This applies especially in the realm of training national pastors. Like the Roman legions, these men should be equipped lightly, so as to be able to make free and complete use of the essential equipment they carry. Abstruse theological material, suitable for doctoral seminars, should not complicate their theology of mission. Too much equipment slows down the rate of march; it is what Caesar called it: impedimenta. The Church on the march needs a compact theology.

Positions which Do Not Demand Constant Rebuilding

Thinkers constantly face this dilemma: shall they make theology relevant (a word often ineptly used for a product that is more relative than relevant), or preserve the fabric of historical and biblical faith. The attempt to "let Christ speak to our day" is profitable only if the voice heard is truly Christ's, rather than the voice of our day distorting His.

In this necessary attempt to speak to the current generation, extreme theological positions develop. If a man redesigns central biblical dogmas to meet the needs of his own small section of mankind, his rendering may cause confusion inside that section and will certainly cause it outside. Special emphases and new fashions in theology demand realignment of all our thinking, and this costs enormous time and effort. If this realignment is followed by another new emphasis, as some other theologian rephrases Christian truth with still another swing of the pendulum, theology becomes, not a girding of God's people for action, but a painful and futile jumping from one new position to another.

A ready illustration is found in the "wholly other" emphasis of Neo-orthodoxy. This developed out of the dismay of Barth with his teachers' "conversation with the world." As they conversed with the humanistic, rationalistic world of their day, they came to positions with little distinctive Christian ground. They were left, for example, without a voice of judgment to speak out on militarism. Their conversation had become surrender to the world rather than proclamation to it. Dr. Barth describes this situation in his *Humanity of God*.[3]

Neo-orthodoxy has rendered valuable service to a world which had lost its spiritual moorings. Barth's insistence on the otherness of God and encounter with God as the stamp of genuine religious experience made it difficult for rationalism to deny vital supernatural truth. However, in achieving this Barth almost made human experience the final criterion of Christian truth. His movement seems in harmony with the earlier one of Schleiermacher who, likewise distressed at the inroads of rationalism, placed religion beyond its reach by making feeling the basic ingredient. Both men rendered helpful service to the world of theology, but it is doubtful if either stood in the midstream of Christian truth, from which a witness to all men could be proclaimed.

Not only did Barth speak to the special condition of scientific Western man, but many, "outbarthing Barth," made him a fad. Teachers of theology rushed to administer his antidote for pre-World War I rationalism to everybody. Some patients to the far left of the theological spectrum needed it badly. Those on the far right, who had never doubted the sovereignty of God, did not need it at all.

The result in Churches of Afericasia was often distressing. In one country where healthy church growth has not been known in

[3] Karl Barth, *The Humanity of God* (Richmond, Va.: John Knox Press, 1960).

several generations, preachers in mission-aided training schools learned to read German in order to know the new German theology—the latest thing! But the people of their land were not rejecting Christianity because of scientific rationalism. On the contrary, they were (and still are) worshiping gods made with hands. Christian miracles did not disturb them. They devoutly believed in bizarre Buddhist miracles. Although some of the elite of the land were reading European books, the mass of the people needed the sure knowledge that Jesus could cast out demons and provide vital relationship with the true God.

Even if we grant that Barth's position is theological penicillin for scientific Western man, it is useless against the diseases of premedieval societies in Africa, Asia, and Latin America. Then, too, Dr. Barth in a recent book confesses that, in seeking to correct a specific ill, he went far past center to an extreme. He now says that God the Father is so inextricably bound in the bundle of life with the human race He created that he must speak of the "humanity of God"!

We have used the "wholly other" emphasis of Barthianism as an illustration, but many other Western doctrinal emphases would have served as well.

Theology in the Younger Churches

What does all this say of Christian theological education in lands scarcely aware of the Incarnation?

It says that many seminaries in Afericasia have prepared students to speak to their people on controversial side issues of Western Christianity rather than about the fundamentals of salvation. It says that Christian ministers of countries which have yet to produce a self-sustaining Christian movement have often missed the basic training which would enable them to engage in fruitful ingathering. Instead they have been prepared to correct ills which *may* develop years later—*if* their churches grow greatly.

This brief review suggests that the theological emphases of seminaries in lands where church members form a majority of the total population may hinder the cause of Christ, if reproduced where the Christian segment is numerically insignificant.

It says, in fact, that special emphases in theology, however novel or corrective, must not replace the foundations on which the entire structure rests, and that any new theological insight should be examined carefully to determine whether it enlarges and clarifies the God-honored New Testament doctrines or discredits and deserts them.

Creative theological thought should be mature, occupied with the major concerns of the faith and properly relating these to the culture of the lands in which churches are to be multiplied. Missionary and national preachers should be alert to the social and spiritual symptoms of their particular peoples.

Major Emphasis on Jesus Christ as Lord and Savior

Wilhelm Andersen makes this statement: "The center of a theology of mission is, therefore, faith in the crucified and risen Christ."[4] Helpful accents on this theme have been sounded by other eminent writers in recent publications. Lesslie Newbigin[5] speaks emphatically about the place of Christ in any faith that is adequate for world need. D. T. Niles[6] is a voice from the East emphasizing the person and work of Christ as the necessary foundation for missions. Edmund Soper's book, *The Inevitable Choice,*[7] is another clear delineation of actuality, by contrast with theory, however alluring, as other religions may express it or borrow it.

Biblical theology insists that Christ is Lord and that He alone is the source of eternal fellowship with God. The truth that Christ is Lord is not subject to variation because of the rejection or accept-

[4] Wilhelm Andersen, *Toward a Theology of Mission* (London: SCM Press, 1955).

[5] Lesslie Newbigin, *A Faith for This One World* (New York: Harper & Row, 1961).

[6] D. T. Niles, *The Preacher's Task and the Stone of Stumbling* (New York: Harper & Row, 1958).

[7] Edmund Soper, *The Inevitable Choice* (Nashville: Abingdon Press, 1957).

ance of men. Even when His Church is persecuted, Christ is Lord.

We must not confuse the "benefits" of Western civilization with obedience to Christ fruiting in God's gifts of the Spirit. Although Western technology, medicine, and know-how may ameliorate the physical misery of many, the rise in standard of living in Western society has been accompanied by a paradoxical decrease in contentment. We have no cause to expect any other result in areas where the technological revolution is now taking place. The condition of the Western world spotlights the inadequacy of the bread that perishes. Our "comfortable" world is filled with hungry hearts enclosed in satisfied bodies, and the concrete jungles of our cities prove conclusively that technology cannot fill man's ultimate needs. Emphasis on Christ as Lord is the only foundation for missionary vocation.

A related problem lies in the vast and helpful carry-over from our Christian past which Elton Trueblood has likened to a cut flower. He shows that our civilization displays lovely "flowers" not in contemporary production. Many in our land no longer live within the primary purpose of Christ, yet display some of the beauty which that purpose created. It is possible for Christian mission to export the cut flowers of Western civilization without communicating the Lordship of Christ. This is a notable current danger. If Christian forces turn their attention to helping others copy such Christian blooms as democracy and education, instead of helping them cleave to Christ, we shall replace vital Christian growth with sometimes unsuitable—always perishable—cut flowers, borrowed bloom without true roots.

Enjoying the flowers of Christianity rather than nourishing the root that produced them is possible for a few generations in a "Christian" society, but scarcely feasible in a non-Christian one. As American missionaries emphasize a higher standard of living, they will do well to recall that the words, "I am come that they might have life and have it more abundantly," were spoken to those who had no access at all to the comforts we now materialistically equate with life. Since Christ is Lord, mission must hear Him declare His purpose and follow His priorities.

There are many implications for Christians in the Lordship of Christ. One is that missions, missionaries, and national preachers stand every day under the judgment of God in Christ. One of the damaging, because often true, accusations leveled against the leadership of missions is that it has withdrawn from careful evaluation. It has been defensive rather than anxious to benefit by corrective assessment. When any enterprise is *called* missionary, it is supposed to stand in its own right without evaluation. This is a most dangerous attitude. When Jesus spoke to the Jews and told them that the Kingdom of God would be taken from them and given to a nation bringing forth fruits, He declared for all time the inability of any set of leaders to freeze the purposes of God around their own conceptions.

What is the will of God for us in our day, in our relationship to world redemption? Can it be other than it was for Christ Himself: to engage in the work of redemption even at the cost of the Cross? If this is God's will, then He judges the Church (and the missionary society) by how well it is getting on with the work of redemption. As He looks at the far-flung and extensive work of Christian mission, He calls for responsible inventory. Christian theology demands self-examination.

Another implication of the Lordship of Christ is that cultures which reject Him stand as fully under His judgment as those that receive Him. Eschatology has an interesting application at this point. It emphasizes the relationship of the sovereign God to all the histories He has created and is creating. He judges them all. They will all stand before the great white throne.

Still another implication is that we must confront men with Christ and His demands regardless of their rejection of or objection to the primary task of mission. He said, "Decide!"—we must not say, "Discuss." He said, "Follow!"—we must not say, "Compare." Men of other religions all too readily compare their theory with our practice and themselves with us—and reject Christ. They are willing to receive benefits growing out of His society, but reject the basic root that produced it. We must make certain that our discussion and effort lead to decision about Him. Christian mission must intend that, through every methodology, men do in fact accept Christ, become living members of His churches, and go on to win others to Him.

Sin As Rebellion

Since the ancient confusion about original sin, theological waters on this subject have been muddy. For some reason hard to understand, a popular impression has been that original sin was the sex involvement of Adam with Eve. Confusion at this point still exists. It is easy also to equate sin with gross expressions in the societies to which missionaries are sent. For instance, the infanticide and *suttee* Carey found in India troubled him. He labored mightily against them, but on the Sunday morning when he translated the edict forbidding the practice of *suttee,* he did not write the death knell of sin or paganism in India. The cessation of widow-burning—however satisfying to those of us who point to it as a fruit of missions—did not save the masses of India or keep them from rejecting Jesus as Savior and Lord.

For an understanding of sin we must return to biblical theology. The words of Jesus are clear: "Ye will not come to me that ye might have life." "Ye must be born again." Many other passages show that the New Testament considers sin as rebellion, a wrong act of will.

Biblical understanding of sin as rebellion makes laughable a parliament of religions to share insights and walk together toward a better world. If a compromise of religions were possible, surely it would have been worked out between the best of the great ethnic religions (Judaism) and the incarnate Son of God. Instead He died in a conflict between this religion and God's provision of His righteousness for sinful man. His words and His death dramatize the depth of it: ". . . Ye have not his word abiding in you; for whom he hath sent, him ye believe not." This was rejection by the best religion of the pre-Christian world. This was rebellion. It is still the root sin of the world.

Pride in self, heritage, and the "religion of our fathers" leads to rejection of Jesus. *Sins* (overt acts from falsehood to murder) degrade whole nations and continents as a result of this basic *sin* (rejection of Jesus as Lord and Savior). Men can and do pride themselves on their freedom from gross sins and yet are guilty of rejecting the love of God and denying His sovereignty. Men—no matter how moral—who thus reject Him should not be held up as shining examples of proper conduct. How often does one hear the expression, "He's a good man but he just hasn't trusted Jesus." In New Testament terms no man is good who shuts from his life the love of God expressed in His crucified Son. Until this is recognized we will encourage men in their self-made goodness—to their own destruction. All theology of mission must ground goodness in obedient discipleship to Jesus Christ.

The original sin was rebellion against God. The world still rebels against God-in-Christ, His revelation and redemption. There is realism in the biblical doctrine of Antichrist. It should be studied outside the context of a millenarian theory. When John says that there are many antichrists, he suggests that this is not an isolated personality but rather a spirit pervading much of our world, which foments rebellion against God the Son. To underestimate the strength of this antichrist sentiment and antichrist power is to make a grievous mistake in our theology of church growth and our mission strategy.

Continuous Emphasis on the Church as a Redemptive Fellowship

Our Lord said, "On this rock I will build my church." In our day the inclination is to count "church" as the significant word. Actually in Jesus' mind "church" meant simply an assembly and the telling word was the possessive pronoun "my." It is only *His* Church which will not be moved.

Because of His presence and the unique characteristics given churches by Him, *they have ability to grow strong and multiply.* One of the ironies of mission history is that we so often distrust the ability of young churches to survive in the midst of world currents. An underestimated or overprotected church has already been wronged and in some measure ruined. The last thing a church of Jesus Christ needs is for somebody to patronize it.

Let it be recognized that we have sometimes given the name "church" to a hothouse plant which is not even a good mission project, and have attempted to pump enough artificial stimulant into it to make it function. Missions sometimes nervously mother an infant organization which is not a church at all. We are not speaking in this book of such psuedo churches, but of churches which are Christ's own assemblies. Can it not be said with truth that real churches will make their own way? With Him, can they fail? One foundation of a viable theology of missions is its emphasis on the church's sturdy independence of men and ever-present dependence on Christ.

In the New Testament the Church served others. It was not a source of goods and services to be given to the members. It made demands upon the members and provided for them virtually nothing except the amazing grace of God—the power to live as His sons. Whatever was given (except the special offering Paul took to the church at Jerusalem) was conveyed in person-to-person sharing. Such assistance is hardly open to misunderstanding, and certainly not to the abuses proceeding from "organized charities financed from distant places."

The churches of the New Testament strengthened the human spirit in relation to the divine by expecting something of the membership rather than weakening it by carrying burdens for it. That the burdens imposed upon the early Christians seem to us impossible to bear reflects our misunderstanding of divine resources. It also reflects our underestimation of the human spirit. With adequate leadership and genuine inspiration the Christian has reached amazing heights of power.

In setting out an adequate doctrine of the Church of Christ as a truly redemptive fellowship we realize that some churches fall far short of the doctrine. Often auxiliary goods and services have constituted their main attraction and have sparked their growth. When growth is based on lures, the members will have a psychology rooted in worldly expectations. Such people have often been called "rice Christians." From the Western point of view a better term would be "apron-string" Christians, for their psychology is created by our desire to keep them closely related to, dependent upon, and grateful to us.

In many lands, including our own, the Church is robbed of its significance by being regarded as impotent apart from the support it receives from institutions which came to life only as a *result* of the vigor of church life in other times. Here again the root/fruit relationship needs examination in terms of basic theology. Is not the Church more important than services rendered in her name? Is not the Church more important than any auxiliary institution? Is it possible that resources and energy required to maintain these services could be used to produce more churches, which in turn would alleviate human misery more basically and more permanently?

Roland Allen insists that ministering or communicating the Spirit effectively meets the pressing physical needs of men on the mission field.[8] He declares that emphasizing the primary function of the Church lays the ax to the root of the tree of evil. Far from expressing indifference to misery in the lives of men and societies, communicating the Spirit eradicates the source of much of that misery and so is the most effective way of meeting physical needs.

An adequate doctrine of the Church will question attempts to "strengthen the church." The New Testament assumes church strength; it talks about the church witnessing—it knows nothing of men's "strengthening the church." Our attempts to provide church strength are like advising a farmer to get exercise by playing golf because he no longer gets body tone from plowing. The main strength of any church should come from daily witness or the discharge of other duties.

A missionary with a long term of service in India said, "We need an outgoing rather than a self-protecting church." We have failed to communicate to people benefiting from the ministry of the

[8] Roland Allen, *The Ministry of the Spirit,* ed. David Paton (Grand Rapids, Mich.: Eerdmans Publishing Co., 1962; London: World Dominion Press, 1960).

missionary the basic imperative that took the missionary to the field. Probably nothing would so strengthen the younger Churches as to measure up to the responsibility of Christian witness.

The New Testament Drive of Outreach

Many are saying we must return to the New Testament, not only for message but also for method. We may profit by examining the basic New Testament drive. Look where we will in the New Testament, we find compulsive outreach toward people and places as yet untouched by the Gospel.

As we read the Book of Acts, we see the Holy Spirit blessing the "people movement" in Samaria with vast response, leading Philip from this ingathering down to Gaza to plant the Gospel in Africa through the converted eunuch, demanding that Peter include Cornelius and other Gentiles in his witness, "robbing" the young church at Antioch of its prime leadership for expansion into all the Mediterranean world, and shutting Paul away from further emphasis on Asia in favor of expansion into Europe. At every one of these departures from the usual plans the Holy Spirit was emphasizing outreach. Human wisdom would have called these movements "premature" or "inadequately undergirded" and would have judged that they placed "impossible burdens on churches too young to bear them." But the Holy Spirit nourished old and new churches alike and drove them on and on to disciple every tribe and tongue and people and nation.

Compulsive outreach is seen in the fact that success was measured in terms of the expectation of Jesus that His disciples would bear much fruit. Timid missions with "limited expectation" overlook the tremendous import of John 15 and 16 and the Book of Acts. Some hold that limited responses to Jesus Himself attend the mission which expects little—and is, in consequence, not disappointed. Yet He commands us to reconcile all men to God and promised that His disciples would do greater works than He did. Pentecost fulfilled this promise in richest measure. The church, which numbered about 120, on that one day received additions to the number of 3,000. Other multitudes were rapidly added to the Lord, and soon the disciples numbered 5,000 men and still continued to increase mightily. Increase occurred because of the power of God and not as the fruit of human wisdom in the organization of the first small church. Growth did not depend on the number or resources of the few original Christians. But note that, though growth dwarfed the original membership, it did not frighten the disciples in the least. They did not stop to "consolidate." They did not limit ingathering. They did not confine church expansion to Jerusalem. They went everywhere making disciples and establishing churches. Christ was glorified in their bearing much fruit.

Mission Rises from Theological Foundations

Mission rises from theological foundations. It is a projection of basic theological beliefs. Its vigor and form reveal what it is based on. Men do not gather grapes from thorns or figs from thistles. Dynamic, growing churches do not spring up from enfeebled or distorted theological roots. If the vast missionary enterprise, proliferating into many cultural and economic activities, would safeguard its life, it must look closely to its theological foundations and make certain that they are found in the New Testament, commanded by Christ, and demonstrated in the growing Churches of nineteen hundred years of Christian history.

IV

IDEOLOGICAL CONFLICTS

EUGENE A. NIDA

Any discussion of church growth is immediately confronted by a serious difficulty: namely, the meaning of the word "growth." In general, in speaking of the growth of the church we are referring to numerical expansion or increase, but the term also carries with it certain biological analogies of maturation (e.g., infancy, adolescence, adulthood, senescence). It is difficult if not impossible to escape from these qualitative dimensions. But even if we restrict ourselves to so-called statistical growth, we really do not know how to count, for in the opinion of some persons one must count only baptized believers (that is, adults), while other church leaders insist that if one is to obtain an accurate view of the significance of the Christian witness it is not only legitimate but necessary to count the total number of persons in the Christian community. Even if, however, we restrict ourselves to counting only "baptized believers in good standing," there is still the problem of the wheat and the tares, and we obviously cannot determine which is which. Further, though we are given a scriptural recommendation to judge men by their fruits, there is no universally acceptable definition of "fruits" by which one can set up rigorous standards of comparative judgment. One thing is quite evident: we cannot judge merely on the basis of so-called doctrinal purity, for there is no such general standard of doctrine.

The recognition of such basic problems in the discussion of church growth might seem to imply at the very outset that we cannot set up any very precise definitions or detailed comparative analyses; and to a certain extent this is true. But such an admission of the essential difficulties involved in considering "growth" may be a very healthy corrective to the tendency to put too much faith in graphs and statistical tables. It may also help us to realize that church growth is a multidimensional affair, reflecting primarily cultural rather than merely numerical factors. Moreover, we soon realize that in analyzing even some of the most obvious forms of Church growth we are only dealing with the outward form and not the inward content. Once prepared to treat the growth of churches in terms of its outward cultural expression, and not presuming to do more than this, we can then proceed to analyze the various features of such growth by applying to the data the principles of analysis used in the study of all other human institutions. This does not mean that we can or should omit consideration of the supernatural or supracultural aspects of the Church's origin or nature; but at present we have no criteria by which we can distinguish the human from the divine, especially when we concentrate our attention on outward increase—and this is the only aspect that can really be studied in any quantitative way.

The growth of the church involves, however, not merely quantitative judgments and measurements, but qualitative analysis. For as an integral element of human culture, religion (in whatever institutional manifestation one may specify) must involve values, and values involve qualitative judgments. In fact, the dynamic of church expansion depends much more upon the value judgments of its members than upon mere numerical increase. Accordingly, we cannot escape from the area of values or from value judgments. But if we are not to be hopelessly confused, we must carefully distinguish between the human elements—which are open to our scrutiny—and the divine (or supernatural) factors—which we presume have been operative, but which we cannot and must not attempt to subject to any statistical treatment.

Without a clear delimitation of our basic problems and without some sensitivity to historical developments, we may be easily led astray by jingoism, in which growth becomes an end in itself, and discipling always seems to have priority over shepherding. Certainly the recent rapid growth of certain churches of the Pentecostal type in Latin America is both encouraging and deserving of careful study. At the same time, there are situations in the history of the Church when shepherding has probably been the only feasible and defensible priority. For example, the resistance of the Greek Orthodox Church to the inroads of Islam was primarily a matter of shepherding, even to the point of becoming identified with national interests and adopting a minority "status quo" role. Something similar occurred in the history of the Orthodox Church in South India. For many persons with an activist American orientation, in which statistical graphs must always go up, growth can readily become a sort of be-all and end-all of missions and the church. There is actually much more involved than mere statistical increase, however.

Conflicting Viewpoints

The question as to whether the Church should always or inevitably grow may be highlighted by two very diverse viewpoints. One insists that "the Church should grow, but it probably will not, at least in the immediately foreseeable future"; the other contends with equal force of conviction that "the Church is growing, but actually it should not be." These contrasting viewpoints may seem here somewhat overstated, but in this manner of presenting them it may be possible to see their differences as well as certain hidden similarities.

The view that the Church should grow but probably will not do so might be called the "liberal position," not as defined by the professional leaders of this wing of the Church, but by many of its lay and ministerial adherents. Actually there is a growing body of Christians, especially in the older and more established churches, who are skeptical about the possibility of effective missionary activity and church growth in these times. More and more persons seem to feel that Christianity has had its day. The constant remarks about the "post-Christian era" reflect this basic skepticism. For if, as seems obvious, the Church is losing out at home (and this is a dominant theme in the thinking and writing of a number of European church leaders), how can it possibly have any significant success within the next generation abroad?

An even more alarming circumstance is the growing number of seemingly only nominal Christians. Secularism appears to be taking an increasing toll in both Protestant and Roman Catholic constituencies. Even though people may retain certain traditional connections with the Christian Church, for all practical purposes they are becoming merely twentieth-century pagans.

The population explosion adds another dimension to the problem of relative size, for though Christendom now represents approximately 27 per cent of the world's population, by the year 2000 it is estimated that Christians will number scarcely 20 per cent of the total.

Even the growth of church attendance in the United States is interpreted by many sociologists as merely a passing phase of our prosperity. They insist that institutionalized religion, that is to say, a religious form increasingly divorced from life (for example, in situations where church attendance increases and public and private morality declines) always flourishes in times of prosperity. Accordingly, if the present growth in church attendance in the United States is based on shallow foundations or is only a passing fad of our prosperity, and if the secularization of life which has gone so far in Europe is destined gradually to spread throughout the world as an inevitable result of a materialistic technology, then certainly one may argue that even our best efforts toward church growth are likely to be only feeble protests against an overwhelming tide of indifference.

Frankly, I wish that I could be as optimistic as Dr. McGavran about the probabilities of church growth. One cannot doubt the statistics on population growth or the gains in literacy, but the ideological conflict with non-Christian forces seems destined to become much more discouraging. Rather than riding the wave of Western colonial expansion (which contributed greatly to the increase of Christian churches throughout the world, but at the terrible cost of confusing Christianity with Western culture and all that this implies), Christianity faces three highly competititve forces: (1) rising nationalism (with little room for anything not strictly indigenous); (2) revived and aggressive indigenous religions (Buddhism is now sending missionaries even to the United States); and (3) secularism, which has adopted the religion of "scientism," thus presuming to make God both unnecessary and irrelevant.

Some of the more radical proponents of the liberal view have even adopted the position that aggressive evangelism is really only a cloak for cultural imperialism, and that to claim that Christianity is unique or ultimate is intellectual arrogance.

For some persons a functional substitute for growth has been the ecumenical movement, though this is certainly not true of most of those associated with ecumenical developments. On the other hand, "getting together" may have provided a false sense of expansion and vitality. Actually, it would seem that most ecumenical movements have resulted more from external pressures than from any basic desire for union; psychologically, the fear of engulfment from outside, more than the desire for fellowship, has prompted these rapprochements.

Nevertheless, regardless of the motivations that have given rise to such developments or the extent to which they may have been shared by all the participants, there are two very important hopeful developments in this liberal view of church growth. First, there is a high degree of self-criticism, resulting from exposure to one another's views and from facing up to the threat of an increasingly hostile world; secondly, there is a growing biblical realism, which insists on taking the Bible seriously, even while often interpreting its message critically and mythologically.

In contrast with this view that extensive church growth is not to be expected in the immediate future, there is the other extreme which would contend that, even though in some places in the world the Church is growing (often at an almost unbelievable rate), one cannot and must not expect any substantial growth in the *true* Church. Many of these persons, some of whom are known as "dispensationalists" of one or another variety, insist that the organized church is basically apostate, and that any growth it experiences is merely a sign of its increasing apostasy. The members of the true Church (by which they usually mean either the members of their own particular denomination or the "invisible Church") are under biblical admonition to "come out from among them and to be separate." Real fidelity to the Lord consists primarily in qualitative perfection and spiritual growth, rather than mere expansion of numbers, since the elect are always a small voice crying out in the wilderness of apostasy. Of course, this does not mean that the members of such churches refrain from missionary work. Quite the contrary; in many situations these persons give themselves far more to the cause of church growth than do those who hold the more liberal viewpoint, for they feel compelled to snatch the brands from the fire and prepare the bride for the coming of the Lord. In fact, the only way that some persons feel they can help to bring about the Lord's return is to guarantee that there is at least one convert from every tribe and nation.

In several instances missionaries with this viewpoint have been almost shocked to find that the results of their efforts were not merely a few isolated converts but real "people movements" in which thousands have accepted the Good News. As a consequence, these individuals have often had to re-examine their theology of the Church. In doing so, many have looked to see what other Churches and missions have done; the result has been a deepening concern for the Church in all its manifestations, and a return to a more central biblical position.

Between these two rather extreme viewpoints there have been a vast number of churches (some with rather diverse theological orientations) which have tried in varying degrees to preserve distinct sets of contrasting views about the nature and function of the Church. For example, they have realized that it is a refuge for the saints (ordinary members) as well as a rescue operation for the lost. It should preserve a model for life, but at the same time be identified with the life of the world for which Christ died. Believers must "come out from among them," but must also "go out to win them." The Church must thus be not only incense but salt; not merely a light on the hill (to which men must climb up) but a lamp for the path; and not only preparatory (what Professor Guy calls "root"), but also reaping ("fruit"). This means that the church must not only build centers, but must diffuse itself out into society. It must have institutions, but only as instruments by means of which it reaches out to men and women.

Too often individuals have attempted to espouse the cause of one or another of these viewpoints to the total disregard of the opposite and complementary element. At times, this may be justified for the sake of a corrective in the development of a particular situation, but one cannot and must not say that it is *either/or;* rather, one must contend for *both/and*. This inclusion of both viewpoints at the same time must not, however, be regarded as merely trying to harmonize the irreconcilable or attempting to work out some balance or compromise. The differing orientations must be kept in constant tension, for the tug one way or another must be determined by the needs of the situation. Different circumstances and different people require different approaches. The cure of a particular problem may not lie with the abandonment of institutions (though this may be required in some extreme circumstances), but in seeing to it that the institutions become truly the instrument of the Church for serving the world and not merely "bait" to get people into the Church.

A Componential Analysis of Conflicting Viewpoints on Church Growth

If we are to understand the real significance of the conflicting viewpoints on church growth, it is not enough merely to argue one position as over against another. We need to apply some technique by which we can obtain some more integrating perspectives, and for this a "componential analysis" based upon certain significant descriptive dimensions is perhaps the most meaningful. Accordingly, in this discussion we have chosen to look at these differences in terms of four sets of binary values: (1) self vs. other, (2) qualitative vs. quantitative, (3) personal vs. impersonal, and (4) individual vs. group.

Certain views as to the proper nature and function of the Church emphasize the "self" in contrast with the other individual. In other terms, certain aspects of the Church's work may be said to be introverted (or centripetal) while others are extroverted (or centrifugal). For example, "revival" in the traditional sense of the term is primarily focused on the "self," while evangelism reaches out to the "other." Similarly, shepherding concentrates on the "self" while discipling extends the ministry to "others."

The qualitative and quantitative contrasts are easily recognized in the distinctions between sanctification (or perfecting) and conversion. Though conversion does involve radical qualitative changes in the individual's life, nevertheless the total effect of a conversion upon "church growth" is essentially quantitative, while emphasis upon sanctification is aimed at qualitative changes as such. Similarly, a program for upgrading the ordained leadership of a church is primarily a qualitative change, while programs focused upon lay activities are generally quantitative.

Contrasts between personal and impersonal foci may be said to concern people vs. institutions, the congregation vs. facilities for worship, and man vs. instruments—e.g., medicine, education, and agriculture. Where people—the congregation—and individual men and women are the primary focus of concern, one may describe the program as person-oriented; where the institutions of the church (e.g., hospitals, schools, demonstration farms) and the church building itself are principal objects of interest, the program is essentially impersonal.

The accent on the individual may be illustrated in the parable of the one lost sheep which is sought after, and for whose rescue there is such rejoicing. At the same time one must recognize that the life of the flock (the ninety and nine) cannot be overlooked; this is the group orientation. When a church highlights the importance of individual decisions and guidance, the focus is on the individual; when the principal concern is for group decisions and the guidance of the "church" as a whole, then quite rightly the group element is dominant.

These four componential descriptive dimensions are of course not mutually exclusive, but actually intersecting and in a sense interpenetrating. A particular organization within a church may be primarily concerned with reaching out for other persons—not essentially for quantitative purposes, but for qualitative gains, as for example in laymen's training programs. The techniques employed by such a group may be largely impersonal, since they depend primarily on published literature and normal educational techniques; the ultimate purpose of the program may be not so much reaching individuals as making them feel that they truly belong to a fellowship.

We cannot expect and should not try to arrange these four sets of factors so that they will be in perfect balance. Rather, they must continue to exist in a constant state of tension, for one is not really effective or valid without the others. For example, the exclusive emphasis upon any one feature (or combintion of them) could result in something rather (1) ineffective or sterile or (2) tyrannical and ruinous. But rather than aim at some passive balance between the two sets of factors, what we really need is a situation in which one factor "sparks" its opposite. That is to say, each leads to the other. Emphasis upon "self" (in revival) should immediately lead to concern for "others" (in evangelism); and conversely, discipling should inevitably develop into shepherding. In a true sense, each element in the binary sets serves its opposite. The ministries of the church in medicine, education, and agriculture should bring men to an awareness of the claims of Jesus Christ, and those who are so reached should themselves seek to discover ways in which they in turn can become instruments of the church in ministering to the world.

Different proportions of these contrasting sets of factors are needed for different situations in the growth of the Church, since growth is never one long steady increase for any long period of time. The Church, like any organization, experiences times of growth and times of retrenchment, waves of expansion and consolidations, reflecting the fundamental laws of entropy—revival followed by cooling off and evangelistic outreach followed by periods of internal strengthening. For both in the individual church as well as in the history of the Church as a whole, growth does not come as a steady process, but in surges of new strength and alternating periods of apparent weakness.

If, as we have suggested, both sets of factors in the descriptive binary dimensions are necessary—that is to say, if one must have both "self" and "other," qualitative and quantitative development, personal and impersonal elements, and individual and group orientations—then true growth cannot and must not be defined merely in terms of such factors as "other," "quantitative," "personal," and "group," as is so often the case. Effective and lasting growth can only be attained through a fully integrated orientation, and accordingly neither the health nor the significance of the Church can be determined merely on the basis of statistical expansion.

At the same time, it must be clearly understood that these opposing factors do not exist merely for each other. That is to say, the group does not exist merely for the individual and the individual for the group. Similarly, the purpose of quantitative gains is not for the sake of qualitative improvement, nor is quality bettered for the sake of further quantitative expansion, though of course in one sense the reciprocity of these opposing factors is important. Actually these single factors exist not for the sake of their opposite number but for the glory of God, for whether the development in a Church at a particular time may be characterized chiefly as "self" or "other," qualitative or quantitative, personal or impersonal, individual or group, the total purpose is not merely for the sake of the Church, but for the higher glory of God's eternal purposes.

Understood in this light, the study of church growth can be something far more vital and valid than is often the case.

PART TWO

Sociological Issues

V

HOMOGENEOUS POPULATIONS AND CHURCH GROWTH

DONALD ANDERSON McGAVRAN

Church growth must be founded on sound theology, as we have seen in the last three chapters. It must also take sociology into account, as we shall see in the next two. God desires church growth; it takes place among men.

The Sociological Fact

Men meet the Church not only as isolated individuals but as multitudinous societies, each made up of interrelated individuals who are often of one blood, skin color, language, dialect, or section of the country. They are apt to have the same customs, economic standing, and general religious outlook. Each of these societies may be considered a homogeneous unit. It is comprised of one kind of people. It conditions the individual, it makes up his mind; to some degree it controls him. It gives meaning to his life. Among the many aspects of human society none is more important to church growth than these homogeneous units of mankind.

This technical term, *homogeneous unit,* is elastic. On occasion it indicates one tribe living in one specific territory and speaking its own particular language, as for example the Tzeltal tribe of Indians in Mexico. On occasion, however, it describes a much larger and less limited population. For example, urban middle-class Japanese could be considered a homogeneous unit, especially in contrast to rural Japanese, living in hamlets and cultivating rice. Indians in the Fiji Islands—as compared with Melanesian Fijians—are a homogeneous unit; but in India itself the homogeneous unit would be, not Indians, but one caste of Indians in one language area.

Some homogeneous units have vague boundaries, as in the case of the upper classes and the masses. Whether borderline cases are classes or masses may be difficult to determine. Nevertheless, the main distinction is clear. There *are* upper classes—aristocrats and large landowners; and there *are* the masses—the burden-bearers and laborers.

Some homogeneous units are tribal populations. The Uhundunis of West Irian (Dutch New Guinea) speak a distinct language, occupy a distinct territory, and believe themselves descended from one ancestor. They marry within the Uhundunis. Other such groups are the Tyal of Formosa, the Uraons of Bihar, and the Karens of Burma.

Some homogeneous units are linguistic. The two and a half million Mandarin-speaking Chinese who as refugees moved into Taiwan in 1949 from mainland China form a society distinct from the 7,000,000 Amoy-speaking Taiwanese. The Hindi-speaking Indians in Trinidad are another example. These populations are not tribes, yet they are homogeneous units.

Orthodox Jews in the United States and castes in India are homogeneous units of great people-consciousness. Though not restricted to any locality, they guard their status as separate peoples. They ostracize any who marries an outsider and have complex eating rules which set them still further apart.

To the foreigner, the inhabitants of any continent often appear all of one sort. For Americans, the uniformity of our own population heightens this illusion. In America all people from Atlantic to Pacific speak English, dress alike, drive similar cars, read the same newspapers, and respond to the same stimuli. If they are females, they curl their hair and paint their lips. But the rest of the world exhibits much less uniformity. There are eighty-eight different Indian languages in Mexico, in addition to Spanish. A typical city of 50,000 in India will have one hundred or more castes in it, each of which intermarries strictly within itself and eats only with its own people. The multitudinous tribes of Congo divide the 13,000,000 people of that land into hundreds of separate "compartments." The Church will grow differently, not only in each different culture, but in each of the many homogeneous units that make up most human cultures.

The Mosaic

The general population may be compared to a mosaic. Each piece of the mosaic is a society, a homogeneous unit. It has its own way of life, its own standards, degree of education, self-image, and places of residence. Even city "melting pots" on examination turn out to be a series of wards or neighborhoods, each occupied by a different homogeneous unit. The *vecindads* of Mexico City are occupied by people from different sections of Mexico, different *haciendas,* different valleys and plateaus. The population of each *vecindad* marries largely within itself and its place of origin. The towns of Ghana have many *zongos* where tribesmen of the Northern Territories come to live—in ghettos as it were—each *zongo* housing people of one tribe. Even in New York City one finds Negro, Irish, Puerto Rican, Cuban, Jewish, and numerous other characteristic areas.

Many Christian leaders accept the fact that primitive populations are made up of diverse tribes, each separate and each a homogeneous unit, but only the very perceptive see that this is also true of many advanced societies. I was talking to a missionary from Cuba who spoke of being indebted to my book, *The Bridges of God*. Surprised, I replied, "*The Bridges of God,* which speaks of tribes and clans, is scarcely applicable to Cuba, is it?" He answered, "Cuba does not have tribes, but it does have extended families, kinship groups, and webs of relationship. Christianity spreads through these just as it does through tribes." Christian mission needs to recognize that homogeneous populations are common and have enormous significance for church growth.

A Theological Straw Man

This sociological viewpoint is factual and reasonable. Men do live in societies. Normal man is man in society. Not only is man enriched by his relationships; in a very real sense he is *composed* of them. As Tennyson says, "I am a part of all I have met." Furthermore, the Bible often considers men in their corporate aspect as homogeneous units. It calls men "peoples" or "tribes." God called Israel out of Egypt—a whole people. Moses blessed tribes —"And of Gad he said, 'Blessed be he who enlarges Gad. Gad crouches like a lion. He tears the arm and the crown of the head.' " Isaiah sings of his people, "Awake, awake, put on your strength, O Zion."

The New Testament also sometimes speaks of Israel's accepting or rejecting salvation (Rom. 9:31; 10:21; 11:26). It speaks occasionally of the Gentiles as homogeneous units (Rom. 9:30; 10:19; 11:12). Luke 24:47 says that "repentance and forgiveness of sins should be preached in his name to all tribes [*ta ethne*]." The Great Commission, using exactly the same two Greek words, commands Christians to "disciple the tribes."

This sound sociological procedure is what John Collier, the noted anthropologist, has in mind when he writes:

> Colonizer, missionary, moralist, idealist, crusader for causes, it is to the hurt of all you love, to the defeat of your own purpose and the ruin of men, if you, plunging toward your aim in terms of individuals, aggregations of individuals, or external material results, ignorantly or impatiently by-pass the society.*

Christianization of groups does not in the least exclude individual conversion. Strictly speaking, individual conversion is both theologically and psychologically the only kind possible. A

* John Collier, *The Indians of the Americas* (New York: Mentor Books, 1960), p. 78.

group, a clan, or a tribe is not a person. It does not have a mind of its own. It can make no decision. It can neither "confess the Lord Jesus Christ" nor "believe on Him." It cannot be "justified by faith." What is commonly called group conversion is really *multi-individual conversion.* It is many individuals believing on the Lord at the same time in shared knowledge of the joint action and mutual dependence on each other. Such multi-individual action has very different marginal meanings and results from lone individual action taken in the teeth of group disapproval.

Recognizing homogeneous units and claiming them for Christ emphasizes the biblical goal of discipling the tribes. This is usually a long road. Seldom does an entire society accept the Lord at the same time—or ever. Usually a people movement is made up of a series of small groups accepting Christ. Each group is well instructed. Each is composed only of individuals who personally accept Christ. Each, while forming, is abandoned by those who do not want to become Christians. Each moves into the Christian faith when it gets ready. In one year three or four groups comprising less than a hundred believers will be baptized. The next year perhaps another three or four groups will be. So, year by year, the movement of a people will proceed in the direction of discipling the tribe.

Many Christians disdain "discipling the tribes." Group conversion seems to them theologically unsound. Influenced by such historical incidents as the conversion of Constantine in 312 and Clovis in 496, they think it implies baptizing a king or chief who is then followed in unthinking fashion by his sheeplike people. But men today do not follow kings. In few tribes does the chief have enough political power to make a decision for his people. In some tribes undergoing a people movement, the big chief even remains non-Christian, fearing that to become Christian might weaken his political power. Without the chief, individuals in each group continue to think through the Gospel and, in *multi-individual decisions,* a series of small groups, come to Christ.

The "theological unsoundness of people movements" is a straw man. Objection to them is based on a false understanding of what actually takes place in tribal movements to Christ. With this straw man out of the way, it should become increasingly possible for Churches and missions to identify the various pieces that make up the general population and to carry out the Great Commission—to disciple the tribes.

Varying Responses of Homogeneous Units

People movements, however, are only one way in which churches grow; the structure of society affects church growth at every level. Even in our relatively homogeneous American society, churchmen are recognizing that certain denominations flourish in certain sections of society and not in others. An inescapable and significant truth is that society not only has a mosaic type of structure, but that different pieces of the mosaic are responsive to the Christian message in different measure.

Our Lord found Galileans much more responsive than Judeans. Eleven of His chosen twelve were Galileans—only the twelfth, Judas Iscariot, was Judean. When the Christian Church started to grow among the Gentiles, despite the fact that Paul considered himself an apostle to the Gentiles and concentrated on them, almost all the church growth described in the New Testament took place in synagogue communities, comprising not only racial Jews but also converted Jews who had been born Gentiles, and "God-fearing" Gentiles who liked Judaism but had not yet subjected themselves fully to the Law. Paul writes to the Romans saying, "I have often intended to come to you . . . in order that I may reap some harvest among you as well as among the rest of the Gentiles." However, the epistle to the Romans could have been intelligible only to such Gentiles as were well versed in Judaism and the Old Testament Scriptures—i.e., to the Gentile fringes of the synagogue. The general Gentile population of the Roman world was a mosaic. Most of its pieces were highly unresponsive to Paul's message. But one piece—the Gentile synagogue community—*was* responsive. The Holy Spirit led Barnabas and Saul to recognize this community and concentrate upon it.

A modern illustration of the responsive piece of the mosaic is the samurai in Japan between 1870 and 1890. Most of the Japanese population was completely unresponsive to the Christian faith. But the samurai, for reasons well described by Winburn Thomas in his book, *Protestant Beginnings in Japan,* were responsive. They turned to Christianity chiefly as individuals, but also in bands such as the Kumamoto band. The degree to which Christianity in Japan began as a middle-class movement, largely among the samurai, is often forgotten. It indicates that social structure operates in advanced as well as in primitive societies.

In the Roman Catholic Philippines, Evangelical missions have built up large Churches, not because they had large accessions from animistic tribesmen, but because the Aglipayans were highly responsive. The Aglipayans comprised the most patriotic Filipinos, including men of culture and wealth as well as those of humble status. At least three millions of them left the Church of Rome in 1902 in a massive revolt. Their leaders took them into rationalistic unitarianism, but some of them longed for something more Christian and heard the Gospel gladly. The existence of this responsive piece of the mosaic made the Philippines a very different mission field from, let us say, Ecuador or Colombia.

The population in India is a classic instance of a mosaic, since it is made up of many different recognizable castes and tribes. Some of these, like the Nagas and Churas, are responsive. Others, such as the Banias and Kayasths, are not.

The beneficiaries of the social order in any land seldom espouse new moves. The *haves* usually resist change more than the *have-nots.* Moses would have had difficulty leading Egyptian aristocrats into the desert; but God sent him to the slaves, who heard him gladly. All populations today are composed (roughly speaking) of the classes and the masses. Of the two, the masses are much more likely to be receptive than the classes.

Each Homogeneous-Unit Church Grows Differently

Rev. O. A. Waltner, Executive Secretary of the General Conference Mennonite Board of Missions, recently made a careful study of the Mennonite Church in India. He found it was not one Church, but consisted of four separate Churches in four separate homogeneous units, each growing at its own rate, with its own problems, flourishing best under its own sons, and needing its own organization. The common parent of all four Churches was the American mission.

The Methodist Church in India, to take another example, is not one Church but a loose assemblage of Churches speaking either Urdu, Hindi, Marathi, Telegu, Halbi, or one of several other languages as distinct as Finnish, English, and Chinese. Indeed, each "Methodist language Church" should not be regarded strictly speaking as one Church but as a fellowship of Methodist denominations, each growing in some piece of the mosaic.

So long as mankind is divided by separate languages, "one Church" can be a reality in a special sense only. For all practical purposes, "one Church" is inescapably a cluster of denominations more or less loosely bound together by common allegiance to a creed, a form of government, or its Head. The desirability of organizational unity is not, however, something I wish to assert or deny; I am emphasizing rather that, no matter how much organizational unity there may be, the functioning organism—the "one Church"—*is in fact* a fellowship of Churches each growing in its own homogeneous unit.

Each constellation of congregations in a separate homogeneous unit is a Church. Each Church grows at its own rate. Its growth potential is determined not only by God's blessing but also by its history, leadership, degree of devoutness, and skill in proclaiming the Gospel. A Church may have great opportunity to grow, but no *will* to do so. Or it may have the will to do so, but be committed to a type of mission work which will not multiply churches. Or it may have the will, knowledge, and skill to grow, but be in a population where the opportunity is very small. Each Church and mission grows, therefore, at its own rate.

Each Church and mission has its own growth problems. Church No. 1, for example, may have arisen from the middle class, with a stress on education, and now—when the masses are open to the

Gospel—may be tied to unresponsive middle classes. Its problem is how to switch from the classes to the masses. Church No. 2, on the contrary, has grown hugely from among the masses. Its growth problem is how to create leaders and lift its members fast enough to keep up with the general increase of learning. Church No. 3 has still another problem. The homogeneous unit it most readily reaches accepts the rich services offered by the Church—education, medicine, agriculture, and the like—but steadily rejects Christ. In order to grow, what should each Church do? Each faces not only a different set of problems but a different set of historical precedents. Hence each has a different growth potential.

Method Influences Unit Growth

Each homogeneous-unit Church flourishes best under its own leaders. This principle is often not understood. Nationalism discerns readily enough that a Church in Africa will grow better under African than European leaders. But nationalism and modern mission sometimes do not perceive that a Church among the Masai in Kenya, for example, will not flourish under converted Kikuyus. Kikuyu pastors are good for Kikuyu churches. They are not good for Masai congregations.

This is why the General Conference Mennonite Church insists that its pastors among Gara Christians be of the Gara caste. Garas speak to Garas better than other castes can. As tribes and castes merge into larger unities, the Christian Church should be careful not to press this principle too hard; but of its basic truth there is abundant evidence. For example, Keith Hamilton, Research Fellow of the Institute of Church Growth, when working on church growth in the high Andes, found that although Spanish-speaking *Mestizo* pastors were better educated and more advanced than Aymara pastors, they seldom made Aymara churches multiply. Multiplying Aymara congregations, he observed, were led by Aymaras.

As Christian mission faces the multiplication of churches in thousands of pieces of the societal mosaic, it must plan not merely to transfer authority from the white missionary to the Asian (for example), but from the "Asian in general" to leaders of the homogeneous unit in which a given Church is burgeoning.

Furthermore, each denomination in each homogeneous unit needs its own organization. The executive secretary of the synod, annual convention, or church union needs to be recognized by the congregations as being "one of us." An excellent example is found in the Baptist Church in Burma. This Church is, in reality, an association of four separate denominations—the Sgaw Karen Church, the Pwo Karen Church, the Burmese Church, and the Hills Tribes Church. Each has its own separate annual convention, with its own elected officers from the constituent denomination and its own year-round offices and executives.

This is not wasteful duplication; this is realistic organization. To merge these separate conventions into one might well place in positions of control men who had no real feeling for the situation and whose leadership would limit church growth in one or more of the denominations. The principle is clear. Each piece of the mosaic develops a Church which grows at its own rate, has its own problems, and flourishes best under its own leaders and with its own organization.

Sociology Commonly Ignored

This detailed statement of the sociology underlying growing and nongrowing Churches has been necessary because Western Churches and missions (and national leaders trained by them) commonly ignore sociology. They speak and act as if, for example, all residents of Mexico were equally immersed in a Spanish-speaking middle-class culture. They plan a course of action as if all residents of India were emancipated members of the higher castes. By ignoring social stratification and disregarding homogeneous units and webs of relationship, they constantly diminish the effectiveness of their presentation of Christ.

They do this with the best of intentions. Some of them believe that Christianity (being a religion of brotherhood) cannot afford to recognize separate clans or tribes. In Christ, they exclaim, there is neither Jew nor Greek! Some feel it a great mistake to permit Christianity to be identified with the lower classes, animist tribesmen, the masses, or the illiterate. They therefore engage in only one kind of presentation—to their own peers! Some believe it sufficient to proclaim Christ to men in general. As this is done, they feel, the Great Shepherd will recognize and call His own. "We are resolved to know nothing of homogeneous units and tribes and castes," exclaimed one pastor. "We preach Christ. Those destined for salvation are converted."

Christian mission today is particularly prone to ignore sociological differences because of the confluence of the ecumenical and Afericasian emphases. Ecumenicists are vigorously engaged in building bridges of understanding between denominations and look with horror on any further division of the Body of Christ into separate Churches. Afericasian Christians have little sympathy with Eurican denominational peculiarities (be these Anglican, Roman Catholic, or Baptist). Facing non-Christian religions, Afericasians tend to think of themselves as simply Christian and to love the strength which comes with unity.

Whatever the reasons, a clear-cut recognition of the fragmented character of society, a realistic acceptance of the fact that some populations are more responsive than others, and a skillful proclamation of the Gospel to the peoples whom God has prepared, is often lacking. In investigations of church growth in many lands, we have found that recognition of the sociological matrix is a key factor. The lack of this recognition is one of the most crucial issues in church growth today.

Recognizing the principle that "each piece of the mosaic develops a Church which grows best at its own rate and flourishes under its own leaders" does not necessarily clash with either the ecumenical or Afericasian emphasis. Just as the Methodist Church in Brazil is a different administrative unit from the Methodist Church in Chile, and these both in turn from the Methodist Church in Angola, so the linguistic and ethnic differences can be recognized and used as highways of the Spirit without breaking the unity of the Church. In 1910 the Anglican Church in India was one Church, but it had a separate diocese for Chhota Nagpur, precisely so that the Uraon and Munda Church there might grow up under its own leaders, facing its own problems and adjusting itself to the unique opportunity to multiply churches among the Uraons and Mundas. With the increasing Christianization of peoples and the continual erosion of local peculiarities, the need for separate administrative machinery (separate Churches) will diminish, not increase. We need neither fear nor fight it.

How Churches grow in various strata of society can be known today with exactness. Churchmen no longer need to be limited to a knowledge of what their own Church and mission have done, and they can readily determine whether their own traditional policies have yielded less growth than they should have. Church growth analyses can be made in any situation. True, up to the present time, not many have been made. The promotional concerns of modern mission—that money be raised and the mission enterprise presented in a favorable light—have prevented realistic appraisal of church growth in many places. In others the conviction that they are doing all that can be done has operated to prevent missionaries and churchmen from conducting a searching inquiry into the question of growth. But today such thinking is giving way to clearheaded determination to find out exactly how much church growth has been obtained and whether any more can be. The place of social structure is being more and more recognized. Magazines such as *Practical Anthropology* are making valuable information available.

It cannot be too strongly emphasized that sociological and anthropological knowledge is *not* Christian mission. Mission is always the proclamation of Jesus Christ and His atoning death and empowering resurrection. Sociology and anthropology serve mission as tools. They help the Church to know where proclamation will be most effective. They identify those social units that are ready to hear the Good News and act upon it.

Bearing on Theological Education

At the present time, scores of thousands of ministers, catechists, pastors, and evangelists are being trained in hundreds of Bible schools, theological training schools, and theological seminaries. These men will soon occupy positions of leadership in the younger Churches.

Theological training should educate them as to social structure. They must be led to see homogeneous units, social strata, and webs of relationship as highways along which the Gospel can advance. Their courses should describe cases where skillful use of the forms of society has led to a rapid growth of the Church and others where a disregard of the *ethne* and the *eicoi* that make up mankind has arrested church expansion.

It is essential that potential pastors study the structure of their own section of humanity. Lutheran seminary students in Madagascar, for example, need to have not only thorough knowledge of the Tanoshi and Tandrui, but also of the ways in which church and mission adjustments to these homogeneous units have either accelerated or retarded the increase of church membership. Even in Japan, where homogeneous units are at a minimum, seminarians need sociological understanding of Japanese society, and especially of the extended families and clan villages. The latter are made up of landowners and so far have been highly resistant to Christianity. Up till now, conversions in these villages have come from the younger brothers who will neither inherit the land nor stay in the village. Seminary students in Japan should know how whole family units in similar clan structures elsewhere in the world have come to Christian faith.

The problem is complicated by the fact that churches in the West during the last century have largely disregarded social structure and yet have grown enormously. This is partly because the West has become highly individualized and highly uniform. Social stratification is minimized by democratic ideals, compulsory education in a standard language, and many other factors. So theological seminaries in the West have not taught how to use social structure in the growth of the Church. When Churches of Africa, Asia, and Latin America imitate this aspect of the West in their theological training, they deny themselves essential knowledge, for their societies are multitudinous and still fragmented and far from uniform. At this point the Churches of Afericasia must dare to be different; at this point they must dare to be themselves. Their ministers in training need careful instruction in homogeneous populations and church growth.

Where Applied Anthropology Is Useful

Examples from various countries show us where and how the use of anthropological insights and sociological skills and habits of work can help Christian mission meet and solve different sets of problems connected with the expansion of the Church.

Often a given Church and its assisting mission will be working with one section of society for purely historical reasons. Eighty years ago, the early missionaries believed that a certain class of people, section of society, or part of the country was approachable. They began to work among them. Since then the people they chose have proved resistant to the Gospel, but the Church continues to "work with them." Thus the Church is not only working with people in general but with a resistant segment of society. It does not obey the injunction of Matthew 10:14: "And if any one will not receive you or listen to your words, shake off the dust from your feet as you leave that house or town." Rather, this Church lays siege to the resistant segment by providing auxiliary services.

"For example," said a national pastor in India, "in 1900 in exploration we hoped the intelligentsia would respond. As a means of winning their affection and respect we opened a school. The people who send children to our school, we said, will become disciples of Christ. As an exploratory move, this was no doubt the wisest thing to do in 1900. But in 1963, when it is clear that the intelligentsia has not responded and that another class is open to evangelization, we continue to work exclusively with the intelligentsia by means of the school. They take our education and reject our faith."

Another good example comes from Mexico. In one of the most resistant sections of Mexico a certain Church and its assisting mission were working with Mexicans in general in about 2,000 *pueblos* and *ciudades*. The Church did not begin to reach all 2,000. But as it dipped in here and there, it found a high degree of indifference. Recently it discovered that a few dozen *pueblos* had fought the Roman Catholic Church on the land issue in 1928 and were still very cordial to the Gospel as presented by the mission. In four or five of the *pueblos* little Protestant churches had arisen in 1929. For over thirty years the Church and mission, committed to working with "Mexicans in general," had not visited most of the few dozen villages very friendly to the biblical faith.

Another crucial point is where a Church or mission is breaking out of the exploratory stage and facing new groups of Christians who need spiritual care and pastoring. Here insight as to homogeneous units and church growth is urgent. Each such Church needs to develop leaders out of the social stratum being discipled, but often it appoints pastors from another stratum.

For example, an old, well-established denomination in a large Asian city finds that one of its mission stations is beginning to get little "congregations" in the countryside. It seems normal to provide "pastors" for these congregations from the "earnest Christian youth" among the "older" congregations. The Church describes the situation in these stereotyped and vague terms, and the new congregations that have arisen in one homogeneous unit get shepherds from a different one. The new churches do not thrive; they grow only a little. They may even apostatize. The Church and its assisting missionaries resign themselves to bearing their cross and working in a very difficult land. They might have had a markedly different experience if they had taken the trouble to create leaders for the "countryside churches" from among countryside people.

In another case a large mission at the end of fifty years has 80 per cent of its work in a small, somewhat resistant tribe of 30,000 in which there are now 5,000 Christians; and 20 per cent of its work in a large, responsive tribe of 500,000 in which there are 100,000 Christians. In this situation there is urgent need for the secretaries of the board and officers of the Church to accept the actuality of sociological facts and differential rates of growth.

Take a case where the bulk of the work is located in big centers —where the Church is not growing and will not grow. By "the work" is meant the church headquarters, the educational institutions, the missionary concentrations, the training institutions, and the like. In these centers the population is composed either of different homogeneous units or of an individualistic industrial society. In both cases the population is different from the responsive homogeneous units where the Church has grown, is growing, and will grow. Church leaders who will not use the anthropological tools described above are likely to miss the key to church growth. They are likely to continue in the hopeful but as yet unproved assumption that churches multiply where much mission work is done.

A final area where education concerning homogeneous units and church growth is necessary is in those places where the civilizing function of Christian mission is confused with discipling. In a certain *pueblo* in Mexico, a small congregation had arisen in an Indian tribe under the Wycliff Bible Translators. It was growing normally. Its leaders, informants to the Translators, had studied the Gospel with great care and felt the Evangelical church was their own. They conducted worship in their own Indian language. They had been leaders of their people and they continued to be leaders in the small, new, nondenominational church. Then the Translators, feeling the need for links with existing Churches and for more effective and experienced leadership, asked a Mexican denomination to send a preacher to the promising young church.

The Mexican minister who came did not know the Indian language. He was quite sure Evangelical citizens of modern Mexico should not be using outlandish Indian tongues in public worship. To do so branded Evangelicals as backward. It kept them from Spanish, the language of the nation. Many of the new Christians had at least a smattering of Spanish. Bible and hymnbook were available in Spanish, not in Indian. So the minister simply instituted—with full approval by the Christians themselves—Spanish as the medium of worship. It was the right move from the point of view of "civilizing." It was the wrong move from the point of view of church growth. Church growth stopped.

The Mexican pastor made the move and persisted in it because he confused civilizing with discipling. Nor did he understand the mosaic that makes up the Mexican population. He considered tribalism an obstacle to Christian progress. In reality it is a highway along which Christ's cause can roll.

In another case, missionaries faced great possibilities of growth in two tribes. Some felt strongly that the emerging Church must have nothing to do with tribalism. "Our task," they said, "is to break down these tribal distinctions. Pastors must forget which tribe they came from. They are Christians. The tribe is the great enemy." Fortunately the majority of the missionaries realized that Christ breaks down the dividing wall of hostility *after* men confess Him and become His disciples. They saw that the wiser policy was to press ahead with building two clusters of congregations, each going forward under its own pastors. They looked forward to the time when both tribes would meet as Christian brethren. In this case substantial growth continued.

The battle for brotherhood and the battle for civilization must not come before discipling. Brotherhood must come as a fruit of the Spirit rather than as a prerequisite for membership. Advances in culture, in use of the national language and the like, are not properly speaking a part of Christianization at all. But where they are considered desirable, every care should be taken that achieving them does not retard the growth of the Church. The mores of each piece of the mosaic are precious to it. Christian mission must avoid not merely Westernization but especially such elements of nationalization as are inimical to church growth. Christian mission exists to bring men into redemptive relationship to Jesus Christ rather than to assist national policies of assimilation.

SUMMARY

I have compared society to a mosaic and pointed out the value of recognizing it as such. Perhaps it will aid Christian mission everywhere to return to and expand the Lord Jesus' vivid agricultural metaphor. Let us view the human race, not as one vast field, all parts of which are planted to one crop, receive the same rainfall, and are equally fertile; but as a patchwork of kinds of soil—sandy and clay, fertile and unfertile, dry and wet, rocky or rich, planted to a great variety of crops in many different stages of ripeness. Christian mission will be more successful as it proclaims Christ with a full and exact knowledge of the types of land and kinds of crops. This is as necessary for the Churches of Afericasia as for the Churches of Eurica. The lack of this background is one of the most crucial issues in church growth today.

VI

CULTURE AND CHURCH GROWTH

EUGENE A. NIDA

Some Christians tend to think of church growth almost entirely apart from the cultural contexts in which it has taken place, as though it were some special supernatural phenomenon involving only the struggle between the forces of God and the wiles of the devil. There is no doubt that church growth is directly related to the total plan and purposes of God; but at the same time it is equally true that God has evidently determined to work within the structures and patterns of human society, even as He works out His purposes for an individual's life in accordance with the physical and psychological principles He has created to govern it. Of course, the cultural factors that influence church growth are not the only elements to be taken into consideration, for the Church is a distinctive phenomenon in the world, in that it is God's chosen instrument for the accomplishment of His will. On the other hand, the history of the Church and its growth or decline in various parts of the world do reflect in large measure the fundamental features present in the rise and fall of any and all types of human institutions. For this reason a careful consideration of the social and cultural issues in church growth can provide significant insights into both what has happened in the past and what is likely to occur in the future.

While recognizing that the Church is in very large measure influenced at many points by the society and culture of which it may be a part, one must also be constantly aware of the fact that it is in a real sense a supracultural institution—in the sense that both its history and its dynamic are the outworking of the plan and purposes of God through the work of the Holy Spirit. Therefore, when we have evaluated some of the human factors involved in church growth, we cannot presume to have said all there is to say or to have described all the relevant factors. We must admit that the operation of God's Spirit cannot be subjected to direct observation, nor can we set up controlled experiments or presume to apply statistical indices of success or failure. The recognition of these facts should make us humble about our judgments and at the same time keep us from undue generalization, whether from statistical or cultural evidence.

The Attitudes of Society Toward the Church

Within any country the attitudes of the society toward the Church are important in determining its rate of growth. If, for example, a given Church is a majority institution of long standing, fully accepted by the society, the official status accorded it and the personal prestige enjoyed by its leaders are apt to result in a Church whose membership rarely increases more rapidly than the over-all increase of population. It often remains almost static. In such circumstances, Christian behavior becomes largely a matter of habit and Christianity itself gradually becomes more and more nominal. If such a Church is threatened by internal heresy or external force, it generally adopts totalitarian techniques to remain in power. Whenever a majority Church resorts to force and totalitarian methods, one can be quite sure that its power is by no means as great as it appears on the surface; leaders generally do not become totalitarian out of strength, but out of weakness.

In most instances, there is an overwhelming reaction against such a Church and its power seems quite broken. But despite its apparent loss of membership, influence or power, the Church usually remains a more significant force than most persons suppose, for after such a rejection it purifies its practices or adjusts its methods, and then often returns with renewed vigor and increased strength. It is such a resurgence of the Church in Russia that apparently so greatly concerns the Communist ideologists; while in Mexico a chastened Roman Catholic Church is gradually undergoing some internal reform and regaining considerable power.

Statistics concerning church affiliation and organizational strength are often misleading. Even when a Church has been apparently discredited and banished, its strength is almost always greater than official statistics would imply; a persecuted minority Church may have several times more "sympathizers" than the number of persons listed on the rolls. On the other hand, whenever there is an "official state Church," the number of active participants is always much less than the number of nominal adherents. Accordingly, the attitudes of people concerning a Church not only affect the number of its adherents; they even tend to mask the true status of its membership and influence.

When a Church is a minority institution, but of long standing—e.g., the Coptic Church in Egypt and the Orthodox Church in South India—it has generally worked out some sort of *modus vivendi* whereby its interests are protected in exchange for a willingness to remain relatively static. Such Churches may actually constitute closed castes, with new members almost entirely restricted to those born into Christian families. Thus, acceptance is purchased at the price of limiting the Church's evangelistic zeal, for growth would induce jealousy and fear, and hence result in persecution.

Where a Church is a minority movement of recent origin and its presence appears to be a threat to the social or political structure in power, it is often completely rejected and systematically stamped out. Thus, at the time of the Inquisition in Spain and Belgium, thriving Reformation movements were almost totally destroyed. Where the rejection does not result in banishment or destruction, one usually encounters a cycle of "adjustment." At first, little notice is taken of the Christian Church. In fact, people may show a kind of esoteric interest in such a novel foreign institution, as occurred for example in the early contacts of the Japanese with Christianity. In fact, until it appears disruptive and subversive, people usually accept a new religious institution as a curiosity—as so many people in Britain appear at present to be interested in Mormonism. When, however, it comes to constitute a menace to indigenous institutions—and opposition may be touched off by imagined as well as by real threats—the reaction of certain power blocs within the society is to destroy, banish, or isolate it; that is, to force it into a ghetto existence.

If a Church is permitted to remain physically within an area, there is often a period of sporadic opposition which tends to diminish gradually. In most instances the initial violence is the worst; later the Church is usually accepted, for as a minority institution, with little obvious power and an ethical standard of turning the other cheek, it generally appears innocuous, even though its opponents see in it no positive value. This acceptance of the Church usually begins by allowing some individuals among its members to enjoy certain privileges in the majority society; then gradually church members are accepted into the local community as a group, first on an economic level, then politically, and finally socially.[1]

Though the Church may be rejected by the majority group within a country, a minority group may find in it a rallying point for opposition to the dominant power. For example, Christianity had a strong appeal to the Karens and other tribal groups in Burma, not merely because these animistic peoples were more "impressionable" than the Burmese, who were Buddhists, but because in their opposition to the Burmese the tribal peoples found in Christianity an ally against their traditional oppressors. At the same time, Christianity enjoyed the prestige of indirect official blessing by the British colonial government, which encouraged the work of foreign missionaries and subsidized Christian schools.

The phenomenal growth of the Church among some minority groups can most certainly be attributed to certain strong cultural pressures. In Formosa, for example, there was only a handful of

[1] Patterns of acceptance on a national level are often quite different.

Christians among the aboriginal hill peoples before World War II, while at the end of the war more than 5,000 were awaiting baptism, and there are now more than 62,000 church members among these Malayo-Polynesian peoples. Their rapid turning to the Gospel is certainly genuine, but undoubtedly their motivation arose partially from opposition to the Japanese. Prior to the war the Japanese had subjected the hill peoples to intensive indoctrination in Shintoism, while discrediting the native spirit worship; but the people quite naturally resisted and resented the highhanded methods of the Japanese military. When the people finally learned about Christianity and realized that this faith was particularly opposed by the Japanese, many became intensely interested in it as a means of showing their opposition to their Japanese overlords, if for no other reason. So widespread was the sympathy for Christianity as at least one form of counterattack against the Japanese that the Christian movement spread, not according to the more usual pattern of family lines, but over whole geographical areas and political entities.

This same story of the appeal of Christianity to minority groups who find in it, not only a defense, but also an opportunity for recognition, has been repeated many times, e.g., among outcasts in India, Koreans under Japanese control, and Bahutus in Ruanda. In a few instances, however, even a majority group has been ready to accept Christianity without a cultural struggle. For example, before the coming of the missionaries to Hawaii the people themselves had become disillusioned with the excessive taboos and increasingly meaningless ceremonies of their own religion. Accordingly, with only token opposition from white beachcombers, liquor dealers, and some ship captains, the Hawaiians adopted Christianity in a unique kind of people movement.

In some situations circumstances prompt a group to adopt a special religious form of expression with alacrity. For example, the Piro Indians, a tribe of about 1,000 persons in the eastern part of Peru, had been won over to Seventh-Day Adventism; but the results were rather disastrous for the people; the extreme dietary restrictions made it almost impossible for them to exist without violating regulations concerning "unclean meats." Accordingly, when other missionaries came and explained to the Piros that observance of these dietary restrictions was not necessary for true followers of Jesus Christ, one entire group left Seventh-Day Adventism almost immediately.

That the attitudes of a society toward the Church can affect its growth is quite obvious, but sometimes it is difficult to realize the full implications of such public opinion. For example, a careful study of the rate of growth of the Christian Church as a whole in Japan parallels quite closely the attitudes of the Japanese toward the West in general and the United States in particular. If church growth can be thus correlated with attitudes not directly tied to the institution of the Church itself, it is natural to conclude that direct opposition or encouragement can have a very marked influence on the rate of growth. Where opposition is direct and intense, it can result in the elimination of a Church, as in Formosa after 1660, when a group of more than 6,000, who had been converted by early Dutch missionaries, simply disappeared during the following two or three generations.[2] In the Mesquital Valley of Mexico, a movement which now numbers more than twenty churches, with more than 2,000 adherents, made practically no progress for the first ten years, for persecution was simply too severe to permit growth.

On the other hand, a certain amount of opposition can be of great value, as was certainly true in the evangelistic campaigns of Dr. Harry Strachan in Costa Rica in 1927. Such opposition has been a continuing element as well in promoting the distribution of the Bible in Latin America. Here, after each denunciation of the distribution of the Scriptures by the Roman Catholic hierarchy, the Bible societies have almost invariably experienced an appreciable increase of interest in the Word of God. Again, the "right amount" of opposition often keeps out of a Church those who have less than worthy motives. As a result, the higher level of consecration and devotion attracts the more sincere inquirers. Moreover, opposition

[2] Hollington K. Tong, *Christianity in Taiwan: a History* (Taipei, Formosa: China Post, 1961), p. 138.

may help to define, more successfully than any preacher could do, the precise differences between a Church and the persecuting religious system.

In general, Christianity suffers less from frontal attacks than by indirect opposition, for the blood of martyrs always attracts the stronghearted; the indirect assaults of syncretism on the other hand (as in Japan), social ostracism (as in Islam), and long-term educational undermining (as in Russia) have been much more effective in preventing the growth of Christianity.

On some occasions the seeming acceptance of the Church, at least in limited ways, actually gives a false sense of growth. In Japan, for example, although for a number of years almost 10 per cent of the graduating classes of many Christian schools accepted Christianity, few remained associated with the Church ten years after graduation. For one thing, their identification with Christianity (including their baptism) was generally connected with the school chapel and not their home-town churches, so that they associated Christianity almost exclusively with their formal education. In addition, Christianity has been traditionally known as "Christ-teaching," so that one could be associated with this "educational" activity without apparently too much personal commitment. Even more important has been the fact that Japanese adults usually take for granted that young people will be intellectually and emotionally "radical." Accordingly, whether in politics or religion, youth is expected to experiment and dabble in strange and esoteric systems. However, once the younger generation is married and takes on the responsibilities of adult life, it is expected to adjust rapidly to the paternalistic patterns of Japanese society and to give up the extravagances of youth. The very fact that the adult sector of society does not usually take seriously the conversions of youth means that reabsorption into Shinto and Buddhist ways of life is more easily accomplished.

In Africa Christianity has, seemingly, often been enthusiastically accepted more for the educational advantages it offers than for the religious content of its doctrines. On a continent where, during the last century, almost 90 per cent of educational programs were undertaken or supervised by missions, it is quite understandable that motivations were desperately mixed. Moreover, it can be readily understood that apparent sympathy for Christianity would turn to hostility when national leaders saw a threat in the alliance of colonialism and Christian missions. These developments do not mean that the work of Christian schools is unjustified, but they should alert us to the fact that church growth which occurs predominantly among students can be an illusory and deceptive phenomenon.

Relationship of the Church to Society

Not only is church growth vitally affected by the attitudes of society toward the Church; the rate of growth is also often closely dependent upon the structure of the society in question. If, for example, a Church is witnessing to a face-to-face society (one in which most of the people of a village, town, or tribelet know one another), it usually either reaches the entire group or splits the society along clan or family lines. Furthermore, as Dr. Donald McGavran has pointed out so effectively in *Bridges of God,* the predominant pattern of growth in such societies is along family lines. At the same time, however, such a system of growth contains an almost automatic, built-in "stop point." In Latin America, for example, a number of churches in small towns and villages tend to grow rapidly to the size of 50 to 100 members, but almost immediately thereafter growth stops, and for a number of years there may be little or no increase. A careful study of such churches reveals that in many instances the church has grown to include almost all the members of one dominant family, including the various ramifications by birth, marriage, and godfather relationships. But when a church is built around one family, it is rare that any equally important family will come in. In fact, in many situations the most critical time in the growth of such a church is the point at which it has included most of the members of one family, but has not succeeded in attracting influential members of other important families. Family connections can thus be not only bridges for growth but also blind alleys of stagnation.

In an urban society, church growth is more likely to follow geographical, occupational, and friendship lines than family ones. Thus, in a class-divided urban society, Protestant churches are likely to consist primarily of a single class. This is so not only because birds of a feather flock together, but also because interpersonal communication, which in social structures is primarily within a class rather than between classes, is much more likely to be effective within a single class structure. In Latin America this class character of Protestant churches is quite pronounced. Such churches also exhibit a great deal of upward mobility, for the adults are generally concerned about saving their money rather than spending it on liquor and vice, and they insist on educational advantages for their children. Accordingly, such a group rather quickly moves up in the socioeconomic scale, and it is not long before it loses social contact with the very class out of which it has been formed; for the people not only aspire to better circumstances, but also rapidly break off the godfather relationships with their extended families. Such groups become increasingly introverted, and little by little the original "bridges of God" are abandoned or destroyed.

The limitations of class and national groups are perhaps nowhere more evident than when one is dealing with minority groups. In one area of northern Argentina, missionaries found that the Argentinians were very difficult to reach with the Gospel; accordingly, they concentrated attention on some Bolivian day laborers, who had everything to gain and little to lose by associating themselves with the Protestant missionaries. Moreover, they were away from their home towns, so that the social pressures and local loyalties which normally would have prevented openness to the Gospel message were not operative. But though the work grew rapidly, the very preponderance of Bolivians in the churches acted as a strong deterrent to the entrance of Argentinians, who regarded the Bolivians as quite inferior. The socially disenfranchised Bolivians were attracted to the churches in some measure as a protest against their own low status, even as the outcasts have been attracted to Christianity in many areas of India. However, the presence of such persons in large numbers within a particular Church acts as a block against further growth among the culturally dominant class.

In discussing these problems of church growth in terms of classes, castes, and families, and the complications that occur because of the social structures involved, I do not wish to imply that the missionary or church leader should coldly calculate the socially most advantageous group or class with which to work. Quite the contrary. The debt of the Church is to all men—Greek and barbarian, bond and free. Nevertheless, one must reckon with the fact that in communicating to all men there are certain inevitable factors, many of which vitally affect church growth.

However, the attitudes of the Church itself toward the structure of the society are often even more important in church growth than is the actual structure itself. For example, a Church may have a "closed attitude" toward its own social structure. Thus the Armenian Evangelical Church, whether in America or France, is not making any significant advance, for it is so tied to its ethnic origins, both in language and culture, that it can only assimilate those who have grown up within the framework of Armenian life. Any appreciable growth can only be at the expense of the Armenian Orthodox Church. Within the United States we have had a number of ethnic Churches—e.g., German, Norwegian, Dutch, French, and Swedish—all of which at various times have faced extinction unless they adjusted themselves to the new currents of life and outgrew their "ingrown" heritage.

Isolation from the world, however, may take the form of ethnic identity or a holier-than-thou Pharisaism which insists upon such complete separation from the world that members lose their vital contacts with the society in which they live. Such groups may succeed in drawing in a few antisocial individuals who are themselves badly adjusted, or whose sense of guilt forces them to expiate their sins by "behavioral escape" from the world—a kind of Protestant asceticism which takes pride in its insulation from evil. But whether the isolation is ethnic or cultic, it almost always results in a static Church.

Some churches, though they neither retreat from the world nor isolate themselves, may nevertheless fail to grow simply because they have little or no concern for evangelization of the communities around them. They are largely self-contained and happy to be counted among "the elect and the elite." Such churches exist not only in some of the smug suburbs of America, but may also be found in such cities as Monrovia in Liberia, or Tokyo.

There are, however, many churches which are vitally concerned with their witness. In fact, they exist primarily for the sake of mission and practice little or no selectivity as to those to whom they appeal. The Iglesia Interdenominacional, with headquarters in Portales, Mexico City, is one such Church. It has more than 8,000 members within the city itself and several hundred churches and preaching points throughout Mexico. This intensely organized church in Portales, under the leadership of a group of lay pastors, has a job for every member, with special concentration on visitation and invitation of people to the church, and with constant follow-up and a "big-brother-in-Christ" program to guarantee the spiritual training and growth of new members. This church, despite its origin in one of the poorer sections of Mexico City, appeals increasingly to a higher class of individuals, with the result that its leadership is of unusual quality and its potential ministry almost unlimited.

External Preparatory Factors Influencing Church Growth

In studying church growth, one is often struck by the importance of certain external factors. Many of these may be largely negative in character, as for example when an area is largely abandoned by a rival religious system. In southern Mexico the Roman Catholic Church had in effect given up the Tzeltal Indian area, because it was almost impossible to support priests on the income received from the Indians. The people were still emotionally attached to their Christo-pagan forms of worship, but they were spiritually undernourished and uninstructed. Accordingly, when Protestant missionaries went in they met with a remarkable response.

The fact that a rival religious system is morally corrupt may also help to stimulate interest in a new religion. All people recognize certain basic ideas of equity and justice and also instinctively react against exploitation, especially when it is carried on in the name of a religion that teaches high ethical standards. Certainly the widespread corruption in the Byzantine Church in the eighth century was an important element in the rapid spread of Islam, for many Christian communities, thoroughly disillusioned with their nominally Christian rulers, welcomed Moslem overlords.

Certain developments seem to trigger interest in the message of Christianity. For example, among the Palawano tribe in the Philippines a Church numbering more than 5,000 members developed within a period of about eight years. Part of the reason for this rapid development was the thorough discrediting of the leadership of the old men only a short time before the coming of the first missionaries. As a result, many of the young men were only too ready to join in this "new way," which seemed to provide the only positive answer to the pressures of the outside world.

Perhaps the most obvious negative preparation for receiving the Gospel exists where a minority group finds in a Church or its missionaries support in their struggle against a majority or dominant group. Certainly this has been true of many peoples, from the Totonacs in Mexico, who regarded Cortez as their savior from the Aztecs, to the Congolese, who often treated American Protestant missionaries with conspicuously greater respect and favor than the Roman Catholic missionaries, who were sometimes regarded as agents of the Belgian colonial government.

External preparatory factors may also be of a positive nature. For example, the famous Karen legend in Burma about deliverance to come through persons bringing a black book on the wings of a great white bird came to be applied to the Bible, as the long-lost and much sought-after book, and the sailing vessel that brought the missionaries, as the prophetic bird. Among the Valiente Indians of Panama the ecstatic utterances of an old medicine woman were undoubtedly important in convincing some of the tribesmen that they should become Christians. Sometimes these so-called preparatory legends or prophetic utterances are manufactured after the event. For example, among the Palawano in the Philippines some old men insisted, after the relative success of the first missionaries, that this coming of a white man with a new message of life was actually prophesied by an old shaman of the tribe. This was prophecy after the event, but its telling certainly encouraged the growth of the churches.

Internal Factors Influencing Church Growth

In general, three internal factors most influence church growth: (1) the effectiveness of the minister or missionary as the source of communication (i.e., his understanding of the people, degree of identification, spiritual leadership, and possession of a winning personality); (2) the relevance of the message; and (3) the qualities of those who receive it—e.g., their fidelity to the message, their spiritual growth, and their aggressiveness in witnessing. There is no doubt about the importance of these three principal elements in any communicative event. The role and power of the communicator is fundamental to any interpersonal relationship. Again, the fact of the message being immediately translatable into personal and community life, rather than remote or unconnected with daily needs, is undoubtedly an important element in church growth. The inherent characteristics of those who receive it are also highly significant in evaluating a group's potential for expansion, for it is obvious that a church made up of culturally dynamic, expanding people is much more likely to increase than one whose members are mainly timid and introverted.

At the same time, it is a mistake to think of church growth too simply in terms of the source, the message, and its receptors, for the situation is actually very complex. One must, indeed, reckon with at least four important sets of factors, each of which in varying degree influences appreciably the character and rapidity of growth. These basic elements in determining culture change are: (1) the nature of the change, in contrast with the existing patterns; (2) the level of change—that is, in this context, the various levels of religious behavior; (3) the types of values involved in such changes; and (4) the kinds of persons concerned. Each of these factors is involved in different ways in all stages of religious experience, from discipling to perfecting. Moreover, these basic factors are spread out over relatively long periods of time, since they not only act as preconditioners to change but also frequently determine the degree and intensity of it. Hence, they must be looked at carefully, and their varying degrees of potential for culture change must be assessed.

1. *The nature of the change in contrast with existing patterns.* The way in which a particular cultural change contrasts with existing patterns of life is often indicative of its potential acceptance. For example, if one is merely concerned with adding a set of beliefs to an already existing system, the change is relatively easy to achieve. Adding Roman Catholic concepts to an underlying Voodooism in Haiti, or inducing Negroes in Dutch Guiana to become Protestants without disturbing their "bush religion," is not too difficult; for if changes are mere additions, involving no conflict with existing patterns of belief or behavior, the task of producing them is quite simple. Unfortunately, in a number of instances it is essentially through such "additions" to existing pagan beliefs that the growth of psuedo-Christian churches has occurred. For example, some of the pseudo-Christian prophet movements in Africa have developed with phenomenal rapidity largely because there has been no radical conflict with existing patterns.

A more complicated type of change involves hybridization, often spoken of as syncretism. I use the term "hybridization" here to highlight the fact that the combining of two or more disparate systems results not merely in a complex synthesis, but in a new and viable union, with its own powers of growth and reproduction. In Japan, for example, one new religion, called "Garden of One Light," is basically a hybrid, since it combines Christian and Buddhist ideals, such as the life of nonpossession, repentance, and abiding in God, the worship of a Supreme Being through all religious truth, a sense of love for mankind without thought of reward, and the establishment of a heavenly kingdom upon earth.

These interwoven strands of Buddhism and Christianity are represented symbolically by the Greek cross and the Buddhist swastika, combined into a circular figure with light emanating in twelve rays. In the Philippines the sect of José Rizal, the great national hero of liberation, is based upon a belief in the reincarnation in him of Jesus Christ, and in the possibility of addressing Rizal in prayer and hearing his voice speak from the inner sanctum of a chapel dedicated to him. This sect has now formulated a belief in his resurrection and has also attributed to him a miraculous birth. Such a hybrid movement, involving dominant themes of Christian ethics and national pride, has had a considerable appeal.

Since a hybrid faith catches on more quickly, there is always a tendency to compromise certain basic tenets of the faith in order to promote rapid development of a Church or a movement. For this reason any rapid church growth must be examined to determine the extent to which hybridization may have been a factor in its growth. For example, the rapid spread among western American Indians of the peyote cult, which identifies peyote with the Holy Spirit, is due in large measure to the hybrid character of the movement.

Substitution, in contrast with addition and hybridization, is a more difficult type of change to introduce. Nevertheless, it is the fundamental principle of all valid mission activity, for in most instances one cannot and should not attempt to eliminate a feature of a culture without first providing a functional substitute. For this reason, missionaries among the Chols in southern Mexico did not try to disabuse the people of their beliefs in evil spirits before telling them about the Holy Spirit. In fact, they explained to these spirit-fearing people how they could be freed from all fear of lurking demons and malevolent spirits.

The fourth, and by far the most difficult, type of change to introduce is elimination. Because of its difficulty, "perfecting" of the faith often comes very slowly, for perfecting involves not only positive ethical behavior, but also the elimination of negative, antisocial action, for which valid functional substitutes may be slow in developing.

2. *The level of change.* Since religion has three main different visible levels—ritual, beliefs, and the behavior sanctioned by the religion—it is not strange that changes in religious expression involve varying degrees of difficulty. Of these three levels, changes in ritual are the easiest to introduce. In the New World, early Roman Catholic priests found little difficulty in instituting changes of ritual, since often the new ceremonies were observed on ancient holy spots, in many instances with pagan idols hidden behind the altars. It is particularly easy to add a ritual, because often it seems simply an enrichment of culture. However, if one desires to change religious beliefs, the process is usually much more difficult, for beliefs involve fundamental aspects of the believer's relationship with the supernatural. Finally, if one attempts to impose a different kind of interpersonal behavior, especially one which conflicts with self-interest, the change is even more difficult to produce. The early Irish missionaries who attempted to evangelize northern Europe met with little resistance in the area of ritual or even of beliefs, but they spent several hundred years trying to introduce a form of Christianity which would in some measure subdue the violent marauding instincts of the Germanic tribes.

3. *The types of values associated with change.* In addition to the particular nature of the change, one must also be concerned with the values specifically associated with the change. For example, if a new form of religion is promoted as based on existing values, it is not too difficult to persuade people to become adherents. This promotion on the basis of values already held is the strength of the Soka Gakkai Buddhist movement in Japan, which, in existence only since World War II, already has an estimated two million members. Not only is it typical of Japanese Buddhism; it also incorporates an aggressive practice of forced conversion to the view that Japan's lost prestige will be regained when the adherents of this militant sect convince the whole world that the Japanese saint Nichiren is the "original and true Buddha." Similarly, the Zion movement in Korea has had a phenomenal growth to at least 100,000 followers since World War II. This semi-Christian movement, begun by a former Presbyterian evangelist, now includes at

least forty separate and remarkably prosperous businesses and a militant group of followers, who do not hesitate to use strong-arm tactics against opposition. The leader has built up his movement largely by appealing to the immediate values of economic security, combined with such typical shamanistic practices as producing rain, exorcising demons, healing any and all diseases, and smelling men's sins burning in hell while the individuals are still alive.

It is a good deal more difficult to build up a movement based on new values, even when these are related to immediate objectives. People are almost instinctively fearful of new values. The old values seem so much more relevant and meaningful to them. Accordingly, church movements that emphasize the essentially new values in Christianity normally grow more slowly than those that try to build a Christian superstructure on the foundation of existing pagan values. Of course, when the new values are shared by other persons, especially those who constitute a group with whom the convert wishes to identify himself, they are gradually assimilated by association. This kind of sharing is a natural fruit of fellowship and the sense of belonging within the church community. Usually little or no progress can be made toward the acceptance of new values unless the existing Christian constituency can give new converts a real sense of belonging. A failure in this regard is one of the acute problems in work among Muslims in the Middle East. Even when a Muslim is won to Christianity, only rarely will a church consisting primarily of converts from the Orthodox or Coptic Church fully accept him, for there is a longstanding and ingrained prejudice against Muslims, based on the suspicion that no Muslim would become a Christian except for ulterior motives. Even former Muslims who have been welcomed into these Churches are often socially ostracized or prevented from assuming leadership in them.

Social Organization and the Structure of the Church

In the study of church growth, analysis of the structure of the society in relation to the organizational structure of the Church is important. Traditionally, missions have had a policy of transplanting church structures; that is to say, the sending Church simply assumes that its own organizational structure is not only the best but the only valid form of church government. Accordingly, Baptists form churches with congregational authority, Presbyterians organize churches along presbyterian lines, and Episopalians quite naturally follow their own episcopal traditions. The result of such a procedure is often extremely confusing, for frequently no one of these organizational structures fits the form of society in the mission area. Of course, what actually happens is that, as long as the mission-sponsored churches are under the control of the foreign agency, they outwardly maintain the structure of the sending Church, though their actual functioning at least somewhat parallels the indigenous social organization. For example, in Japan churches may be developed formally along congregational, presbyterian, or episcopal lines, but they all tend to function like most Japanese social institutions—namely, under the paternalistic control of the pastor. Similarly, in Latin America there may be various forms of Protestant church organization, but in most instances these Latin churches reflect the strong tendency to *caudillismo* (domination by a strong personality) typical of Latin social institutions.[3]

The artificiality of imposing our own patterns is probably never more conspicuous than when, to take an extreme instance, Robert's *Rules of Order* is thought to be an indispensable part of indigenous church organization (one missionary in Africa actually translated Robert's *Rules of Order* before he had translated any of the New Testament); or when double-entry bookkeeping is regarded as an integral element in church stewardship. In fact, one missionary in Southeast Asia insisted that a Church of several thousand members could not be given freedom to make its own decisions because there was no "native" who knew how to keep books.

The basic tragedy in this discrepancy between form and function

[3] I do not wish to imply that in setting up a form of church government for a particular society one should blindly adapt the church structure to the forms of society. Quite the contrary, one should seek to introduce necessary correctives, but this can only be done by giving careful attention to the indigenous structure and by formulating long-range modifications.

is that it makes the Church appear to be an artificial organization, formally expected to operate in one manner but in reality functioning quite differently. This ambivalence not only introduces an element of hypocrisy into the Church itself, but also inevitably results in serious malfunction. The ill-fitting formal structure is often so strange and unwieldy that its very operation takes all or most of the energies of the local leadership, while the more important aspects of church growth are neglected.

On the other hand, it is possible for a form of church government to fit the local social structure so closely as to stifle new and creative leadership. For example, in certain areas of Africa, presbyterianism, which places extensive control in the hands of elders, has brought about a situation in which younger pastors and laymen find themselves almost entirely frozen out. Similarly, a Church which places considerable power in the hands of bishops can be readily subverted by self-seeking men, with a bishop assuming all the authoritarian prerogatives of a local pope.

Despite the obvious difficulties and opportunities for exploitation inherent in social structures congenial to indigenous forms of leadership, one must nevertheless regret the enormous amount of time and energy wasted in foisting ill-fitting church structures upon those who neither understand nor appreciate them. It is particularly unfortunate when such an organizational structure is presented as the only biblically sound method for developing a satisfactory church.

Perhaps the most instructive manner of studying the proper relationship of church organization to social structure is through an analysis of the ways in which indigenous Churches have developed, as to both form and function. By this, however, I do not mean indigenized Churches—that is, those which, begun by missionaries, have gradually been turned over to national leadership. Rather, the phrase "indigenous Churches" in this context designates those which have grown up without missionary guidance and direction. Although such Churches are often only one spiritual generation removed from the missionary cause, as it were, in the sense that their leadership has often been led to the Lord by someone converted through missionary enterprise, they are for all practical purposes entirely indigenous. In Mexico, there are four relatively strong Churches which fall into this category: *Unión de Iglesias Evangélicas Independientes, Iglesia Cristiana Interdenominacional, Movimiento de Iglesias Evangélicas Pentecosteses Independientes,* and *Iglesia Apostólica de la Fe en Cristo Jesús.* These organizations each have several hundred congregations, and though they were founded only about twenty-five years ago, they are all structured more or less alike. They have relatively strong leaders who represent a close psychological approximation to the old *patrón* system, but are for the most part amazingly close to their people. In general, the church structures are very loose, with a good deal of local authority and considerable vagueness about statistics. In fact, some of the leaders cannot provide adequate information about the very movements they head up, for their leadership depends far more on their personalities and spiritual gifts than upon well-organized and disciplined church structures.

In Japan, the Spirit of Jesus Church, founded by the Rev. T. Murai, claims 40,000 members and as such is the third-largest church organization in that country. Mr. Murai studied for some time in a Methodist seminary (though he did not graduate). However, he soon became dissatisfied with foreign-dominated church work and began his own Church, largely along Pentecostal lines, with strong emphasis upon healing, the Second Coming of Christ, and a literal interpretation of the Scriptures. In terms of church organization, Mr. Murai is sometimes spoken of as a "super-bishop," for he has the same complete control over his organization as do the leaders of some other new religions of Japan who exercise almost totalitarian authority. In the Non-Church Movement in Japan the organization is entirely informal, for it is in large measure a protest against the formal structures of the denominations. Nevertheless, in the strong influence the various Bible teachers have within the Non-Church groups one finds a ready parallel to the influence and control exercised by important Buddhist teachers, who demand and receive a large measure of loyalty and support from their personal disciples or adherents.

A rapidly growing Pentecostal movement among the Tobas of Argentina has a very loose structure by which the local churches are related more or less in the same manner as were the scattered hunting Toba bands before these Indians were subdued by government forces. In these churches there is a kind of personal attachment to the local "preacher," a relationship almost identical with the earlier dependence of the people upon their medicine man for spiritual guidance and healing. Such a Church is an easy victim of self-appointed prophets who create sporadic waves of enthusiasm, just as in pre-Christian times certain local shamans developed a wide following among those impressed by spectacular cures or prophecies.

Essentially the story is the same with all strictly indigenous Churches. Whether prophet movements in Africa or such Churches as the Little Flock or the True Jesus Church in China (both of which are now flourishing in Taiwan), their organizational structure closely parallels the patterns of the society out of which they come and of which they are a part. This parallelism has been characteristic of the Church throughout history; for the governing forms of the earliest church in Jerusalem were certainly a reflection of the Sanhedrin, since the leadership consisted of a self-perpetuating group of elders. As the Church expanded, especially among those acquainted with the governing structures of the synagogues in the Diaspora, the forms of church government, as indicated in the Didache, closely paralleled certain democratic forms of the Jewish synagogue. However, as the Church later moved out fully into the Greco-Roman world it readily adopted a type of episcopal structure which matched in remarkable detail the authoritarian elements in the Roman administrative organization. Later, at the end of the feudal period, some Churches in western Europe took on a presbyterian type of structure, modeled in large measure after certain aspects of the canton and clan structures of Swiss and Scottish life. At about the same time some minority Churches, which had imbibed a number of ideas from the Age of Enlightenment, insisted upon a congregational form of government, for the face-to-face relationships of the members were readily structured into the democratic organization of an extended family. These historical developments have not hindered some church leaders from a selective interpretation of the New Testament record which exclusively validates their own form of church organization. But the facts of history make it quite clear that indigenous Churches have almost inevitably patterned themselves after the social structures of their day. One must also recognize that over a period of time the organizational structure of a Church may have an appreciable effect upon a governmental structure, for there is a mutual reinforcement and reciprocal interaction in all such relationships.

For effective church growth, the organization of a Church must be (1) understandable to the constituency (most implanted church structures are entirely too complex to be easily manageable); (2) congenial to the social structure (it needs to fit the known patterns of human interaction); and (3) efficient in its correlation of form and function (otherwise it is artificial as well as deceptive). If a Church tends inevitably to develop a system of government paralleling the local social patterns, then it is highly important that these factors be recognized in the initial attempts to organize churches, so that they may develop in accordance with the social structure and not in contradiction to it. Further, if the church is organized along lines understandable and congenial to the local society, it is often possible to build in safeguards against abuse. If, however, the form and function of a church organization are too diverse, unscrupulous individuals "in the know" are able to use such discrepancies for their own aggrandizement, since they soon learn how to twist the forms to serve their personal ends.

PART THREE

Methodological Issues

VII

DEVELOPING BASIC UNITS OF INDIGENOUS CHURCHES

MELVIN L. HODGES

Indigenous churches and their basic units, so often talked about in missions today, are not primarily the result of organizational manipulation. Nor will organization develop basic units of indigenous churches. They are the result of life, of growth, of seed and harvest.

The Parable

Matthew 13:24, 37 reads: "The kingdom of heaven is likened unto a man that sowed good seed in his field. . . . He that soweth the good seed is the Son of man; the field is the world; the good seed are the children of the kingdom. . . ." The figures of speech used in this parable are of critical importance for the growth of the Church and for developing indigenous churches.

"The field is the world"—what clearer statement of purpose and scope could we ask for? In this world God intends the seed to produce a harvest. God wills harvest. This is the first essential for church growth. In spite of slow progress for the Gospel in some areas, and the discouraging fact that more people are being born into the world than are coming into the Church of Jesus Christ, yet we are promised a world harvest, which includes not only presently responsive areas but also the presently unresponsive. All the world is included: Africa, Latin America, Asia, the United States, and Europe; Roman Catholic, Protestants, Moslem, Hindu, and pagan worlds are all part of this field. Christ said there would be a world harvest. I encourage my faith by accepting this statement as a sure promise. God's mission of redemption to the earth is destined to triumph!

Good Seed

Good seed is the second essential for harvest. "A man sowed good seed." This figure of speech is rich in meaning for church growth. The seed here is not simply the written or the spoken Word as in the case of the Parable of the Sower earlier in the chapter. This seed is the Word made flesh, germinated to life by faith in the heart of a man. Children of the kingdom are seeds.

Seed produces a harvest. God's seeds are men. Converted men and women are His means for expanding His kingdom. Far too often we forget this! Some Christian publications give the idea that buildings are the chief requisite in church growth. In mission circles we often give the impression that money is the primary factor. What we could do, we say, if we had $50,000 to spend in our area! Then the Church would really grow! I am not one to say that buildings and money are not necessary for the growth of the Kingdom. However, the early Church started without either. Peter could honestly say, "Silver and gold have I none." The early Christians met in borrowed buildings, synagogues, schools, private houses, and the open air. No mention is made in the New Testament of building a place of Christian worship, nor is there any exhortation of Christians to do so. The emphasis all the way through was on the *seed*—men and women, Christ's men, the seed of a new kind of life. Christ did not say that He would build His Church if He had enough money at His disposal. He did say He needed seed. With the right kind of seed, we shall have church growth.

The comparison of spiritual life to seed is a happy one. Seed has within it a germ of life. A grain that loses its power of reproduction may be all right for flour but is worthless as seed, for it is unable to reproduce its own kind. Someone has said a small object can be made which cannot be distinguished from a grain of wheat by its looks, smell, or the quality of flour into which it is ground. But if sown and left for a day or for a thousand years, it will not produce a plant. It is not seed; it lacks the germ of life.

Seed produces according to kind. The first requirement for church growth on the mission field is for the Church at home to produce and send the right kind of seed abroad. As I have indicated earlier, the missionary, as the first seed of the Church, will reproduce his own type of faith and spiritual vigor in the life of his converts. Perhaps the reason that there is little church growth in some areas is because the seed sown has little vitality. Vigorous Christians produce vigorous converts. Yet many of us expect prayerless, feeble missionaries to produce strong, spiritually vigorous converts. I am fully aware that most missionaries are dedicated, hard-working people. But a person may be sincere, honest, dedicated, and hard-working, and still not have a vital spiritual life. Dedication to a task and fruitfulness are not the same thing. The first step in church growth is to have missionaries who are vital Christians, who will inspire in converts a true spirit of sacrifice for the Gospel and a burning passion for souls.

No good farmer plants seed and fails to cultivate and fertilize it. Yet how seldom do we take the time to nurture new converts in the things of God! We take their name and address, tell them to attend the new converts' class, and in due time baptize them. Do we take time to pray with them until the things of the Spirit are made real? Converts must be nurtured in a spiritual atmosphere. Teaching them a catechism is not enough. Only the Spirit of God can reveal the things of God. One way or another, we must provide the time and means for converts to learn of Christ through the Spirit. Let us teach them to really pray. In the atmosphere of a praying church the converts learn to partake of God's Spirit and thus become a good-seed-producing harvest!

Living Local Churches

Vital local churches are a third essential for church growth. Individual Christians must be bound together as working local units of the Body of Christ; they must together become the Church. The local church is God's chosen agency for evangelism and extension. This truth is emphasized in the New Testament. We are many members, but only one body. We must work together. This organism, the local church, should be just as vital and strong as the individual convert. I remember visiting a certain area where a mission had been active. A good number of converts had been won. Believers were scattered over the countryside, but there was no real church! These converts were helpless to carry on without the missionary. Only when the missionary came to their villages were there church services. Only when he spoke was there any evangelism. This condition existed for years. A great potential for the Kingdom was lost.

Jesus said that where two or three gather together in His name, He is there. Two or three are enough to begin a local church. They can meet together for worship. They can build themselves up in the Word of God. They can make a united effort to reach their unsaved neighbors. The church they form will be just as vital as their experience in following the Spirit and their knowledge of the Gospel permit it to be. What a shame to stop a group like that from growing because there is no mission-trained pastor available to lead them, or no missionary to visit them. Often we overlook something vital when we think of a church. Perhaps part of the trouble is lack of a true concept of what the Body of Christ is and how it functions.

Basis of Common Understanding

Now, if two or three persons or more are to work together, there must be some basis of agreement. This I consider a fourth essential. "Can two walk together except they be agreed?" the prophet asked. To walk or work together there must exist a basic common agreement of faith and objectives, understood by all concerned. The methods of working together must be agreed upon by those who participate. The Apostle Paul, writing to the Corinthian church, which had abundant manifestations of spiritual life and gifts but lacked unity and discipline, expressed his concern "that ye all speak the same thing . . . that ye be perfectly joined together in the same mind and in the same judgment." (I Cor. 1:10).

In the Assemblies of God in Latin America, our *Reglamento Local,* or "Standard of Doctrine and Practice," has proved invaluable to both individual Christian and the local church unit. The *Reglamento* is a collection of Scripture texts and statements concerning the Christian way and church life. It teaches every new convert the essentials of the Christian faith. He learns his responsibility as a Christian to the Church and to the world. This simple basis of agreement has proved to be so vital in our church expansion program that our missionaries in El Salvador attribute the rapid growth of the Church there to "Two things, first the moving of the Spirit; and the second, our *Reglamento.*"

The local church cannot be effective in its outreach if built on shaky foundations. It is like the man who put one chair on top of another and, standing insecurely on this shaky base, tried to drive a nail into the wall, but could give it only ineffectual taps. His wife said, "Strike a brave blow, husband!" He answered, "I cannot strike a brave blow on such a shaky foundation."

Converts cannot strike a brave blow in evangelism if they are on a shaky base. Such a standard as the *Reglamento,* in whatever form it may be presented, provides a basis for agreement among the members of a church, and indeed, a basis of fellowship for the churches in a given area. It provides a standard by which new members may be received into the local church and new groups into the fellowship of the churches in the area.

Objection may be raised that this imposes a foreign pattern on the local churches and therefore does not allow the Church to be truly indigenous. Paul had no scruples about giving the churches instructions. To the Corinthian church he gave teaching on morals, discipline, lawsuits, marriage, meat, the support of ministers, proper appearance in the place of worship, and the manner of partaking at the Lord's table. It is noteworthy, though, that he did not invoke the authority of the church of Jerusalem or even of the council. He worked out church problems by appealing to the authority of the Old Testament Scriptures, the words of Jesus, the conscience of the believers, and their sense of propriety. Paul saw to it that each Christian should find an answer that he himself understood, and accepted (see I Cor. 6:1–5; 9:9, 10; 11:13–15; 11:22–25). A standard imposed by the missionary may be observed as long as the missionary is present, but is likely to be disregarded as soon as he leaves. It is something foreign and has not taken hold of the mind and conscience. Converts should reach an agreement as a result of their own convictions by searching the Word of God and through the illumination of the Holy Spirit. It takes patience to sit down with men and lead them on until they find the Christian answer to their own problems, which are so often vitally related to their own culture. But there is no other way, if we are to have a strong Church which will truly be a "city set on a hill" in the midst of pagan wickedness.

Another objection which has become popular more recently is the concept that creeds, doctrines, and organizational patterns divide the Church rather than unite it. Strong voices today, raised in the interest of church unity, present the theory that doctrine is after all of secondary importance; that we must unite in service. There is, therefore, a tendency to reject doctrinal emphasis as divisive. In considering this, we must go to the New Testament for our answer. There were deep differences of opinion in Paul's day; yet Paul certainly did not omit teaching doctrine to the infant churches for fear of causing division in the Body of Christ.

One must regret differences which disturb the unity of the Church, but we cannot heal divisions by following patterns contrary to Scripture. Teaching doctrine to converts and uniting churches on a common agreement of doctrine and action is certainly the New Testament method.

Biblical Purpose of the Church

A fifth essential to church growth is a fully biblical understanding of the purpose of the Church. According to the Bible the purpose of the Church in the world is twofold. It is to be at one and the same time the "city set upon a hill"—the gathering together of the faithful, *and* the "salt of the earth"—the scattering of the faithful throughout the world. It is a "tower" of strength and refuge *and* a disciplined army going out to battle with a numerically superior enemy (Luke 14:28–31). To return to the figure of the parable, the Church is the barn into which the grain is gathered, but it is also *the granary from which* the seed is to be taken and sown in the field.

Here, then, comes a vital question: Is the seed to be stored or sown? Is the Church only a place where missionary or evangelist brings the sheaves he has gathered, knowing they will be kept safe until the coming of the Lord? Do we think our task is to win all the souls possible in one area and conserve these results by bringing them into a church, and then begin the process again in another area? Do we leave evangelism to a professional class of missionaries and trained pastors, forgetting that the entire Church is composed of children of the Kingdom who are the seed for future harvest?

In those areas in Latin America where the Church has truly progressed it is notable that the entire Church is fruitful seed. There is always a special emphasis on lay activity. Every convert is a witness and every Christian works not only within his church but in outstations and branch Sunday schools. He is a personal witness of his belief, extending the Church by his work.

Two methods of church growth may be illustrated by the strawberry plant. First a bird picks the ripe berry covered with little seeds and flies with it to a nearby tree. A portion of the berry drops to the ground, the seed germinates, and a new plant results. This corresponds to the planting of the Gospel in an area where there are no Christians, and might be called missionary evangelism. The other way the strawberry reproduces is by means of shoots or runners. As these reach out, perhaps a foot away from the parent, leaves grow up and roots go down into the earth. For a time the young plant receives nourishment from its mother. Then the connecting runner dries up and the new plant is on its own. Presently it also begins to send forth shoots. Each runner produces one, two, or three plants, until the whole area is covered with strawberry plants. This method corresponds to the activity of a church in raising up branch churches—a mother church producing daughter churches through lay workers' activity. The Church as a whole grows by both reproductive systems: seeds and runners. We need both to multiply trained missionaries and evangelists in new territories and to release the vital life in every group of truly converted people and help them reproduce Christians and churches.

A Christian friend in Estelí, Nicaragua, illustrates "runner reproduction." His work required him to travel by horse from the town of Estelí to San Juan de Limay, a distance of about twenty-five miles. As he stopped along the road for water and food, he was faithful in his witness for Christ. He usually spent the night at a rancher's home about twenty miles from Estelí. One Sunday, after this had continued for several months, the rancher saddled his fine horse and rode into Estelí to attend the church service. He surrendered his life to Christ that night.

The next Sunday he was back with his foreman, who also surrendered to Christ. I visited the rancher's home shortly after this. These two men were standing alone for Christ. The wives had not yet made their decision. After three days of instruction, we baptized the two men. Then the rancher opened his home for a young worker just out of Bible school. Within two years the church established in the rancher's house had grown to about 60 members. The believers were personally taking the Gospel message to the entire countryside within a radius of fifteen miles. The church moved into town and exists today. Another church has been started not far away.

The rancher himself was a quiet man. We could never persuade him to say a word in the church service, more than to request a favorite hymn. One day, when I was visiting his home, a cattle buyer came to transact business. There was an exceptionally fine yoke of oxen for sale. I came upon the two of them in the corral and, thinking to get an intimate glimpse of native life, drew near. The rancher was leaning on the back of one of the oxen and talking earnestly. Instead of praising the merits of his animals, his first words to reach my ears were: "What you need is to surrender your life to the Lord Jesus Christ as your Savior." I withdrew quietly. With a corral for a chapel and an ox for a pulpit, the rancher was preaching Christ in his simple way. Here was the secret. A runner from the church in Estelí took root and established a new church in a rancher's family, and then that new church was putting out new runners—reproducing churches of Christ.

Let me give you an instance of seed reproduction. A young lady in the eastern section of El Salvador who had fallen into a life of sin went to visit some friends in San Miguel. The friends took her to one of our services conducted by the local pastor. After ten days she went back to her home in the hills, a changed person. At home she could talk of nothing else to her family. Such wonderful songs they sang there! Such joy in the heart! After a few weeks the father hitched the oxen to the oxcart and the family went to the city for a week. They attended the services and the joy of salvation became theirs. As they were about to return, the man said to the pastor, "Now we have been here for a week. Now it is your turn to visit us. Up where we live there are many people that need the Gospel." So it was arranged, and in due time the pastor visited this family in the hills. The first word we had of what was happening was through a telegram sent us by the pastor: "Come and visit, revival." We went! The memory of that visit is still with me. Several families had been converted, and they welcomed us with the enthusiasm of newborn sons of God. Once again living seed had dropped into fertile ground and reproduced.

Often we erroneously regard each church as a storehouse for converts instead of a distributing agency. We think, sometimes unconsciously, that only people trained in our institutes and carrying our credentials can really win souls and establish churches. We overlook the tremendous potential in live seed. In order to realize the harvest, each convert must find his place in a church functioning as a soul-winning agency rather than as a storehouse—shall we say, at times cold storage?—for Christians. Every convert must become a Christian witness. Every church should be a center of evangelism. Every church should consider itself responsible for all the surrounding territory at least halfway to the next church.

The local church may send out its runners in the form of outstations and local workers. Outstations are established throughout the area wherever openings are found. The church officials designate stable converts able to give a clear Christian testimony. These local workers carry the Gospel once or twice a week to the outstations, which then develop into churches. Local workers develop into full-time workers and become students in our Bible schools. The young people's group, the ladies' society, and the Sunday school may all contribute to the extension of their church.

So much for the parable and the teachings that arise out of it. Let us now consider the creation of these basic units of indigenous Churches. What kind of training produces the kind of seed, church, and field God desires?

Training the Entire Church

The first most important task is to train the entire Church rather than a select few devoting themselves to full-time ministry. Our training must fill the artificial gap between clergy and laity. The whole Church is the Body of Christ and should function as such. Every individual Christian has his place and his ministry. All are not called to be preachers or teachers, but all are called to witness. The whole Church is an evangelizing organism. We have drifted very far from this concept in our churches in America, and it is therefore difficult for us to inaugurate New Testament church growth on the foreign field. We tend to train only the few who will become ministers. We neglect the entire Body, the army of witnesses God intends to bring the Gospel to every creature. Can we let such immense manpower go to waste and still expect to succeed?

Jesus sent out both the Twelve and "other seventy also." What place do we have for the other seventy in our training program? According to Acts 8 the apostles stayed in Jerusalem after the persecution that followed the death of Stephen, but the *disciples* scattered abroad and, fleeing for their lives, went everywhere preaching the Word. The Church was spread by refugee Christians.

We are missing a tremendous opportunity for the Kingdom by failing to develop a lay ministry. Let us remember that the worker is not required to have all the available knowledge before he begins to witness. One who teaches needs to be only one step ahead of those who are taught. The new convert can witness to the unsaved. Older converts can help the new converts. The pastor can help the deacons and local workers. Missionaries and Bible-school instructors can help pastors. Converts can become Sunday-school teachers; Sunday-school teachers can become lay workers; lay workers can become pastors. If all birds refused to sing because they could not equal the nightingale, the forest would be a silent place. One of my missionary friends, Ralph Williams, put it this way:

> When a farmer is harvesting tomatoes, he needs not only a truck with a driver, but for each truck several men with baskets who will hand-pick the fruit and bring it to the truck. There is no advantage in multiplying the truck drivers above the number of pickers. We need more lay preachers—more pickers out on the field. We have too often concentrated on training drivers.

A church in El Salvador was begun through the vision of a brother not in the least outstanding as a preacher. He did have a concern that his community hear the Gospel and for this purpose set aside a plot he owned. He worked ten years to build a chapel. During this time he and those working with him preached the Gospel. By the time the chapel was completed, it was filled with Christians. By our standards this man would be considered dry and uninteresting. He was not a creative thinker. He went over and over the doctrinal truths in the little *Reglamento*. He would preach on all the fundamental truths given there as well as on the responsibilities of each Christian to live as a testimony before the world and tell others of Christ. He would repeatedly have members of the congregation look up the texts and become familiar with them. Because he was not a strong preacher himself, he surrounded himself with men from the congregation who could help in the work. He had from ten to sixteen men who went around the countryside preaching the Gospel. As a result, every local worker and every deacon as well as most of the members knew how to teach the vital truths to a convert and how to prepare him for baptism and membership in the local church. Because they knew how, these deacons and workers went out and established churches.

The mother church became hedged in with churches planted by these men. Even so, during some twenty-five years the church did not lose its vigor. Local workers would enter the Bible Institute, but others would take their place. Thirty-five full-time ministers came out of that one church. Its sons are among the leaders of the national church. If one church that never had more than a hundred members can produce such results and contribute in this degree to the growth of churches in a country, what would happen if all churches could catch this same vision?

The Church of the Assemblies of God in the little country of El Salvador has grown from 78 congregations in 1954 to 270 in 1962. In the capital city in 1956 there was one church with approximately 100 in Sunday school. Today there are 27 churches in the same city, with 9,500 in Sunday school. In addition the local churches care for approximately 150 branch Sunday schools and outstations. This great harvest has been brought about largely by training members of the Church and pressing them into service as Sunday-school and lay workers.

Training All Possible Laymen

The Christian and Missionary Alliance in the Philippines has given us an excellent example of church multiplication by laymen. Byron W. Ross in 1960 writes:

> In the Sarangani District, the missionary found an impossible task before him: no roads, trails inaccessible to horses; no boat to reach the 250 miles of coastline. He leaned heavily on the Lord for guidance,

and God suggested the laymen of the area be gathered for teaching. Thus, Sarangani Lay-Preacher Training Institute came into being. At that time there were 9 churches and 5 backslidden laymen plus one Bible School graduate in Sarangani. As a result of the Sarangani Institute, there are now over 50 churches, 5,000 baptized believers, over 40 trained lay preachers, and this in seven years!

This growth resembled germlike multiplication. A layman would come for training, and on his return home be so enthusiastic for Christ that many would be saved in his home area, and a church was born. Other laymen, newly saved, desired training so they could serve Christ. They, too, joined Sarangani Institute, and when at home, went much farther into the interior to win souls and establish a new church.

The result of Lay Preacher Training—which means training all possible laymen—is first-century in magnitude. An Indigenous Church is developed which is:

Self-supporting. The laymen have their own farms or businesses, hence need no support from their local church. Offerings go 50 per cent local, 50 per cent district, in a specified ratio, toward building, and to help with district expenses.

Truly indigenous. The students stay in their own environment. They are not taken out to strange city life for long periods, only to be so changed that they do not want to go back to their former simple living. The Lord Jesus did not take His disciples out of the world to shut themselves up in the cloistered halls of a seminary, but led them right into life situations.

Self-governing. The lay preachers and their churches form an integral part of the district organization.

Self-amplifying. Neither the national Church, nor the district, nor the missionary makes any assignment of these lay workers. They are Spirit-assigned. If He asks them to go 15 kilometers on foot every week to pastor a church without pay, they gladly do it. From among those they pastor, others come for training, and repeat the process of spiritual reproduction.

Self-teaching. These trained men, standing in that wonderful relationship of New Testament prophethood under God, are capable of teaching in the Lay-Preacher Training Institute and communicating God's good truth to others. They can get along without a missionary in case of international tension.

This program of training the whole Church demands our best thinking. This is true evangelism, resulting in local churches which are living cells of Christ's Body. It is, in my opinion, the best hope for significant church growth and for evangelizing the world in our generation.

Producing Reproductive National Spiritual Leaders

The second most important part of training for church growth is producing reproductive and spiritual national leaders. Thriving churches cannot depend on the foreign missionary to provide the teaching and guidance needed by new congregations. The New Testament pattern is for the leader to come from among the converts. Missionary work does not end with winning converts, nor even with organizing the converts into churches. Paul's ministry produced leaders like Timothy, Titus, Luke, and others. We must train men not simply to maintain the churches, but to multiply them.

Many pastors and workers produced by mission schools have neither turned out real soul-winners nor manifested true spiritual leadership. While there are notable exceptions, many workers lack initiative and depend too much on the mission for guidance and financial support. Something has been missing, and it may be that neither the missionary nor the worker knows what it is. It is not necessarily lack of consecration, or lack of the love of God, or yet failure in diligent and energetic service—although few of us would claim we could not improve in this regard! What is this "something" lacking? I often find it can be explained by one or more of the following gaps in our training program.

There may be a gap between the intellectual and spiritual development of the worker. Too often we have trained the mind and have not been able to lead the student into the full life in the Holy Spirit.

There may be a gap between knowledge and practical ministry. We place a student in school and nurture him in a somewhat artificial climate. He is often too far removed for too long a period of time from the rugged life and problems he is to meet in the ministry. Some workers seem to feel that after they have been to school they are above pioneering a church or working in rural areas. Perhaps this is a reflection of the general modern movement toward the large cities. However, we cannot doubt that there is a measure of failure in our training program if the men we are training are unwilling to return to the churches and areas with which they are familiar and which present a great spiritual challenge. In this case, we are at least partially training them away from the task instead of for it.

We may have left too wide a gap between the clergy and the laity. Our training program should aim to put the entire Church on the march for God.

Our concept of the role that training workers plays in the development of the Church may be an inadequate one. Some train only to fill vacancies. A minister of a Latin American country voiced his criticism of our Assemblies of God workers' training program. He thought we were training too many prospective workers. His own denomination looked ahead and saw it would need seven more pastors. This is the number it trained. When a class finished seminary a place was assured for each one. There was no question of support or what this pastor would do. The well-intentioned criticism here was that we train more pastors than we have openings for, so that many have to fill inferior places or get along without support.

My answer to him was, "We are training workers for expansion. We do not expect merely to hold our own, but to train far more workers than we have churches. We believe this is the way that new churches will come into existence. A man trained under your static concept would not be expected to exercise personal initiative. Someone else would do the planning for him and finance his efforts. Can we hope to evangelize the world in any generation if we follow such a concept?"

What Must We Do?

I have the deep conviction that every deficiency in our work can be traced to a failure to follow the New Testament pattern. True indigenous church principles are in reality New Testament church principles. We may be completely orthodox in our *theology* and yet be a long way from the New Testament example in our *prac-*

tice. How easy it is to accept the established pattern as the right one! Yet experience is teaching us that the traditional pattern of modern missions is not sufficient to meet the demands of the day. We will never reach the world for Christ if we simply follow in the groove worn for us by our predecessors. The New Testament approach is *flexible.* It leaves room for the guidance of the Holy Spirit. Are we spiritual leaders of sufficient stature to be able to determine the mind of God for the problems of our particular field?

We must integrate our training program with the national Church. Its pace should be synchronized with the tempo of the national Church and its program should meet the true needs of that Church. There is a tendency for institutions to become an end in themselves instead of a means to an end. A missionary may feel that the Bible school is his particular sphere of influence and carry on quite independently of the national Church. The Bible institute may become an island isolated from the mainstream of the life of the national Church. But the Bible school must serve the national Church. The Church should feel that the training program is its own and that the trained workers produced are its own, not the mission's.

The workers should be trained to the task, not away from it! Some institutions seem to have for an objective the sealing off of the student from his ordinary life. The directors feel that it is necessary to separate him from communal life so that the school's spirit can be infused in him and his character can be built under the direct supervision of the school. Such separation may have advantages, but it is difficult to know how a student kept in the artificial climate of a theological school for three years or more can make the proper adjustment to the demands of rugged pioneer work when his schooling is finished. In the New Testament we read of effective on-the-job training. Jesus taught His disciples, but He also took them with Him. When He said, "Look on the fields, the harvest truly is great," He was in the midst of human beings who could be won. The harvest field was not something found on a missionary map of the world, but visible in the needs of the sick and sinful surrounding them on every side. Jesus taught His disciples, then sent them out to preach and to heal the sick. When they were confronted by failure, as in the case of the man with a lunatic son, He gave them further instruction. He taught them "on the job." In the 19th chapter of Acts we find that Paul had a training school in Ephesus. He taught them two full years. Lest anyone think this was classroom instruction only, the statement that follows reads, "So all Asia heard the word of the Lord." Certainly Paul himself did not take this message personally to all Asia. He taught others. With on-the-job training, the workers and elders raised up under his ministry accomplished this tremendous task.

Tailor the Program to Fit the Need

We must tailor our training program to fit the need. If unlearned converts feel the call of God, we must provide the elementary training needed so that they can fulfill their ministry. We should not neglect the older converts. In New Testament times, the Church laid hold of the more mature converts and these became the elders. Some had ministry in the Word and others helped govern the Church. Because we cannot give these men proper training under our present set-up, we are inclined to neglect them. By so doing we set back the development of an indigenous Church by ten or fifteen years, perhaps longer. Consider the benefits of short courses in Bible schools. For years the Assemblies of God have experimented with terms of varying duration. At present we have settled for a four-month term. This particular period has proved its worth. Note the advantages: (1) mature workers can attend, since it is for a short period out of the year; (2) the worker does not need help to support his family, since he can return to his farm and raise a crop between school terms; (3) he does not lose contact with his people and customs; (4) he gets practical experience while he is learning; (5) if he is pastoring a small group, this relationship need not be terminated, but only interrupted, while he attends school.

In El Salvador the present course of study includes four such terms of four months each. In order to make better use of our buildings and take care of a greater number of students, we have divided the school year into two sections—the first and the third terms study at the same time, but in separate classes, for four months; then, later in the year, the second and the fourth terms come in. We do not allow the first term student to go immediately to the second term of studies. He must leave the school and be active in the churches for an interim period. This gives him sixteen months out of school before he takes his second course of studies.

To come to the first year, the prospective worker must show promise of usefulness. To qualify for the second term he must have had experience as a local worker. By the third year, only pastors of experience are attending. Often it requires five to eight years for a man to finish his studies, but we do not lose him from his area, and his studies mean much more to him after he has had several years of experience in the actual ministry. We shall probably add two more terms to this curriculum as the workers develop further.

Our students are required to have a weekend ministry. As a result of their activities, many new churches continue to come into existence. In 1960 every student who left school had a pastorate already prepared by his own activities during school. Within thirty miles of Santa Ana, where the school is located, we have now about one hundred churches. Some of this has been accomplished by Bible-school students during their time. The greater part, of course, is the result of the self-multiplication of the local churches.

Three Areas of Training

The local church. The training of workers does not begin in Bible school or seminary, but in the local church. Pastors carry on a regular workers' training program in every church, instructing lay preachers and establishing outstations. This is on-the-job training where it counts! A part of the Bible-school institute program is to furnish the pastor with materials for this local training.

Regional short courses. These take lay training to areas and workers that cannot come to the central Bible school. Several churches in one region get together and send students who will become Sunday-school teachers, deacons, and lay workers. Each church contributes its share to the support of the course of perhaps two weeks. Bible-school classes are held in the morning. The afternoon is dedicated to visitation in the area, with each student passing out literature, giving invitations, and in other ways doing personal work. Each night an evangelistic rally is held. This is a most fruitful program. It gives teaching to men who cannot otherwise receive it. It strengthens the local churches. It combines classes with a great evangelistic outreach. Prospective workers have their appetite whetted for more serious study in Bible school.

This plan is being used in several countries to good advantage. It is a practical way to train lay workers and find candidates for the ministry. Courses may include fundamental doctrine, personal evangelism, church life and responsibilities, Christian life, simple homiletics, Sunday-school methods, and the like.

Finally, *the central Bible school* is itself an instrument for evangelization. Referring again to El Salvador, our missionaries there are asking to move the Bible school to another city simply because they have so well carried out their commission that the students have to go long miles on weekends in order to find their preaching places.

Sacrifice and Death Essential to Productiveness

A last reference to Christ's parable brings me to my final point. To produce, seed must be sown in the field. As long as it stays in the barn it will produce nothing. Of course, the seed prefers the barn to the field. It is so comfortable in the barn—hearing the sermons and having fellowship with other Christians. But seed is destined for the field. In the field it must lose itself in the earth. Jesus said, "Except a corn of wheat fall into the ground and die, it abideth alone, but if it die, it bringeth forth much fruit." Jesus was the great example of this. He gave Himself to the world and for the world on the Cross. The corn of wheat fell into the ground and died, and what a harvest has resulted! Sacrifice is absolutely essential for the growth of the Church.

A missionary in Chile told about trying to arrange for a great evangelistic meeting which later was held and produced considerable results. When the committee from various denominations met, a pastor who had received his salary from the mission all his life became quite agitated when it was suggested that the Christians should bear the expenses of the campaign. He said, "You cannot ask our people to sacrifice like that, that is not according to the Gospel!"

How often national church leaders and missionaries have felt that way about the converts: we cannot ask these to sacrifice. It is not right to ask a man to suffer. I wonder what Paul would say to such a statement. I wonder what the real answer of the Cross of Christ is to that? We cannot reproduce New Testament results in church growth unless our people—pastors, converts, and missionaries alike—are called to total dedication. The "corn of wheat" must still fall into the ground and die.

There are many examples of such sacrifice today among both nationals and missionaries. Swollen and bleeding feet of brethren who have walked for miles for the Gospel's sake. Stripes on the arms and back of a worker placed in prison and beaten because he dared to preach Christ. Mud-covered clothes of the Christian who climbed on hands and knees over the hills to people waiting to hear the Word of God. The corn of wheat falls into the ground. When it gives itself completely, it does not abide alone.

There will be world harvest. The only answer to the world without Christ, experiencing a tremendous population explosion, is seed that will multiply, seed that will yield "some thirty, some sixty, and some one hundredfold." The Son of Man Himself is the sower and the seed is in His hand. God help us to make a new surrender and dedication to Him who is our Lord and Master. Every Christian is seed in the hand of the sower, and Christ has a right to place each where he can do his part for a world harvest.

VIII

ELIMINATING THE UNDERBRUSH

ROBERT CALVIN GUY

In any planting, valuable timber trees grow best when the tree farmer cuts out useless underbrush. Missions, too, have underbrush. Sentimentality, outgrown ideas, nonessential duties, and overgrown personal involvements flourish. Eliminating them would make for more effective mission. How to accomplish this elimination is a crucial issue.

The first step has already been discussed in relation to the theology of missions. Careful evaluation of mission aims and methods is not only a theological imperative; it is a pragmatic necessity.

Unfortunately, evaluation of matters relating to faith and practice is far from easy. People tend to react emotionally when any area of their religion is questioned. This is understandable. The detachment of the philosopher is neither possible nor profitable for the man of faith. Religion calls for attachment; the stronger the bond, the less welcome is question or evaluation.

Difficulty results when attachment, proper to faith, is transferred uncritically to methods of work. Missionary leaders must have a deep loyalty to the essential doctrines. Unfortunately, they often have the same attitude toward methods of work. They receive any questioning of these as though it were an attack on them personally, their motives, or the basic tenets of their faith. Conversely, dedicated persons often expect the personal respect they earn by their dedication to carry over to their methods, which may or may not be equally admirable.

For these reasons, discussion of missionary practices should be prefaced by pointing out that it is possible to hold missionaries in high regard while asking probing questions about their theories and activities. The following illustration defines the two entirely different spheres. Several years ago a mature, well-balanced student asked me to help him. He felt a clear call to mission service in Japan, but had one child whose health would suffer in the damp Japanese climate. The board was refusing to send the family to Japan. He and his wife were convinced that their place was on the mission field and had reached a decision which would, they hoped, enable them to get there. It was to give this child, one of four, to a brother and his wife, take the other three children, and go on to do the Lord's bidding.

Such obedience and unself-conscious sacrifice demand a high degree of respect. Yet, when that is said, there remain other areas in that missionary's and every missionary's life abroad about which questions may legitimately be raised. Give missionaries a grade of 100 in dedication, but freely raise questions about the effectiveness of their service, the fruit of their ministry, and the wisdom of their procedures.

Missionaries and mission administrators must, I think, grant the privilege of discussing effectiveness. They should not deny discussion because of possible hurt feelings. Discussion of mission policy is not remotely related to fellowship, friendship, or personality. It is a simple necessity thrust upon us all by the magnitude of the mission task. Evaluation of methods of work should always be open to intelligent people. Such evaluation, even when the conclusions differ, does not involve rejection of the motives and worth of the persons involved in it.

Is it not true that any live enterprise demands constant evaluation? A corporation not able to adapt to new conditions will stagnate and disappear from the scene. Ineffective mission policies are not subject to the violent but necessary examination of the market place, yet they should not be justified and kept unchanged simply out of respect for good men and women. Maintaining the confidence and support of the constituency also calls for utter openness in evaluating programs.

The last decade in medicine has produced more progress than any half-century prior to it. Physicians are continually evaluating effectiveness and adopting more efficient methods. The doctor who does not read his journals and keep up with the latest thought in his field is soon hopelessly behind. This was illustrated when a young physician presented a paper describing a new method of treatment. An older physician rose to discuss the paper and said, "Young man, I've practiced forty years of medicine and know that won't work." The young physician replied as courteously as he could, "Sir, you may not have practiced forty years of medicine. You may have practiced one year of medicine forty times." Administrators and missionaries in the most important business known dare not continue practicing patterns of work set years ago, especially if the degree and quality of church growth is less than may legitimately be expected. Some of the needed changes involve clearing away false or half-true ideas and philosophies of mission, such as the following.

Substitution of Sentimentality for Biblical Realism

Sentimentality of various kinds produces a lush growth of underbrush. For example, Christian compassion for people is a soil which can grow sturdy trees of immense value. Often, however, failing to receive continual cutting out of useless vegetation, it produces only tangled, nonproductive undergrowth. While the desire to help others is truly Christian, deciding *how* to help may be so influenced by consideration for the things of the flesh that the needs of the spirit are grossly neglected. The elimination of useless underbrush in favor of useful growth can be carried out only by clearly defining mission purposes in terms of biblical realism. The soil of concern is peculiarly suitable for the growth of energy-sapping, diversionary practices.

One example of substitution of sentimentality for biblical realism is the drive to gain good will and popularity. A normal person wants to be popular. No one likes to be called a foreign devil or a proselyter. An insinuation that the missionary has gone overseas because he can make more money there may cause a sensitive soul to break out in hives! Scorn and derision may make an honorable man devote much energy to self-defense. He wants others to recognize the purity of his purposes. Disciples, exhorted to aim at what is honorable in the sight of men, naturally desire to be favorably received by their fellows.

Nevertheless, the feeling that we must gain popularity and good will must be tempered by Jesus' warning that the world will hate His disciples because they hated Him. The reasons for that hatred may be varied and the hatred itself can be intense. The Apostle Paul in his early life hated the name of Jesus and all who revered it. Perhaps this hatred prepared him to endure the stripes and imprisonment meted out to him by those who formerly took the greatest pride in his accomplishments and his prospects.

As a Christian, Paul often became a prisoner. He did not enjoy the imprisonment but was at peace in it because he knew it came from the opposition of the world. He never tried to stir up opposition, but in the places where the greatest change was wrought by his message he always encountered it. One may almost say he was doing the most good when he was encountering the most opposition. What a compliment was paid him when he was accused of turning the world upside down! Paul, who learned to glory in tribulation, should turn us away from the modern emphasis on being "accepted."

Another contrast between biblical emphasis and modern sentimentality is seen between the determination to stay and build a church for "these poor people" and the New Testament admonition to shake the dust off the feet when a town refused to receive Christ's messenger. A. R. Hay notes that when Paul and his fellows entered a town "it was to establish a church there and they remained until a sufficient beginning had been made. Where there was no response they did not stay."[1] The modern feeling often seems to be that everybody deserves a church. The New Testament indicated instead that those who would receive the message and its responsibilities were to be sought out. The rejecters were to be passed by because receptive towns deserved to hear.

Another sentimental doctrine nowadays is that this is our "day to serve the world." Matthew 25 describes the acts of the Christian moved to compassion; but Jesus exercised compassion within the limits of spiritual responsibility. For instance, He fed multitudes of people only twice. In each case it was under circumstances where the normal channels of securing food were closed, and people before getting home would have fallen by the wayside. The five thousand were fed when it was evening, in a desert place. The four thousand had been with Him three days—many had come from far and had neither the strength nor food left to get home. This compassion of our Lord, shown under special circumstances, has become the justification for much routine mission charity—these two isolated incidents become the reason for decades of life devoted entirely to meeting physical need.

Several comments need to be made about such misapplication. He was not instituting a relief program. There were multitudes of hungry people. A ready-made relief program was available to Him. He could have obtained bread every morning and broken pieces off it all day long. He would have been popular indeed, in a land where an able-bodied man, competing with slave labor, was able to earn barely enough in a day for one good meal for a large family.

In addition, Jesus distrusted people who hunted Him out after He fed them. According to John 6:26–27, He said, "Verily I say unto you, ye seek me, not because ye saw the miracles, but because ye did eat of the loaves, and were filled. Labour not for the meat which perisheth, but for that meat which endureth unto everlasting life, which the Son of man shall give unto you: for him hath

[1] A. R. Hay, *New Testament Order for Church and Missionary* (Audubon, N.J.: New Testament Missionary Union, 1947), p. 395.

God the Father sealed." No doubt can be entertained either of Jesus' compassion for people or of the clear distinction He made between the bread that perishes and that which endures. He set clear limits to the degree to which He would meet the physical needs of men.

We often hear men claim that they are building firm foundations for the future instead of reaping a transient harvest in the present; but we do well to judge what is firm and what is transient in the white light of biblical realism. The Bible declares that God judges every church—and shall we say, every mission?—and some have no future. To one church the Lord said, "thou hast a name that thou livest and art dead." And to another He said "Repent . . . or else I will come unto thee quickly, and will remove thy candlestick out of its place."

Sentimentality is no substitute for biblical realism. If we defend sentimentality with a bland quotation, "Judge not that ye be not judged," we not only misapply Scripture but also fail to fulfill our Lord's demand of fruit from all His disciples.

Eliminating Outworn Ideas

Another case of dense underbrush which stifles church growth is the supposition that missionaries still encounter the strange unknown world that Schmidt, Morrison, and Carey found, and must therefore use the same methods with which they began our modern mission era. These pioneers traveled almost without a map, began without a pattern, and blazed trails for which Christians will always give them honor. But the world of these men is not that to which missionaries currently go, either in transportation required, in its reaction to new ideas, or in its ignorance of the rest of the world.

Unlike the pioneers, today we know almost every land very well indeed. Extensive studies in geography, language, history, anthropology, and sociology have been made in every country. We honor the progressive, daring spirit that drove the missionary pioneers on, but we do not honor them by fearing to examine the patterns they set to meet the world of their day, and hesitating to change them for patterns more appropriate to our own time.

Another flourishing weed which chokes the expansion of churches is the comfortable feeling that we have plenty of time to do the job. During the "great century," European empire seemed to promise the missionary an eternity in which to carry out his task. The West was supreme in commerce, arms, and science. Nonoccidental peoples, impressed by the possessions and boundless energy of their new rulers, seemed willing to learn from them indefinitely. The Pax Britannica encouraged programs that prepared for harvest decades later.

Today all this has changed. Who can say what will happen ten years from now? A vast uneasiness possesses the world. Everyone has modern weapons, and some backward nations are forward in the use of them. In few places can the missionary expect long contact with the people. The patience of the colored nations with their white rulers was wearing thin long before the Communists began their march toward world conquest. Gradualism in mission work —doing something else now so that churches may be established fifty years hence—is risky business today. A psychology which assumes ample time to give our witness violates present-day reality and biblical urgency. "Now is the day of salavation."

A part of the underbrush is an easy opinion of the state of man without Christ. No one can describe the terrible lostness of men without Christ—yet in regard to man's eternal destiny a vapid sentimentality has replaced biblical realism. Paul firmly believed Israel was lost because it rejected Christ. He wrote, "My prayer to God for Israel is that they might be saved." John maintains that "He that believeth not the Son is condemned already." How much plainer can language be?

Men are brought to redemption in their brief life's span, or they are eternally without God and without hope. This truth is obscured by the fog created by Universalism, Eddyism, Russellism, and the supersentimental outlook of our day. Men who would not die on a cross for anyone's salvation make bold to declare that the One Who did is cruel and unfair to make relationship to that atoning death a *sine qua non* of eternal life.

Another impediment to church growth is the feeling that Christianity has always been a minority movement and always will be. Denying this, Peter affirms, "The Lord . . . is forbearing toward you, not wishing that any should perish but that all should reach repentance." It is hard to believe that God wills Christianity to continue as a pitiful minority. On biblical grounds it is more reasonable to assume that in every land multitudes will become disciples of Christ. In many countries this has already occurred. Some societies have been transformed by the movement of most of their people to Christ. Recall the inscription on the memorial plaque of a South Sea Island missionary: "When he landed in 1848 there were no Christians here; when he left in 1872 there were no heathen." Recall the conversion of Norway and the Reformation in Scotland. Granting that after most people in any land have become "Christian," Christianization has only just started, still, how else can it start than by thousands becoming responsible members of His Church? Making disciples of nations is the biblical goal.

The statement, "Christianity is a minority movement and always will be," is made by men who accept the present perspectives of history as the verdict of God without stopping to examine the human frailties that have contributed to the historical outcome; and without seeing into the broad possibilities of the future.

Finally, hardly any idea has limited church growth more than the affirmation that quality is more important than quantity. Many thoughtful men have answered that in the Christian Church quality is closely linked with quantity. A static congregation, neither bringing men into the redemptive relationship nor longing and trying to do so, lacks not merely quantity but the essence of quality. It is not concerned that men know the Savior, and it does not become a channel for divine grace.

Careful Pruning of Mission Activities

If rank growth of outmoded ideas has somewhat choked church growth, multitudinous mission activities have choked it more. Many missionaries believe that the work they are doing, far from accomplishing the primary purpose for which they were called, actually prevents them from accomplishing it. Until some of these secondary and tertiary activities are diminished or eliminated, much progress toward primary goals cannot be made. Principles valid for examination of the entire mission program will be applied here to a few parts of it.

Is it fair to ask about the results of various parts of a field program? (Discussions along this line are impossible without referring to the clear definition of the goals of missions set out in *How Churches Grow*.[2]) Primary goals are: converts won and churches established. All others are secondary, either ministering to these or growing out of them. The relationship of everything else to these primary goals needs to be understood in the light of this further question: Are these other activities of the nature of root or fruit?

For example, is *medical service* a root of churches? Does it win men to Christ and multiply churches, or is it a fruit of compassion in a Christianized population? Medicine has been widely considered an integral part of most mission programs. Many missions carrying on a medical program speak of it as "medical evangelism." They believe it is a most effective way to present Christ. They expect medicine will open the hearts of men to receive the Savior.[3]

These are high aims. Where they are held, should not we check performance against expectation? Several questions should be asked. How many converts come from the medical program? Is there any difference in the quality of spiritual life of people won through medical evangelism and those won otherwise? What comparison can we draw between the number won in a given area through a medical program and in another area without it? Is it fair to compare costs in money and personnel in medical evangelism and straight old-line evangelism?

How valuable is the good will created? Does it lead to conver-

[2] D. A. McGavran, *How Churches Grow* (London: World Dominion Press, 1959; New York: Friendship Press, 1959).

[3] A few missions carry on medical work entirely as a philanthropic enterprise and declare it ought to have no evangelistic purpose. The following discussion does not deal with their position.

sions, or to permission to create more good will? How much of the good will gained in medical work is directed toward the missionary and how much toward the Gospel? Does it result in willingness to commit life to Christ? Many people at home and abroad have kind feelings toward the medical missionary but express marked hostility toward Jesus. Good will toward the messenger may eventuate in good will toward the message, but Christians must remember that "the offense of the Cross" often keeps men from Him we proclaim, even when they are friendly to us.

Someone has recently coined the term "air-wick missions," meaning those that create a good atmosphere whether reaching primary goals or not. How much medical work is "air-wick" and how much is truly medical evangelism? In evaluating medical missions, the great contribution to the health of both the Christian community and missionaries must, of course, be placed on the credit side of the ledger.

As the underbrush of multitudinous activities is considered, a question must be asked about the results gained by the *operation of schools.* These are sometimes considered an evangelistic tool and sometimes a means to train Christian children. Many writers in the field of methods believe schools for Christian children are more justified than those having an evangelistic purpose. Roland Allen is particularly insistent at this point. He says it is impossible to give Christian education to a non-Christian. He reasons that, regardless of the intention with which it is offered, education can be received only in the student's own frame of reference. A pagan can receive it only as pagan education, even though it may be conducted by Christians and have some Christian content.

One great danger involved in mission schools is that education is a most alluring form of bait. It is the golden key to the middle classes. Boys will endure anything to get an education. They may even comply superficially with the forms and rituals of their teachers, though usually they take the education and reject the faith it is supposed to introduce.

If schools are carried on as agencies of evangelism, we must find out whether they do in fact fulfill this purpose. That a mission school is old, influential, and honorable often has little to do with its missionary effectiveness. An illustration of this is found at Serampore College. Recently one of the staff there, in answer to my question about how many students had been converted since entering the school, replied, "Two." Obviously one of the oldest and best-known mission schools has now no really effective evangelistic influence.

Even if a school is an active evangelistic tool, we still need to ask whether such evangelism could be carried on without the school, and whether the cost/result ratio is favorable by comparison with churches as evangelistic agencies.

Some people connected with missions become indignant at the mere mention of "the cost/result ratio." They exclaim, "One soul is worth all that can be spent upon it." Their objection would be valid if there were unlimited resources and it were necessary to spend vast sums to win one soul. Actually, of course, resources are always very limited, and many lands are more responsive than they have ever been before. Lavishing great expenditure upon the conversion of one or two seems hard to justify. Moreover, expressions of widespread soul-hunger suggest that it is not necessary in our day.

Another question involves the quality and the durability of converts. Are those who come out of evangelistically effective schools durable in their Christian commitment? Are they reproductive? Do they furnish strong leadership to the Christian movement? If so, there is argument in favor of evangelistic schools. If only a small percentage of those trained in Christian schools come to Christ, and they neither spread the faith nor follow through into a lifetime of Christian leadership, then the worth of schools as evangelistic agencies may be seriously questioned. The following statement is distressingly current in some lands: "they graduated from school and church in the same ceremony."

David Paton says the schools he knew (in China) came nearer to unfitting their students for the fellowship of the churches available to them than securing them for it. Yet in some lands (notably Africa) Christian schools have greatly added to the Church. One cannot pronounce about mission schools in general. Each group of church or mission schools should be most carefully studied to determine its evangelistic effectiveness. Records of such surveys are now almost entirely unavailable. One is forced to the conclusion that no one has had the concern to conduct them.

Mission and nonmission schools which provide leaders for the Christian movement should be studied to determine what proportion of students become (1) effective preachers in local congregations, (2) Christian teachers influencing the people of the country, and (3) lay leaders in their churches. If any school must train 100 students to get 5 church leaders, one may question the wisdom of pouring more money into it. A school which handles so many before finding enough for church use is scarcely efficient. The proportion of graduates who are indifferent to Christ and His Church—or even hostile to Him—is one measure for recognizing a school system as genuine timber or underbrush of the mission movement.

Mission schools cost money. Consequently Christian mission as a faithful steward should always investigate the possibility of developing leaders from less expensive operations. It may be that under some circumstances schools, financed in part or whole by mission boards and churches, are the best way to create Christian leaders. A careful cost accounting, proving that this is the case, would amply repay the investment. Any more effective way of doing the basic work of missions should, however, be considered seriously. Mission schools are a means. Like all means, they are subject to inquiry as to how efficiently they achieve their announced ends.

The same basic questions should be asked about the *church program* in any land. Just to label it "church" does not automatically make it spiritually effective. Churches should be subjected to the same searching inquiry bent on other aspects of mission. How many and what quality of converts come from the church program? Are these converts independent, able to carry on their own affairs, and anxious to propagate the faith among their fellows? Or are they dependent for their very life upon the "mother instincts" of the missionaries? Are they aggressive or passive, actually remaking their environment or nearly beaten to death by it? Do Christians reproduce the missionary motivation or simply accept the service provided by the church or mission?

One fears that some activities on the mission field (in all three departments—evangelism, education, and medicine) are carried on because no one knows how to administer the *coup de grace* and start something more productive. Just as surely as new enterprises ought to be started, some old enterprises ought to be stopped. Which to start and which to stop can be determined only by careful evaluation.

Act in the Light of Information Obtained

Conducting a survey is worthless unless Churches and missions are prepared to act on the information garnered. Often this is not done because much good money has already been poured into the work shown to be nonproductive. Could it be set out as a principle of missionary administration that, when evidence shows a piece of work is inadequate, it must not be maintained just because much money and devoted life have been poured into it? King Amaziah of Judah once hired one hundred thousand soldiers from Israel for a hundred talents. Then a prophet told him these men would do him not good, but evil. Amaziah asked, "What shall we do about the hundred talents I have spent for these men?" The prophet answered, "The Lord is able to give you much more than this." In effect he said, "Forget the money already spent, send the men home, and go on to victory without them." Amaziah heeded the prophet, lost his hundred talents, and won a victory. It is seldom wise to pour good money into failing enterprises. Continued use of personnel on unproductive projects just because they are part of an existing mission program should always come under serious scrutiny.

When evaluation requires stopping an enterprise, losses in property should be taken calmly. One large mission board lists all its property overseas as worth one dollar in order to say emphatically that everything is expendable for the sake of discipling the nations.

I sometimes illustrate the need for clear thinking by asking my unsuspecting students how many legs a mule will have if you call his tail a leg. They usually answer "Five." I point out that he will still have four, since calling his tail a leg won't make it one. The application is clear: church and mission enterprises need to justify themselves in fact rather than in bland statement. Yeast is not yeast through being called by that name, but because it makes the dough rise. Many projects are commended as effective missions, but honest evaluation shows that such commendation is in the realm of propaganda rather than fact.

Evaluation was often made in the New Testament churches. Paul left Tarsus and went to Antioch. He left some synagogues and went elsewhere. He left Athens and went to Corinth. He shook off the dust of Antioch of Pisidia and went to Iconium. When evaluation showed a situation was not favorable for planting churches, he went elsewhere to seek one that was.

Eliminating Underbrush of Personal Involvement

Just living makes considerable demands on the missionary's time. If the minutes spent in shopping, residence upkeep, maintenance of the auto, radio, and other Western conveniences were added up, the total would in most cases be staggering. Questions are being raised from many quarters about the missionary reducing his standard of living to free him from the onus of distrust and jealousy of the much poorer people he has gone to "serve," and to give him more time for his work. D. J. Fleming's book, *Living as Comrades,* pleads with missionaries to make community with the people. Dr. Herbert Jackson, adjunct Professor of Missions at Union Theological Seminary and Director of the Missionary Research Library, in his inaugural address in 1962 suggested that a missionary monastic community would be much freer than today's missionaries to give itself completely to mission. Today's vast opportunities call for effective measures.

Where missionaries have spent much time providing for personal comfort and well-being they ought to examine their procedure. One difficulty in suggesting such examination is that many

Christians who stay in their homelands are not willing to reduce their standard of living to supply resources for attempting vast harvest abroad. They cannot, then, demand that the missionary do what they themselves are unwilling to do. Most discussions of standards of living end in a stalemate, with consciences still uneasy and the witness clouded. Paul, on the contrary, because he himself endured hardship, was heard when he exhorted his converts to endure hardship.

Further underbrush consists of running errands for people on the field. Since most missionaries have automobiles and most of the people they serve do not, the missionary easily becomes a taxi-driver. Of course the mission taxi earns good will for its cause; but how much does such good will really further the Gospel? The perplexing question as to use of cars should be answered according to whether cars advance the real work or retard it.

Personal involvements are also subject to misinterpretation. One missionary operated a generating plant and, using the excess electricity from the few hours a day of its operation, froze ice for his own use. He sold the surplus to defray the cost of operation of the plant. When someone asked what his business was, a national replied, "That American? Oh, he is in the ice business here, and does some preaching on the side." It would be interesting to probe the thought processes of nationals to find how many think the missionary as being a church-planter "on the side."

Paring Responsibility to Essential Mission Function

What is the role of a missionary today? There are many. They range from the simple function of a man with pulpit and Bible to the complex one of administrator of a large organization. It seems likely that in most roles, rather than having a planned sphere of work and leadership, missionaries are victims of an unplanned accumulation of activities. Various responsibilities, both essential and nonessential, have become part of their duty. Many missionaries are so beset by things that go along with the office, rather than the direct responsibilities of the office itself, that they are in despair. Some leave the field because they cannot fulfill the missionary vocation as they think it ought to be lived. Many more meet the conflicting demands of the work but lose part of their effectiveness. Day by day they prove that a man can live a long time under serious frustration.

The accumulation of so much underbrush stops church growth in two ways: it diverts the energies of men on the field to unproductive activities, and it prevents other able men from considering the missionary calling at all. So many missionaries on deputation among the churches present the periphery rather than the center of mission life that, without even knowing why, the man with a strong thrust toward a creative spiritual ministry is not moved. He does not define his reason for lack of enthusiasm; he simply invests his life in other enterprises.

In running hospitals and schools, aiding churches, preaching the Gospel, and training future pastors and lay workers, Christian mission spends money. All must be accounted for. Books must be kept; but who will keep them?

One of the most difficult problems a board administrator faces is how much time a man called to communicate the good news of redemption should spend in bookkeeping. It is no good to tell a missionary chained to account books, "You are doing this for the good of the missionary movement." As long as his major role is bookkeeping, a man with a sense of a more direct spiritual ministry will feel seriously limited. Aside from the fact that a lifetime missionary is an expensive bookkeeper, we must ask how much bookkeeping is essential and how much is merely the complex business procedure of our day.

A week spent in hearing missionaries plan their next year's work is illuminating. Budgets, salary scales, repairs, rents, and scholarships take hours. While the bulk of their planning ought to concern the spiritual thrust, most of it deals with matters material and mechanical. Part of this is an outgrowth of the subsidy system, part a product of the American environment transferred overseas, and part a failure to understand the essential function of planning sessions.

How much of a missionary's time is spent in "ministering the Spirit"—praying with fellow Christians, deepening spiritual life, preaching the Word of life, training church members and lay preachers, and activities of a related nature? Missionaries who have discussed the question with me suggest that the average missionary spends no more than two weeks out of fifty-two in "communicating the Spirit."

Much discussion is being given in America to a similar problem: the role of the pastor. His return to a prophetic calling is demanded. The difficulty in both cases lies in defining a method by which this return can be effected.

However much justification we may find for the involvement of the missionary in things on earth, the fact remains that it affects the spiritual health of national Christian leaders. Missionaries sometimes express regret for the lack of faithful, day-by-day witnessing on the part of national pastors. But is it not possible that national pastors have learned too well from missionary example? Have they perhaps observed that missionaries in this or former decades played an administrative rather than a basically spiritual role, and deduced that they should do the same?

Roland Allen ascribes involvement in "other things" to an unconscious attempt to avoid the harder task of ministering the Spirit. These other things run all the way from spending Saturday with a mimeograph in order to have a Western-style bulletin for a church service on Sunday to planning weddings and assuming grandfather responsibilities with the people in and out of the churches. The question here is not whether such activities are interesting and helpful; it is whether they dissipate energies sorely needed for the main purpose of Christian mission.

Two books of satire on situations like this may add a light concluding touch to this somber discussion. *Parkinson's Law*[4] is a hilarious study in administration. It deals with big business and big government, and the jungle of increasing organization which makes for decreasing effectiveness of the man involved in it. *The*

[4] C. Northcote Parkinson, *Parkinson's Law* (Boston: Houghton Mifflin Co., 1957).

Gospel Blimp[5] is a parody on the search for souls by a group which seeks to win one man by the indirect route of purchasing a blimp to tow Scripture texts over his house. Blow by amusing blow, rather painful to all of us involved in creating organizations which tend to become ends in themselves, it shows how the original purpose is forgotten and how shocking in the end is its realization. Both books make us laugh even while thinking deeply about eliminating underbrush—that jungle of competing, nice, but inessential activities so well known to us all.

[5] Joseph Bayly, *The Gospel Blimp* (Havertown, Pa.: Windward Press, 1960).

IX

KNOWING EACH VARIETY OF CHURCH GROWTH

DONALD ANDERSON McGAVRAN

The General Background

As regards church growth, Christian mission works in a fog which obscures all other issues. This is caused by the multiplicity of good ends sought by mission, constant thinking together about widely different situations, and lack of scientific terminology. A kind of "missionese" or technical jargon marks modern mission, which has come into being as a result of these forces. Leaders use missionese in discussing "common" problems regardless of the variety of Church involved. Missionese makes possible conversation between widely different kinds of mission, and rules out promotional shock.* It also renders impossible exact thinking about any specific church.

It is as if Christian mission had resolved to talk about carrying out the Great Commission without ever examining the degree of discipling achieved anywhere. This is not a conscious conspiracy, but rather the outcome of far-flung enterprise, promotional need, theological reticence as to the value of numbers, and recognition

* Caused by assessments of mission which might discourage or offend supporters or in any way lessen giving.

that often years of sowing have been required before harvest can be reaped. The net result is a vast miasma which envelops modern mission and keeps the growth of the Churches from being clearly seen anywhere. To recognize this fog and get out of it is one of the crucial needs of modern mission. Unconscious acceptance of this clouded view is natural—but highly regrettable. To think intelligently about Christian mission and the coming day when every tongue shall confess that Jesus is Lord, requires exact knowledge of each variety of church and each variety of church growth.

Physicians have to distinguish hundreds of types of disease and describe the stages in each—exposure, incubation, onset, crisis, and recovery. The science of medicine would be heavily handicapped if its practitioners had to discuss health without a precise terminology. Without it, the most crucial issue in modern medicine would be to get an exact knowledge of each disease as speedily as possible. The application to missions should be plain. Christian missions do not have exact descriptions of the many varieties of church growth, and should get them.

All through this and other conversations on church growth, people are handicapped by the various meanings inherent in the word *church*. In 1956 I wrote Dr. Pierce Beaver, at that time head of the Missionary Research Library, asking whether 50 per cent per decade (i.e., 5 per cent a year) of church growth would be a good minimum to set for Christian mission.

He replied, "Growth of 50 per cent a decade would be a nightmare." I had mentioned this minimum, thinking of Churches which had achieved good sound growth of 500 per cent a decade and more. He was thinking of different populations, different missions, and different Churches. What I considered minimum he thought wildly excessive.

Missionaries to Moslems object to a definition of missions that stresses the physical increase of the Church. Under their circumstances this is quite understandable, but the present temporary unresponsiveness of the Moslem world—and some other mission fields—must not be allowed to set a norm of petty expectation for Churches in other, more responsive areas. Nor do we help our colleagues in resistant populations by retreating into foggy "missionese" which studiously avoids reference to numbers of converts and, indeed, denigrates such a thought as worldly. Some of my British brothers have even suggested that to expect multitudes to become disciples of Christ is a typical American point of view, originating in the kind of mind that created the mass production of the Ford factory in Detroit! To them I can only reply that God so loved the world and all its multitudes that He sent His only Son. God's passion for the salvation of multitudes (nations, *ta ethne,* the tribes) is the basic authority for church growth. That there are unresponsive populations must not diminish our belief in God's purpose or our zeal to fulfill it.

Physical Size and Shape Essential

Christian mission must discover and set forth with great care the numbers of Christians, rates of growth, and many other facts about each Church that can reasonably be called a homogeneous unit. The physical size and shape of each Church is an essential part of it.

A terrific amount of discussion and writing has taken place about "the nature of the Church"—the *theological* nature of the Church. Now the Church as a whole does have a theological nature, but its multitudinous homogeneous units also have multitudinous physical forms. They deserve equal interest, discussion, and description, if the welfare and extension of the Church—the Body of Christ—is our aim. Those who discuss the nature of the Church today should remember the many visible Churches. What is said about one is probably not fully true of another.

A striking illustration of this point is found in the *C M S News Letter,* a little magazine discussing basic mission policy in broad and statesmanlike terms, to which many of us are indebted. In the June 1962 issue Canon Warren writes about urbanization in Africa and the part the Church should play in it. A man from the cities of Asia would read with increasing puzzlement, for the Canon's assumption throughout is that a major part of the

Church's work lies in solving the problems of urbanization. He writes as if Christian congregations could and should do something about them. "This," says the missionary from Singapore, Calcutta, or Cairo, "is impossible. Christians in our cities are .1 per cent of the population. Is Canon Warren writing about urbanization in England? Has his cultural overhang projected onto Africa the duties of congregations and missions in a European land where the Church is strong?"

Puzzlement is resolved when the missionary reads on page 5 that, "most of the inhabitants [of these cities] are nominally Christian." Suddenly he realizes that Canon Warren is speaking about a section of Africa where Christians form a large part of the population, and Churches have power and influence. For that kind of population and that kind of congregation, his statement suddenly becomes reasonable.

Whenever one writes or speaks about Churches, he should, in the interest of clarity, state what the physical size and condition of the particular Church is.

As we study the three main varieties of church growth, the five kinds of mission, and the many kinds of Church, we shall realize the manifold varieties of church growth concerning which Christian mission ought to have exact knowledge, and by thinking more precisely we may be better able to dispel the present fog.

Three Main Varieties of Growth

At the outset, three main varieties of church growth are constantly confused.

There is biological church growth. Christians beget children who grow up in "the nurture and admonition of the Lord," confess their faith in Christ, and become full members. This is a necessary type of church growth, but will never win the world to Christ; for while Christians are begetting their hundreds, non-Christians will beget their thousands. True, persistent encouragement of Christians to have more children than non-Christians might in the long run extend the faith; but this is counsel of dubious wisdom.

There is also transfer growth. I have ten dollars in my right pocket. I take it out and put it in my left pocket. My left pocket is now ten dollars richer—but the right pocket is ten dollars poorer and I myself am no wealthier than before. Much "growth of the Church" in cities is transfer growth. City churches grow, but country congregations die. However important it may be that Christians who move should join churches where they go, it is obvious that such transfer growth will never disciple the nations.

Conversion growth is the third variety. Extension of the grace of God "to more and more people" depends ultimately on conversion growth. That is why, when Silas and Timothy returned from Macedonia, they found Paul arguing in the synagogue every Sabbath and persuading Jews and Greeks to become disciples of Christ, testifying to them in every way that the Christ was Jesus and none other. (Acts 18:4, 5). Paul was working for conversion growth. Biological growth and transfer growth come through shepherding existing Christians. These are necessary activities but mission has to do primarily with extending God's grace to those who are not yet disciples. Lack of clarity at this point is fatal.

When the United Church of Christ in the Philippines invited me to study it, I was told that the churches in Manila were growing greatly. The fact was that, as Protestants—students and others—moved to the capital city, Protestant membership increased by transfer growth, yet there was little conversion growth. The religious emphasis week in a Manila college I visited resulted in many "decisions for Christ," but no one knew whether these were mostly decisions of Protestant youth made for the first time, rededications, or conversions from the world.

The missionary society, to take another example, that takes comfort in and gives promotional publicity to the fact that its Asian Church last year had 4,000 "adult" baptisms, is deceiving itself in a dangerous way. For its Asian Church of 200,000 souls has about 5,000 boys and girls turning fourteen each year. If it merely holds all its own children it will get 5,000 baptisms. But the Church is not conserving all its children. How many of the 4,000 baptisms are biological growth and how many conversion growth no one in Asia or America knows—a specific example of fog at work. If this Asian Church and its assisting missionary society want to think accurately about their opportunities and responsibilities, they must record baptisms from the Church and from the world separately. If their field totals read as follows:

Baptisms from the Church	4,000
Baptisms from the World	0

we should deduce that this Church was losing to the world about a fifth of its children every year and was, missionarily speaking, impotent.

When the kinds of church growth are known, suitable action can be taken. When the facts are not known, all one can do is carry on church and mission work faithfully and hope for the best. This last phrase is in itself a wonderful example of cloudy missionese: "all one can do is carry on church and mission work faithfully and hope for the best."

The widespread use of "least-common-denominator"—or most vaguely general and overused—words such as "work," "outreach," and "witness" is part of the misty mission jargon of the twentieth century. Multitudes of activities of missions and Churches are indiscriminately called work, outreach, or witness. Praying for the victims of a landslide in Peru and building a church in the Philippines are alike outreach. The common factor in teaching the landless poor of the Gangetic plain how to raise more chickens and baptizing believers in Nigeria is that both are "pieces of mission work." Even those who are successfully planting scores of churches are so habituated to the fog that they will not say, "We are multiplying churches among the Kambatta in the Hosanna Hills of Ethiopia." Instead they say, "We are carying on work among the Kambattas" or "We are reaching Kambattas with the Gospel."

"Least-common-denominator" words generate fog because they are so inclusive and have such slight real meaning. What the "work" is, what it attempts, whether it issues in relief of suffering, teaching illiterates, or reconciling men to God, all this is obscured.

Whether "outreach" to the Kambattas results in a church in every village or tract distribution to an indifferent population cannot be known. To what end one reaches out is not stated. Whether men, believing on the Lord Jesus, become partakers in eternal life or not is not set forth. But wonderful "work," "outreach," and "witness" are going on. The careless use of these words keeps Christian mission from seeing church growth and makes it easy for missionaries and Christian leaders to operate in the fog.

Five Kinds of Mission

Rather than talking of "work" and "outreach," we should distinguish carefully between the following five kinds of missions: exploratory, mission station approach, scattered Church, people movement, and large younger Church.

Every mission on fresh ground begins as an *exploratory mission.* There is no Church; the missionaries (whether these be Korean Christians working in Thailand, Indian Christians working in Kenya, or American Christians working in Congo) are learning the language and the culture, making their first mistakes, and meeting their victories, and—we hope—baptizing their first converts.

In the past, if an exploratory mission met a hostile, indifferent, or unresponsive population, it made a few converts around the place where the missionaries lived and settled down to serving all life—street preaching and evangelism, a wide program of service, literacy, refugee assistance, and discussions of church union and comity. Such a mission carries on "splendid mission work." Devoted missionaries and national churchmen succeed each other through the decades. In the first fifty years—let us say—18 churches are founded, with a total of 2,400 communicants, and the mission hopes to add another 2,400 in the coming fifty years, thus achieving a Church of about 5,000 at the end of the first hundred years. This inch-by-inch progress I call the *mission-station approach.* It has been extensively described in *Bridges of God* and is the dominant kind of mission today; it sets the common image of what a mission is and what a younger Church is.

In Latin America and the Philippines a third kind of mission is found—one *assisting a scattered Church.* In nominally Roman Catholic lands the biblical faith has a self-validating quality that brings about a situation in which the Church propagates itself out beyond the mission, yet without a people movement developing. Sometimes the scattered Church grows greatly. Often it is static. The mission carries on many of the same activities as in the mission-station approach, but the churches are not closely clustered at or near the station.

The fourth variety of mission is that which *assists a people movement* to Christ. Some caste, tribe, or kinship web finds flowing in it a Christward surge and begins to turn to Christ in chains of families. A series of small, well-instructed groups of closely related people become Christians—a few groups each year. When a people movement to Christ occurs, the mission is concerned, first to multiply churches in a receptive population, and second, to create a leadership for them. All other concerns are secondary. People-movement missions are a distinct variety, but their uniqueness is often blurred and their effectiveness lessened by applying to them the techniques, slogans, and goals of the dominant mission-station approach.

The fifth variety of mission is that *assisting a large, well-developed Afericasian Church.* The Church has its own ministry, both of local churches and of the national Church; is properly jealous of its prerogatives; wants assistance but is fearful of domination; and limits its missionaries to tasks it cannot do. It prefers money rather than missionaries; but also values ecumenical links. This fifth variety of mission must help the younger Church discreetly—keeping out of its way as much as possible.

Each of these five kinds of mission is quite different from the other four. Each can normally expect a different variety and degree of church growth. Growth which appears impossible to men carrying on a mission-station approach is commonplace to those giving aid to a scattered Church. Exploratory mission would not know what to do with a vigorous scattered Church or people movement. On the other hand, consider a people movement like that in Timor, where, in 1956, 200,000 souls were getting along with three national ministers of seminary education, ninety catechists of eighth-grade education and three hundred of less than eighth-grade education, plus only one European missionary—and 10,000 baptisms a year. Men in a people movement of this sort look with incredulous eyes at the missionary concentration in Ecuador, where in 1960 there were 400 missionaries, 4,000 evangelical communicants, and a very, very slow rate of growth.

Until it becomes commonplace for missionaries and national churchmen to identify the types of mission they are speaking of, we shall have confusion in Christian mission. There is no valid reason to continue in this confusion and add to the fog.

Many Kinds of Churches

Turning now from the kinds of mission to the kinds of Church, we readily see that missionaries and their supporting Churches and missionary societies (both Afericasian and Eurican) are working with younger Churches of many different kinds. Gertrude Stein wrote that a rose is a rose is a rose, but younger Churches are all different.

For example, the Mangyan Church of Mindoro, written up in the July 1962 issue of *Frontier,* is a beginning people movement numbering only 250 full members of the Church among an entirely illiterate tribe in the Philippines. Not one of the leaders of this younger Church has been to regular school a day in his life. How totally different from the Kyodan in Japan, with a communicant and highly literate membership of 180,000, and 2,000 seminary trained ministers, many of whom are more competent to discuss Barth and Brunner than their American or English counterparts would be.

The following schematic chart demonstrates the actual complexity of the Churches of Afericasia. Churches differ in four visible elements—size, ordained leadership, stewardship, and reproductive record—and each element may be present in one of four degrees of difference. There are many more qualities than the four selected, and more than four degrees of difference in each could easily be distinguished. The reality, therefore, is much more complex than this simplified chart, which nevertheless well illustrates the large number of really different kinds of Churches.

THE COMPLEXITY OF CHURCHES IN AFERICASIA

	A	B	C	D
	SIZE	ORDAINED LEADERSHIP	STEWARDSHIP	REPRODUCTION RECORD
		Proportion Who Are Missionaries	*Days' Earnings per Year Given to Church*	*Net Yearly Gain per 100 Communicants*
1	1–500	All missionaries	2–5	1 person or less
2	500–2,000	9/10 missionaries	6–14	2 to 3 persons
3	2,000–10,000	1/2 missionaries	15–24	4 to 10 persons
4	10,000–100,000	1/10 (or less) m's	25–50	10 to 30 or more

The four qualities are listed in columns A, B, C, and D. Take size, in column A: Afericasian denominations may be classified according to their size. Tiny denominations are of 1 to 500 members. Keith E. Hamilton, in his careful study, *Church Growth in the High Andes,* has pointed out that in Peru there are 36 denominations with an average membership of 235. These tiny Churches would rank A-1.

A-2 denominations run from 500 to 2,000 members. Many younger Churches fall in this category. They are found on every continent. Many are static little enclaves of Christians who barely hold their own in an expanding population decade after decade. They increase very slowly, with generous amounts of mission assistance. The few A-2's which are growing pass rapidly out of this classification.

A-3 denominations run from 2,000 to 10,000 members. These are, for the most part, Churches which have had a period of rapid growth in some homogeneous unit. Sometimes a church merger of A-2's will produce an A-3, which characteristically has numbers of educated leaders, some large congregations, and a few men and women of national note.

A-4's are the Afericasian Churches we often read about. They have 20,000, 50,000, or 100,000 or more members. They have sometimes arisen through merger, as in the case of the 180,000-member United Church of Christ in Japan (1961). Sometimes they are the result of long mission effort, as with the 17,000-member United Church of Christ in Thailand (overwhelmingly Presbyterian in origin). Most commonly, however, they have come into being through a people movement to Christ as in the case of the Baptists in Burma, the Anglicans in Uganda, the Seventh-Day Adventists in Peru, and the Christian and Missionary Alliance in Congo.

Churches may also be classified according to the proportion of the ordained leaders—column B—who are fraternal workers or missionaries. This classification does not parallel that of size. The ordained leadership of some very large Churches—A-4's—is nine-tenths missionary, and that of some very small churches—A-1's—is nine-tenths national. It would not be difficult to find a Church which was A-3 and B-2, with—say—4,000 communicants, and missionaries comprizing nine-tenths of its ordained leadership. On the other hand, many Churches today would be A-2 and B-4, with up to 2,000 communicants and only one-tenth or less of their ordained leadership consisting of missionaries.

Obviously the kind of growth possible to any Church is enormously dependent on these two factors. Exact knowledge of the variety of growth possible means knowing that a given Church in Afericasia is, let us say, "A-2, B-4" *and whatever kind of growth is possible to A-2, B-4 churches.* Pronouncements about "younger Churches," or "the mission field" often sound as if all Afericasian Churches were of the same sort and all mission fields essentially the same. Such pronouncements have at best a thin meaning. At worst they become meaningless jargon. In all cases they contribute to the confusion about church growth.

Stewardship and Reproduction

Churches may also be classified by the number of "day's earnings" their members give to the church—column C. To obtain this figure one takes the total income of the denomination in cash and kind received from the members and divides it by the number of members. Then, on the basis of the average day's earnings in that country at that time, one can calculate how many days' earnings church members are accustomed to give.

Let us be clear that a high rate of giving, while usually desirable, does not correlate with church growth. A denomination in Brazil, let us say, whose members give twenty-four days' income per year to their church, does not necessarily grow faster than one whose members give three. Some fully self-supporting Churches do not grow, while some whose giving is very sketchy do. Subsidy sometimes helps church growth, sometimes hinders. While these things are true, nevertheless the indefinitely reproducible pattern of church growth whereby a Church spreads across a whole countryside generally includes self-support by the congregations as one of its characteristics.

Precise thinking about the amount of growth possible to a Church will take into account its level of giving. We need to know whether the members of a Church are giving from 2 to 5, 6 to 14, or 15 to 24 days' earnings a year.

Finally, Churches may be classified by their reproduction record —column D. A few Afericasian denominations add one member per hundred or less per year. In a decade they experience a growth of 10 per cent or less. Such denominations can demonstrate plenty of good church and mission work and the devoted labors of many fraternal workers, but they do not experience membership increase. They do not even keep their own children.

Many other denominations have a net gain of 2 or 3 persons per hundred a year and grow at a rate of 10 to 30 per cent a decade. This commonly means they are conserving many of their own children and adding a sprinkling of converts. It may, however, mean large numbers of converts and large loss of children of the Church.

Still other denominations add 4 to 10 persons a year per hundred of existing members, and a few add 10 persons a year and more. A brief way of indicating this reproduction variable is to label these four types of Church D-1, D-2, D-3, or D-4.

The growth potential of each Church varies according to its nature. Granted that all Churches are—theologically speaking—the Body of Christ, their ability to reproduce depends very much on their visible nature, some aspects of which I have been describing. All administration needs to think about church growth in specific terms. It should always be the growth of one specific homogeneous-unit Church. Only so will it avoid the pitfall of carrying on "good work" in the vague hope that somehow, sometime, the Church will grow.

Administration's Knowledge of Church Growth

Administration is a four-level affair. Each ordained person (man or woman, national or missionary) is an administrator in his own bailiwick. District superintendents, union secretaries, and secretaries of Christian education, social action, evangelism, and the like are also church administrators. Executives of the denominations of Afericasia and of the Missionary societies in Eurica (that is, Europe and North America) are also missionary administration. All levels of administration need to think exactly about church growth, Churches, and missions.

On a visit to Haiti, during the eighty-mile drive from Port au Prince to the mission station, I queried my host, Mr. Shirer, about the Churches. He knew them well and answered the questions exactly. A young missionary who had been in Haiti for a year was the third passenger in the front seat. As we drew near our destination he said, "How do you know what questions to ask? I've learned more in the last few hours about the Churches here than I did in a whole year of residence, though I've been living with Mr. Shirer all that time."

For a year the young missionary had been seeing splendid church and mission work without realizing the exact structure and nature of the Church. This is quite possible. I lived for twelve years in India, engaged in Christian education and general mission administration, before I became vividly aware of the nature of the Churches in Central Provinces, where I was working. During all this time I could have described these Churches in a fashion to please my teacher of ecclesiology at Yale Divinity School, but I did not know much about the varieties of Indian Churches and the *growth potential of each.*

Foundational Knowledge

Let us consider the matter of exact knowledge of each variety of church growth from the vantage point of a different analysis. Every churchman connected with the younger Churches needs *foundational knowledge about the physical churches.* Unless he has it, he will continue to operate in a fog as far as the Great Commission is concerned. He may be full of good works, but he will also probably reconcile few men to God.

Of first importance in foundational knowledge is awareness of the spread of the Church and the shape of its congregations. I remember with what a shock I first realized what my host in Orissa was calling a church. In his field there were 84 "churches," some over thirty years old, running from 10 to 55 members and averaging 27 members each. These 27 members moreover, lived not in one village but, on the average, in three! The average congregation was very "spread out." Three little bands of nine illiterate Christians living from one to five miles apart constituted the normal church in that area. I have since learned that a "spread-out" pattern is characteristic of many Afericasian Churches. They live as small groups very much surrounded by the world.

This "enworlding" of the Church has both advantages and disadvantages. In some circumstances such a Church will grow amazingly. In others it will wither. At any rate the "spread-out" Church is not like a great people-movement Church in Fiji or in the Republic of Congo, where the shape of the large congregations is something else again. The physical length and breadth of a congregation, the number of houses, the number of full families, half-families, and single persons who make up its membership—all are vital to church growth and constitute the first part of foundational knowledge. Every level of administration should know both the physical shapes of many kinds of Churches and what each shape means for church growth.

The second part of basic knowledge is that of the societal foundation of the Church. What section of the population is becoming Christian? And how much of that section has become Christian? Churches do not grow in the general population. Except in "melting pots" they always grow in homogeneous units, in webs of relationship. A typical rural Church in Nigeria, for example, is not made up of "Nigerians"; it is made up of Yorubas, Egons, Tiv, or Ibos—not all four, but one of the four, exclusively. In Bolivia the typical congregation is not made up of Bolivians, but of Aymaras, Quechuas, or Mestizos. In Abra Province of the Philippines, a church does not consist of undifferentiated Filipinos; it consists of Ilocanos or Tinguians. If a missionary society is concentrating on a segment of society where no one becomes Christian and slighting those where people more readily become Christian, it can expect scarcely any church growth. The relation of each embodied Church to the society from which it came is most important.

The proportion of church members who have affectionate relatives in the old societal structure is a matter of enormous importance for growth. So is the proportion of members who have so thoroughly departed from their old society that they have no intimates left there at all. Both should be known.

The Very Useful Graph

The third part of foundational knowledge of the physical Church consists of its rates of growth. Every churchman, national and missionary, and every executive of every board ought to know the precise facts of the rate at which his Church or Churches have grown. The easiest way to obtain this information concerning any Church is to make an accurate graph of its growth. The membership figure for each year is readily obtained and portrayed in a graph. At a glance it will show how that Church has grown from the beginning. Every spurt of growth, every revival, every loss through epidemic or war, every variation due to some notable churchman's arrival or departure, will be faithfully portrayed.

Are such graphs reliable? One hears much about the unreliable nature of church membership figures collected and recorded by the denominations. It is true that for any one year these may be in error, but when the figures for fifty years are plotted, they give a general trend which is highly reliable. The errors of one year are corrected in the next. If error runs along for several years it is finally wiped out in a thorough revision of the rolls. The general trend is as firm as a rock.

The most revealing graphs of growth are of homogeneous-unit Churches. When a homogeneous-unit Church is large and varied, graphs of significant clusters grow in different fashions. Denominational "field totals" which inevitably cancel losses of one cluster against gains of another and come up with an over-all average have limited usefulness. They hide what is happening.

Graphs of growth ought always to be compared, not with what the Church or mission is achieving on other fields, but with what other denominations and missions are experiencing in the same population. Thus a mission at work in Kenya should measure itself, *not* by how its Church in West Pakistan is growing, but by how other Churches in Kenya are flourishing. The Methodists in Costa Rica need to study their record in the light of the Latin American Mission and the Assemblies of God at work in Costa Rica—not that of Methodist Churches in Panama or Mexico. Graphs portraying comparative growths of several homogeneous-unit Churches are extremely useful. They redeem denominations from complacency.

In the fourth place, a good basic knowledge will include facts about the salaries of ministers and catechists in terms of the average income of *the section of society becoming Christian.* A ministerial scale of recompense possible to the one segment of society becoming Christian is an absolute necessity for church growth.

Foundational knowledge of the physical Church, of the sort I have been outlining, is essential to dispel the fog in missionary thinking about church growth.

Misleading Statistics

Before suggesting a system for obtaining such data as a regular thing, let me pause to observe that exact knowledge of church growth frequently fails owing to erroneous statistics. A good example comes from Japan. Various interdenominational agencies have been gathering and publishing statistics of Churches in Japan. These have come out in the *World Missionary Atlas* of 1925, the *Interpretative Statistical Survey* of 1938, the very useful *World Christian Handbooks* of 1949, 1952, and 1957, and other summaries. The figures in these books for the communicant or full members of the Episcopal Church in Japan yield the following table.

INTERDENOMINATIONAL FIGURES

1925	12,017	World Missionary Atlas
1938	26,818	Interpretative Statistical Survey
1949	45,900	World Christian Handbook, 1949
1952	28,236	World Christian Handbook, 1952
1957	38,538	World Christian Handbook, 1957
1960	46,317	Japan Christian Handbook, 1960

Note how in the twenty-four years between 1925 and 1949, during which Japan passed through the flames of World War II, the membership according to these figures almost quadrupled, from 12,000 to 46,000. Then in the wonderfully responsive postwar Japan, in three years, 1949–1952, the Episcopalians lost half their members; then the Church climbed back to an all-time high of 46,300 in 1960. The trouble with these figures is that—though true in a way—they are meaningless. Different categories have been reported in different years.

The Episcopal Church in Japan records membership accurately in four columns, as follows. For the six years in question I give figures furnished to Tetsunao Yamamori at the Institute of Church Growth by the Episcopal historian Rev. Francis Matsudaira.

OFFICIAL EPISCOPAL FIGURES

	Active Communicants	*Total Communicants*	*Active Members*	*Total Members*
1925		12,017		
1938	11,605	18,192	28,606	47,244
1949	9,971	12,950	19,891	25,522
1952	13,199	16,749	25,568	34,970
1957	16,237	20,224	29,532	40,802
1960	17,418	21,659	30,713	43,891

"Total Communicants" means all those who, if they wished to, could commune. "Active Communicants" means those who do commune at least once a year. "Active Members" means all baptized persons (including infants) who come to church or whose parents come to church. "Total Members" means all the living baptized on the roll whether attending church at all or not.

In 1925 the interdenominational figures for "Full Members" (12,017) were taken, as they should have been, from the "Total Communicants" column. In 1938, however, the interdenominational figures for "Full Members" (26,818) were taken—as they should *not* have been—from the "Active Members" column of the table just above. In 1949 the interdenominational figures (45,900) were taken from the "Total Members" column. A further source of inaccuracy is that interdenominational figures usually take two or three years to get printed, so that the 38,538 of the 1957 *World Christian Handbook* comes from column 4 for 1955 or perhaps 1954. The 26,818 in the 1938 *Statistical Survey* are in fact "Active Members" for 1936, not 1938. The 45,900 "Total Members" reported to *World Christian Handbook* for 1949 were not for 1949 (after the war) but for 1937.

Changing categories (columns) is a frequent source of error in membership records. As demonstrated above, it makes weird reading. Denominational figures gathered regularly year after year and obtained direct from Church and mission headquarters are relatively free from this error; but interdenominational figures gathered at intervals (and impossible to check against figures of the previous year) are particularly susceptible to it.

Responsible Membership Accounting

The work done at the Institute of Church Growth by men of baptist and pedobaptist, congregational, and episcopal ecclesiology indicates that it is now quite possible to obtain responsible membership accounting, with all its advantages for all denominations. Only three small steps are needed.

First, Christian mission needs to work out a *uniform way* of recording those facts which have a vital bearing on church growth: the numbers of catechumens, members, believers' baptisms and confirmations, infant dedications and baptisms, kinship webs, causes of loss, and the like. All branches of the Church can use the *same basic forms and definitions*. Three research fellowships at the Institute of Church Growth should be given by widely separated but representative branches of the Church Universal. Suppose the Assemblies of God, United Presbyterian, and Protestant Episcopal Churches were to assign a man apiece to work out, in co-operation with each other, a form to be used by all Afericasian Protestant Churches. Within five years after the perfected form was put out, half the congregations of the Protestant world would be using it and within the next five years half the remainder would be. Using the same basic forms is a type of co-operation and common sense which will benefit every younger Church and every missionary society.

The second simple step is for missionary societies to make continued aid to younger Churches, whether in Eurica or Afericasia, dependent on a thoroughly accurate system of keeping all records having to do with church growth. Missionary societies already insist on businesslike accounting for funds. It is more important to keep track of church growth than of money. All boards already require annual statistical reports. A small move in this direction would achieve the desired end.

A third simple step is for Christian world mission to invite denominational missionary societies, faith missionary societies, and Afericasian Churches to appoint one missionary statistician per hundred thousand communicants. This man should always serve out of his country. His hundred thousand communicants might be found in a hundred branches of the Church Universal or in one. His would be an ecumenical enterprise in the best sense of the word. He would be available to all Churches of his area desiring his services; would travel throughout the churches of his hundred thousand members making sure that the recorded facts about membership and church growth were accurate, meaningful, and up to date. He would lecture in Bible training schools and theological seminaries so that catechists and ministers, as a part of their preparation, might know the universal system of membership accounting.

The appointment of these missionary statisticians would not burden the missionary movement. For example, in Ecuador, Peru, and Bolivia there are over 1,200 missionaries and fewer than 100,000 communicant Evangelicals. The appointment of one of the 1,200 for this area would seem to be well within the range of possibility.

Many branches of the Church may want to amplify the basic form for their own use. Nothing would prevent their doing so. As long as they made out the basic form they could gather as much additional information as they wished.

This uniform responsible system would immediately give to Christian world mission a firm, comparable, and significant measure of accomplishment. No longer would Churches and missions grope in a fog; they would know where they stand, and where their comrades and fellow Christians stand. They would not take refuge in "pieces of mission work" and vague "outreach." They already yield full allegiance to the theory of winning men to Christ and multiplying churches throughout the whole earth. But they would then know how in actuality they are getting along with that aspect of God's commission.

Summary

I have stressed the need for understanding the exact nature of each homogeneous-unit Church: its physical shape, its history, its social links, its past rate of growth and probable future rate of growth, and other facts that bear on membership increase. Continual research into and study of these matters is an urgent necessity. Seeing the structure and antecedents of church growth in each cluster of churches is a crucial issue in Christian mission today.

That this summary is in line with some serious thinking about the Church is evident from the weighty closing words of Bishop Wickam's Introduction to his book, *Facts and Figures about the Church of England.*

> The strategy of mission, wise deployment of manpower, the right orientation of the mind of the Church, the training of the clergy and laity appropriate to the tasks, these require both statistical and depth studies. The location of the "areas" of such studies, the theological interpretation of their findings, and the consideration of possible policies consequent upon them is a specialized task, and it is to be hoped that in due course there may be a . . . group . . . concerned to do this for the Church.

X

DYNAMICS OF CHURCH GROWTH

EUGENE A. NIDA

Growth, whether of the individual or of a social structure, is always a series of increasing and diminishing surges. That is to say, it is never one continuous expansion at a steady rate for any long period of time, but reflects fluctuating changes in the essential tensions that always exist between an orderly expanding structure and the disorderly inroads of random behavior—what sociologists have described as "social entropy," on the analogy of the second law of thermodynamics.

Theoretically, we would like to think of churches as expanding at a steady rate of 10 per cent per year, so as to make possible an effective assimilation of new converts as well as to provide a significant challenge to the unreached world. But neither history nor the nature of human behavior provides any basis for such a theoretically desirable mode of growth. The best we can hope for is a series of undulations with continuously higher crests. If, however, we are to understand what is involved in the dynamics of growth, we must give some careful attention to the processes of change that occur in innovations of group or individual behavior and then analyze certain principal factors which are present in the "cooling-off" stages.

Some of the major characteristics of the dynamics of change may be diagramed in the following way:

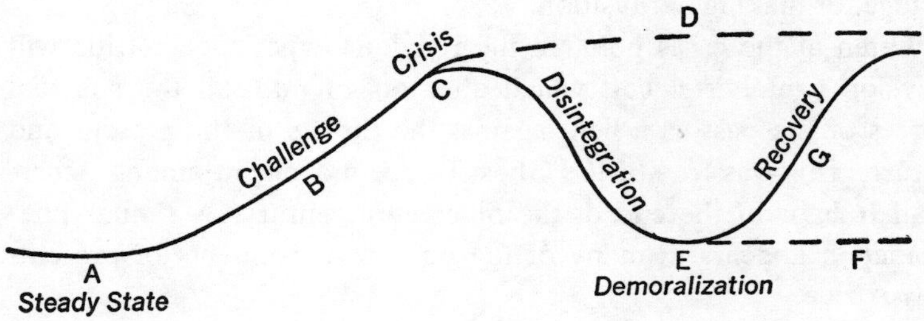

A movement toward change normally begins with what may be called a steady state, at least with regard to the type of change under consideration. From position A the change or pressure toward change progresses, slowly at first and then with increased momentum, until at point B or C the society experiences a crisis. Among the Karens in Burma the challenge to become Christians may be said to have occurred at B, for there were many cultural factors which positively influenced many of the people to enter the church. In large measure those groups that espoused Christianity were able to proceed through the crisis C, and by the bridge of D adjusted readily and effectively to the outside world; for they adopted a positive attitude toward education and responsibility for community life.

In the case of the Tobas in Argentina, many of whom adopted Christianity after defeat by the Argentinian armed forces, and of the Hawaiians, who had become disillusioned with their own religion, one may say that the decision to adjust came just after a severe cultural crisis, but before demoralization had set in. For the Tobas, there is considerable demoralization because of a failure to adjust to the socioeconomic demands of Argentinian life; their former nomadic "buzzard culture," which was based on a pattern of "stuff and starve," has had to undergo some radical shifts to accommodate itself to a system of "slave and save" as required in a money economy. Though the people are far from accomplishing their goals, many of the Evangelicals have found in their Christian faith their one sustaining influence and the most important cultural bridge for making a transition.

Often at the crisis point in the religious experience a tribe will develop a nativistic cult which attempts to rally all the spiritual forces of the past as a help against the threats of the present and future. This was true of the Ghost Dance movement among American Indians at the end of the nineteenth century. A similar phenomenon appears in many of the prophet movements of present-day Africa.

When a society fails to meet the challenge of a superior cultural force, utter demoralization may result, expressed religiously in escapist cults, such as peyote worship among the Indians of the Middle West and group drunkenness among the Indians of the Altiplano in South America. In some areas of Southeast Asia the cargo cults, whose adherents believe that by magic they can bring to their shores great steamships filled with refrigerators, cars, motorcycles, guns, and radios, reflect certain elements of nativistic defense cults, together with escapist tendencies. The Khmus in the interior regions of Laos believe, not in magic cargos, but in a magic cave in which they will find all sorts of Western luxuries—a belief skillfully exploited by some Communist propagandists.

Again, among the Indians of the Altiplano of South America socioeconomic circumstances have been such as to keep the people in a state of demoralization for several centuries. However, where a positive possibility for adjustment exists and a few persons offer leadership, a society can usually begin the long struggle up toward reconstruction. If, in the meantime, the tribal culture has largely disappeared, as for example with a number of the Great Plains Indian tribes, the reconstruction will involve primarily isolated individuals. Where there is a group orientation, however, the entire society may gradually work out its salvation, as in the case of the Navajo and Hopi, who are now beginning to adjust themselves to the white culture.

For the individual member of a culture, there may be a similar pattern of behavioral crisis, demoralization, and readjustment. However, changes in an individual's life are usually accomplished more rapidly than in an entire group, especially if the individual is in a new cultural environment or in a group which is in process of rapid change. Accordingly, evangelistic work is more likely to be successful in a new town, or even in a new suburb of an old town, than in an old town; for in such new situations traditional socio-religious ties are not so strong. Often a person in such circumstances is not suspicious of intruders, but rather is looking for new friends. Likewise, in a population already in the process of change, even when the latter is apparently unrelated to religious values (e.g., change of employment or political structure), it is possible for people to adjust more rapidly to changes of religious values; for culture change then acquires a snowball momentum.

The Cooling Off of Christian Movements

After a period of rapid growth all movements experience periods of "cooling off," even when external conditions continue to appear quite propitious. The Naga Hills churches of India have already leveled off in growth, and more recently even the spectacular increase among the Mountain Peoples of Formosa has greatly abated. This same experience of cooling off has occurred in all religious movements, Christian and non-Christian, for it is a basic characteristic of all human institutions. It is essentially a form of entropy, as stated in the second law of thermodynamics. That is, all other things being equal, any group activity will in time tend to diminish in intensity, since familiarity with the patterns of behavior results in loss of dynamic impact. For example, the same message that brings a tremendous spiritual experience to one generation, as the people move from fear-ridden paganism into Christianity, becomes matter-of-fact to the second generation, which has never experienced the earlier intense conflict or crisis. Thus the impact of the original message is greatly reduced by long acquaintance with it, and perception of the contrasts between the old and the new way of life becomes increasingly dulled by habitual contact and adjustment. Moreover, what at one time was obviously "news" is no longer new, hence the motivation to share it is weaker and the desire to hear about it significantly less acute. Accordingly, although the Church still possesses the "eternal Gospel," the members of the Christian community experience less and less concern for its propagation, while non-Christians are less and less impressed with what they hear.

A number of factors increase entropy or speed up the cooling-off process. For example, if a movement lacks leadership or organized direction, it usually disintegrates rapidly, for there is nothing to channel the energies of the individuals involved. At the same time, however, overorganization can also increase entropy, for the organizational structure may be so heavy, cumbersome, and awkward as to require practically all the energies of the individuals to keep the machine going, with the result that the organization is not able to do more than keep the wheels going around. If there is no innovation within a movement it will likewise collapse of its own weight, since organizations must bring in new elements if they are to remain living organisms. When the goal of an organization has been reached, entropy often sets in rapidly, for once the objective is realized, those concerned feel that there is no need for the organization. Again, entropy may come into play equally fast if the goals of a movement are regarded as utterly unattainable.

To reduce entropy—that is, to prevent cooling off and sustain the power of growth of a movement—one must adopt counteractive measures. These include: (1) a balance of organization vs. work; (2) new leadership with fresh vigor; (3) new information, which can serve to introduce new goals and better ways of attaining objectives. There is thus a constant need for prophet and pastor, for discipling and perfecting, for justification and santification.

Growth in an organization occurs as a series of periodic advances, followed by slackening of the pace, during which time the organism gathers new power and momentum for a further increase. This fundamental law of individual and social life must be recognized in dealing with all problems of growth, including church growth. When the crowds are surging in, one must not be so optimistic as to think that this pace will continue forever; nor should one be unduly pessimistic when growth ceases and preparation for revitalization must begin. During the upward phase of the cycle one should anticipate these developments and prepare people for the tapering off of growth by emphasizing the qualities necessary for steadfastness; in periods of decline, one must anticipate later opportunities for growth by helping people to learn how to extend their witness and expand their fellowship. In other words, we should be ahead of the fluctuations, rather than lag behind them. By anticipating the downswings we can often reduce their severity and at the same time prepare effectively for greater growth in the future.

Basic Factors Influencing Church Growth

The two great factors influencing church growth are (1) the supernatural (i.e., the work of the Holy Spirit) and (2) the human. The work of God is not, however, an isolated element in church growth, but one that completely interpenetrates the basic human factors, which are primarily (a) communication, (b) economics, in the broad sense of the term, and (c) leadership. Since the work of the Holy Spirit is considered fully in other chapters, it is not treated here, but one must constantly bear in mind that none of the factors affecting church growth can be fully understood apart from a recognition of the role of the Spirit.

Communication

The dynamics of a social movement greatly depend upon the information that gives rise to its distinctive character and also largely determines the direction of its development. Church growth must therefore be studied in terms of certain fundamental aspects of communication. Such communication is of two types: (1) the communication that takes place within the church structure, and (2) the communication of the Church to society.

Communication within the Church. This is of two principal

kinds: related to the internal functioning of the organization and the life of the people within the fellowship. Effective communication among various functioning units of a church organization is essential to church growth. Without it there is little or no possibility for co-operation in an undertaking. The real difficulty arises when, as often happens, internal communication multiplies more rapidly than growth advances. In other words, the organization becomes bound up in its own internal red tape. Unfortunately, within the bureaucratic structure of many church organizations with a multiplicity of committees, boards, and related secretaries, internal communication may become an excuse for lack of growth. That is to say, even though a department or institution is not expanding or extending its ministry, it can give a semblance of efficiency by multiplying its forms and increasing its interoffice memos—a typical example of Parkinson's Law. In general, however, such excesses of internal communication do not so much prevent church growth as signal the end of it, for the mushrooming of a bureaucracy normally marks the close of a creative period. During such a latent period organizations may concentrate their energies on writing their history and tidying up their statistical reports. During times of rapid growth, on the other hand, the leaders are usually too much concerned with growing pains to be worried about recounting the past or even taking stock of the present.

Moreover, preoccupation with internal communication can so stifle efforts to develop new modes and illuminate and elaborate the content of the Church's message that the more important matter of communication to society is seriously impaired.

More important than communication that merely serves the internal functioning of an organization is that which provides its members with the dynamic information guiding their conduct and discipline; namely, their liturgical and ritual practices and their interpersonal conduct. In a sense it may be said that the Church has always lived in tension between the priestly and the prophetic functions of communication: whether, for example, communication is to be primarily related to the people's worship or to the daily behavior of the religious community. In either case, an organization with a long history tends to develop its own distinctive vocabulary and modes of expression. As a result, such a group becomes more and more isolated from the larger society surrounding it and ultimately tends to become a kind of inbred, esoteric community. The distinctive vocabulary developed by such a group becomes increasingly a sign of belonging and of group identification, rather than a means of communication with the world or of serving practical human needs. Such a development is almost inevitable when a persecuted minority stops growing, since protection from the overwhelming majority seems to demand a kind of distinctive, introverted terminology. Such a terminology unfortunately becomes less and less useful in talking to or about the world in which the majority of people live.

Some Churches have traditionally encouraged a specialized form of language, not only to promote unity but also to inspire awe. Thus Latin, Old Church Slavonic, *Koine* Greek, Old Armenian, Ethiopic, and Syriac are all used today by different church groups. Even within Protestantism, which has so emphasized prophetic communication to the world, there has been an increasing use of Latinized vocabulary—e.g., *sanctification, justification, predestination, propitiation, expiation, conversion,* and *salvation.* All these terms have perfectly good dictionary definitions, but they are words not often found on the lips of laymen. Nor is there any significant improvement in the present tendency to use such words as *confrontation, ecumenical, koinonia, kerygma, Heilsgeschichte,* and *eschatology.*

It is a notable fact that during its times of greatest creativity and growth the Church has tended to employ the language of the common man to explain "uncommon" truths. This practice was certainly a dominant element in the life of the early Church, and was boldly exemplified in the Reformation as well. Fortunately for the continued vitality of the Church, such language is increasingly employed in present-day translations of the Bible into the principal European languages.

Communication of the Church to society. This involves three important elements: (1) the role of the source, (2) the nature of the medium, and (3) the type of audience to which the message is directed.

Of these factors, the source is probably the most important; for in the communication of a living message the life of the communicator is inevitably a critical factor. Often it poses a difficult problem. Thus, in Latin America the missionary's role is usually difficult. Though he would like to function as a teacher, he is forced instead into the role of *patron* as the head of an enterprise which hires workers and carries on a business. Similarly, in Africa many a missionary who has set out to be a "prophet" has ended in competition with the chief. Intending otherwise, he nevertheless becomes involved in endless palavers involving his employees and the people living on or near the mission.

But in some societies the formal role of the communicator is less important than the personal and charismatic qualities of the source. In the Philippines, for example, Felix Manalo combined a number of qualities important in the oriental religious leader: (1) a dynamic personality, (2) a prophetic distance from the people, which tends to make his person sacrosanct, (3) a capacity for identification with the people's problems by solicitous concern for their daily needs, (4) an emotionally charged manner of speaking, and (5) the conviction of being a divinely appointed messenger of the truth. Again, in Korea some of the most successful leaders of the semi-Christian "prophet" movements have personified the role of magic-working and spirit-invoking shamans, though with Christian overtones and symbolism.

Nor can the role of a communicator be properly analyzed without considering the social class of which he is a part. Most societies expect and require the source of religious information to be from a class superior to those whom he wishes to reach, for the authoritarian nature of religious instruction seems to imply the need for information coming down from an upper to a lower class. In other words, religious information descends socially. Within a complex culture, the network of religious communication quite naturally involves certain significant barriers, e.g., between urban and rural persons, between competing ethnic groups, and between hostile socioeconomic factions. Within a face-to-face society, communication flows readily along family and clan lines, but tends to encounter suspicion and resistance when it flows between groups.

It is, of course, possible to employ a proper source of communication but still use the wrong medium. For example, a truck-mounted loud-speaker employed to broadcast a religious service to a Hopi village would be regarded as a complete outrage, since the Hopis regard religion as something which should be discussed only in the intimate secrecy of the *kiva.* In American life the value of radio for evangelization has undoubtedly been exaggerated. Though the theoretical audience is great, the actual number of otherwise unreached persons significantly influenced by radio is probably startlingly limited. Particularly is this true when a program attempts to reach the "lost" while depending for support upon those who are not "lost" but favor hearing the message explained in the old-fashioned language and standard clichés employed by the radio preacher. On the other hand, in certain situations radio can hurdle cultural barriers and reach beyond social and political curtains; but the living reality of a faith must generally be communicated by and to living men and women who meet in a direct interpersonal context.

Some of the most acute problems in church growth involve the question, not only of what the Church should say and how it should be said, but also of the type of audience to which the message should be directed. In a day of mass communication and demographic thinking, it is customary to think primarily in terms of the masses and to evaluate the impact of the message in terms of listening-minutes or viewer-minutes. But the Gospel is neither soap nor breakfast food, and response is not calculable in terms of audience size. In communicating the Gospel there is also the qualitative and spiritual dimension; for men witness to the truth, but it is the Spirit of God that "communicates" this truth to the life of the believer. A study of the communication of the Church to society that fails to take into account this supernatural factor is bound to be meager and impaired.

While recognizing the limitations of mass techniques, however, it is important not to exclude mass evangelism as a legitimate approach to the problem of church growth. Although the end results of large mass meetings are seldom proportionate to the energy expended, the real answer to this problem appears to be, not to choose between mass and personal evangelism (or communication), but to employ both, each in the circumstances where the method seems to have the best chances of eliciting a significant response.

But a Church must not depend primarily on mass evangelism. No Church can excuse its lack of growth merely by citing the fact that people no longer respond to the evangelist's pleas. Even in the cultural context that exists in so-called Christian lands, the professional evangelist's efforts are confined primarily to those who are already attracted to the Church. Any real church growth must depend upon the witness of the laity, who in their daily contacts are in vital relationship with the world. The evangelist can confirm the saints and restore the backslider, but the lay believer is the indispensable communicator to the world outside.

Types of Communication. Because of a preoccupation with the verbalization of our faith, we Protestants tend to think of religious communication as essentially a technique for communicating or transmitting words. At the same time, we generally focus our attention upon the formal elements of verbal communication, including ritual or liturgical formulas and theologically approved explanations of belief given in sermons, books, ritual prayers, and devotional literature. But formal communication is rarely as important as informal sharing—for example, the casual remarks people make about their faith and the opinions and rumors that spread about the behavior of church members. Such informal communication is immeasurably more important than formal methods, both in promoting and in church growth.

Unfortunately, with the increasing growth of professionalism in any movement, many new believers think they cannot serve as communicators because they do not possess the technical knowledge required for formal communication. They may even be encouraged in this idea by missionaries or church leaders who, either because of a latent feeling of insecurity as to their own indispensability or because of some exaggerated idea of the need for theological exactness, insist that recent converts should not attempt to witness to their faith until they are fully instructed. In actual practice, of course, they are teaching such persons, not to witness, but to preach sermonettes, which are often both doctrinally and experientially beyond the convert's capacities. In one area in Mexico where missionaries worked for approximately ten years, there was never more than a handful of believers and no significant growth took place, because the missionaries insisted that the converts were never quite ready to witness to the people in other villages. When another group without such exaggerated ideas of doctrinal purity came into the region, several churches were formed almost immediately, but not from among those who had been in contact with this esoteric handful of overnurtured individuals.

Nor is communication limited to formal and informal means of transmitting verbal symbols. In fact, nonverbal symbols are often much more persuasive. Certainly the observable "sermons" of unselfish behavior speak louder and more effectively than any polished discourse. Religious systems may, of course, differ radically in their communicative emphases, and visual and behavioral symbols may be much more than isolated objects and acts. In fact, they may constitute entire systems of communication. In Roman Catholicism, for example, a primary purpose of communication is an emotive reaction to a set of nonverbal symbols, to be found not only in the images, pictures, and emblems of the Church, but also in the pageantry and ritual of the Mass. Such awe-inspiring visual symbols are powerful elements in communication. It is not without interest, therefore, that in many of the rapidly growing indigenous movements in Latin America one finds a dramatic use of nonverbal symbolization in warm colors and bold architectural forms; participation of the laity in the service (e.g., standing whenever God speaks to man through the Scriptures, kneeling whenever men speak to God in prayer); an indigenous hymnody; and dramatic pageantry (e.g., in filing forward to give their offerings, group prayer for the sick, and laying on of hands).

One highly important form of symbolization is to be found in music, which, though often containing verbal elements (the words to the music), manifests its power principally by means of its melodic pattern, tone color, and harmonic structure. All creative and extensive periods of church growth have been characterized by an appropriate indigenous hymnody, for the musical expression of praise and gladness is one of the universal forms of corporate religious activity. It has been said that more people are sung into the kingdom than are preached in; and though this may not be entirely true, there is nevertheless enough truth in the assertion to make it certain that an indigenous hymnody can be an integral and important part of any significant program of church growth.

Communicative Roles. To transmit a message to a society involves the use of a complex network of communication, in which different people have quite different roles, the nature of which depends upon their complex, multidimensional interrelationships. Effective transmission of the Christian message and subsequent growth in the Church in response to this message depend largely upon the manner in which the message is channeled. In general, there are four roles in communication: (1) censors, (2) creators, (3) purveyors, and (4) receivers.

The censors of information are usually the chiefs, rulers, elders, and upper-class leaders—all those who decide whether or not a particular message is to be accepted or rejected. Members of the ruling class normally do not create information, but they do determine which one of several alternative courses of action is to be followed. In general, they make their decisions on the basis of the traditional values and mores of the society, accepting what seems to reinforce its traditions and maintain the status quo, and rejecting whatever seems to threaten or undermine the group's heritage or position.

The creators of information within a group are usually not the leaders themselves, but rather those who in various ways are competing for leadership. They are generally the intellectuals, whether in a sophisticated European society or in a small Indian tribe of the Amazon, who are in rebellion against things as they are and desire change. Among the Palawanos of the Philippines, they are the young men who have traveled outside the tribe. In the Congo, they are the young évolués, whose French education has caused them to rebel against tribal authority and customs. In Latin America, they are the poor university students who are determined to turn society upside down and are only waiting for a *caudillo* to lead the way.

The purveyors of information in a technological society are the reporters for communications media—newspapers, radio, and television. In primitive villages, they are the town crier, drummer, or chief's messenger. In small towns of the Western world, barbers, taxi drivers, bartenders, and itinerant tradesmen are often the most important purveyors of information. In central Africa, the truck drivers and petty inspectors produce a constant flow of information from one place to another. At the same time, of course, everyone serves to some extent as a purveyor of information. Similarly all persons are receivers of it, but some play only a limited role as purveyors—e.g., children, the poorly educated, and the socially isolated.

In evaluating one's approach to a society, it is important to determine just what communicative role is essential for the spread of the Gospel. Those who are principally censors of information are not likely to take much initiative in communicating the message to others, for they sit in judgment on information rather than broadcast it. On the other hand, those who are primarily receivers of information may be attracted to the message, but they are not likely to be strategic disseminators. In some societies, and in certain restricted circumstances, children can be very useful in providing an entrance to the family, but by and large proportionately too much time has been spent on children rather than on the total family group.

For the most effective church growth, messages should be directed primarily to the creators and purveyors of information, who in general belong to the dynamic middle of the society, rather than to the upper or lower extreme.

Patterns of Support

Hampering the growth of a Church as much as any other single element is its failure to adjust its economic patterns to those of the society in which it attempts to work, for the economic factors are crucial. In the first place, no church will consistently pay its pastor more than the average salary of its lay leadership—not because the group is unable to do so, nor because a missionary cannot convince the people that their pastor should be paid more, but merely because the lay leadership does not think in such terms. Of course, under pressure of mission subsidy the lay leaders may agree to pay a relatively higher salary. Nevertheless, left to themselves they will almost inevitably revert to a pastoral salary that is no higher than the average of their own, though they may quite happily pay one that is lower. In the second place, it often happens that churches which are in the greatest need of well-trained leadership are precisely those least able to support men with the requisite training. In the third place, systems of formal education of the ministry often stimulate aspirations for income which are disproportionate to what the churches can provide.

In the sending Churches it is taken for granted that a pastor should give full time to the ministry and should be paid accordingly. As a result, mission boards have generally felt that subsidizing "native workers" is the only means of developing a Church. However, the problems in this procedure are enormous. Obviously no local church wishes to take on responsibility for a pastor's salary as long as the mission will provide it, and any attempt by the mission to withdraw its support is regarded as a policy of stinginess. On the other hand, when a local pastor is paid from foreign funds, the church tends to feel that he is an employee of the mission and hence has sold out to foreign leadership. At the same time, the laity within a church may insist that, since the pastor is paid to do church work and they are not, all the work of the church is his responsibility, and they are accordingly relieved of any necessity to witness or promote the cause. Moreover, salary arrangements which are known only to the mission and the local pastor and not to the church as a whole tend to raise suspicions, not only within the church constituency but also among those outside it.

Instead of gradually taking on the support of a full-time worker as a church feels the need for such a person, usual mission practice is to give full support at first and then gradually withdraw funds, leaving support to the church. The practice more often than not provokes resentment, especially if the congregation has been "given" a building which is more expensive to keep up than the people can afford.

In general, missions provide three types of financial support for local national workers: (1) fully paid salaries from foreign funds, administered by the foreign mission; (2) fully paid salaries, with a graduated scale of less and less subsidy from the mission, until eventually the salary is paid entirely by the local church; (3) indirect and partial support of workers through housing, education of children, medical help, or land to cultivate.

On the whole, the first type of support—fully paid salaries from foreign funds—should never be undertaken if the mission is truly concerned with effective church growth; for nothing so stifles local enthusiasm and leadership as foreign-paid ministers.

The second system—fully paid salaries gradually taken over by the local church—has the dubious advantage of cutting off the dog's tail an inch at a time, under the assumption that it hurts less. In point of fact, the process can be very painful to the church program and utterly disruptive of interpersonal relationships and loyalties. Of course, if a mission has begun with the first type of support—fully paid—a complete cutting off can be both unjust and unwise; but it is rarely satisfactory to start with the second system. If, however, such an arrangement is made, the funds for the salary should be paid to and administered by the national Church and not by the mission.

The third type—the indirect partial support of the ministry through special benefits—often constitutes an important and effective contribution by the mission, for it does not seem to damage the local sense of responsibility to the same extent as the other two methods. However, it may under certain circumstances bring about grave misunderstanding.

In the most rapidly growing indigenous Churches no foreign funds are available, and it is left entirely to the local congregation to decide when and how they will support their ministry. In general, this support is given in three steps, depending upon local circumstances: (1) cultivation of the pastor's garden, carrying his water, herding his sheep, providing gifts of food and lodging, and so on; (2) giving the pastor special gifts of money for travel, for attending conferences, and for obtaining the benefits of training institutes; and finally (3) full support, when and as the program grows. Though this system of support is not only ideal but necessary for an indigenous movement, it is difficult for a mission to sponsor it. In the first place, missionaries are usually very anxious that the work should grow rapidly, and heavy subsidies seem the best possible kind of investment to this end. At the same time, the individual missionary is usually not in a position to refuse to grant a subsidy. He cannot plead poverty or lack of funds, for even what seems to him a modest living standard usually makes him appear a relatively rich person in the community. Furthermore, his attitudes and behavior almost inevitably mark him in the community as belonging to the class of landowners or businessmen and only rarely to the role of "prophet." Accordingly, not only because of his own relative affluence but because of the role assigned to him by the local people themselves, he soon comes to be regarded as the manager of a big business.

It is obvious, of course, that subsidies for the salaries of nationals do pay off in the immediate growth of a program. When a mission can come in and hire an abundance of national workers (often "stealing" them from other Churches, and more often than not getting some of the spiritual outcasts into the bargain), the mission can obviously count on a rather rapid expansion of its work. However, the rate of growth will almost inevitably level off rapidly, and even fall off appreciably during the subsequent period of adjustment in subsidy. Sometimes a mission-sponsored program never regains its original momentum, while time after time indigenously led and supported programs, though much slower at the start, rapidly push ahead and in time outstrip the mission-supported undertakings. Some of the most obvious examples of this can be found in Chile, where the number of indigenous Pentecostals is four times as great as all the other groups combined; in Brazil, where indigenous Pentecostals have just laid the cornerstone for the largest Protestant church in the world, to seat 25,000; and in the Philippines, where the Iglesia ni Cristo founded by Felix Manalo has rapidly outstripped all Protestant Churches, both in total growth and in the value of church properties.

Patterns of Leadership

Qualifications for leadership differ considerably from culture to culture. For example, in Latin America the leader must be a strong personality, capable of both charming his followers by his presence and influencing them vitally by his words. In the United States a charismatic public appearance is certainly an asset, but the ability to organize and manage is thought even more important. In India, on the other hand, the religious leader has been traditionally the ascetic prophet—the holy man who has little or none of the external appearance considered indispensable to the successful Western leader. In each of these situations leadership is defined ideally in terms congenial to the culture. In actual practice, moreover, the leadership within the churches has developed along quite different lines in these different cultures.

Patterns of leadership are also influenced by specific historical developments. For example, one reason for the phenomenal growth of the Christian Church in Korea prior to World War II was the opportunity it offered Koreans for leadership. At that time the Japanese controlled practically all institutions and Koreans were kept almost exclusively in secondary roles or were mere puppets. In any case, they were functionally subordinate even when they were formally heads of institutions. The one exception to this monopoly of leadership by the Japanese was found in the Christian churches; and accordingly many young men anxious to express their capacity for leadership were attracted to the Church. Furthermore, the Christian Church became a symbol of anti-Japanese sentiment, and hence adherence to or leadership of such an institution fulfilled secret as well as manifest longings for both personal and national recognition.

Though social psychologists are still not able to define absolutely the characteristics of personality that make for leadership, one thing is certain: leadership ability is not the exclusive or permanent possession of certain families or of a single social class. The dynamic changes constantly taking place within any and all societies make for a constantly changing pattern of leadership structure. In an urban society, families constituting the ruling class do not remain permanently in power, because of their opposition to changes. By and large they are content to maintain and preserve the status quo, since their position and power depend upon it. Thus they tend to favor traditional institutions and to foster a static power structure, with little or no adjustment to the realities of change being forced upon the society by technological or ideological evolution. At the other end of the scale are the lowest classes, who have drifted to the bottom and given up the struggle, convinced that the chances for substantial improvement in their condition are nil. Such persons are the ready accomplices of revolution, for they cannot conceive that their circumstances could be worse; they are quite prepared to risk their crumbs of bread for the loaves promised by revolutionary leaders.

The potential for dynamic change in any urban society normally exists, not in the largely static extremes of high and low, but in the seething middle. The most dynamic part of this middle class is usually not the upper bracket, which often identifies its interests with those of the upper class, nor the lower bracket, which may be relatively content with having risen above the level of indigence. Rather, the dynamic core of society is concentrated in the aspiring middle, where there is little to lose by change and much to gain by the possibility of catapulting into leadership. It is in this group that one usually finds a number of highly intelligent rebels who are determined to change their world. Such persons are often convinced that their personal potential is much greater than present circumstances will allow to be fulfilled, and that only by radically changing the situation in which they live can they adequately express themselves.

In a face-to-face society there is no such class structuring as I have described in the foregoing paragraph. However, there are similar tensions, not only among the various clans or family groups but also between the young men and the traditional leadership, usually headed by a chief and his advising elders. Espousing new ideas about the world and determined to profit by the developments of a "new day," the young men seek to upset the reactionary power of the old men and to undermine the forms that thwart their efforts toward change.

In its approach to a society the Church has adopted two different courses: (1) that of winning over the present leadership by (a) giving gifts or offering political advantages to the people in power, or (b) compelling compliance by use of military force (a widely employed and defended method of church expansion in the sixteenth century in Latin America); or (2) influencing a significant segment of the "dynamic middle" of the society to produce the desired changes, first in the lives of believers and then—as the Church hopes—within society as a whole. The first method (which might be called the glass-beads or gunpowder approach) produces quicker and more evident gains, but the results are generally superficial, for religion is the most resistant of all cultural features. The second method (which may be symbolized as "leaven") is much slower, but the gains are surer. By influencing a small segment of society, one may either plan a violent assault against the existing leadership (as in political revolutions), or foster the slower method of gradually but surely leavening the whole lump.

This method of leaven is the one most widely used by Protestant missions. In country after country subjected to such a method an examination of the Church's growth indicates that the most significant leadership in the process comes from the dynamic middle of the culture. For example, in Latin America an overwhelming number of Evangelical pastors come from families in which the father was an independent tradesman—carpenter, shoemaker, baker, plasterer, stonemason, or small merchant—men not identified with the powerful ruling caste or class and at the same time to some extent economically independent of it. These persons are often the first to see in the Evangelical message a source of hope for a new life, and to be willing to make the necessary sacrifices to identify with it.

Types of Leadership Training. The development of an indigenous ministry is almost always worked out by missionaries in terms of schools, institutes, and seminaries—institutions of formal education with a three- or four-year educational program built upon minimal requirements in the national school system. Such programs closely parallel the educational standards of the sending Churches, though an implicit paternalism usually justifies the watering-down of the standard of instruction to accommodate the educational deficiencies shown by the students. Such educational programs send out into the ministry a group of neophytes, usually not older than twenty to twenty-five, often with expectations of a salary considerably higher than local churches are able to pay. As a result, the mission is usually called upon to subsidize the support of such persons for a number of years.

In most indigenous Churches leaders are normally trained by informal educational methods, primarily through apprenticeship systems. For example, in some indigenous movements in Mexico a congregation which has grown to 50 or 100 members under the tutelage of another church is encouraged to elect a local person as "pastor." He is then ordained by leaders of the movement and authorized to administer the sacraments. This local pastor is often the best-educated person in the congregation; but even so, his principal qualifications are spiritual, not intellectual. Once he has been appointed, he is expected to gather with other pastors weekly or monthly for a period of Bible study, prayer, fasting, and discussion of church plans and programs. Also, he is encouraged to attend frequent conferences of the churches, where he continues to learn more about how to preach, what to teach, and how to organize and develop his church. The salary he receives will depend upon the extent to which the local group is able and willing to support him and to make possible for him both the necessary travel and taking the necessary time from his work as a farmer, carpenter, or mason to give to the church. By selecting a pastor from the community it is possible to develop leadership on a viable economic basis. Such a local person is also likely to be more faithful within his own community than if he were sent into a new area, where there would be fewer social pressures to cause him to conform his life to the new standards he has openly espoused. Moreover, a man who has lived for years in a community has no problem of knowing the people or understanding their problems. Though admittedly it is hard to be a prophet in his own country, a local person will be, at the same time, much less likely to turn renegade.

In the large urban centers as well, training of leadership in the indigenous Churches follows an apprenticeship system. However, because of the larger churches and the greater specialization of functions, the young person with leadership potential is usually given a variety of jobs—ushering, praying for the sick, conducting street meetings, organizing visitation, and caring for the poor. When, at thirty-five to forty years of age, he is given full responsibility as pastor of a church he has had a number of years of training and personal Bible study and presumably is qualified to minister to the needs of the people in both spiritual and temporal ways. In this way, by the informal structuring of training through a series of increasingly important responsibilities, potential leaders are both prepared for their work and constantly screened by the test of practical accomplishment. As a result, the leaders in such indigenous movements are often highly competent.

In general, it is not until the man takes over full responsibility for an important church that his salary is fully paid by the church. Meanwhile he has had a regular secular job by which he earns a living, and by the age of forty has more or less established his appropriate salary level within the economic system. Accordingly, if the church wants him to give up his secular job and devote full time to it, there is no problem in determining what such a man is worth. If, on the other hand, the church cannot afford to support him at his established economic worth, he can either accept the reduction in income or retain his secular job and continue to help as a layman. In these conditions, many laymen in Latin America are actually carrying heavier church responsibilities on a part-time basis than some full-time pastors whose salaries are subsidized by mission funds.

Certain mission-directed programs have in some measure incorporated the apprenticeship system. For example, in Latin America a number of missions have short-term Bible institutes for laymen, with well-integrated programs. If followed over a period of years, these institutes give the students an excellent comprehensive introduction to biblical content and churchmanship. Some formal seminary training programs are purposely interrupted at intervals in order to provide for periods of practical work. During this time the students often travel and live with their missionary leaders in a kind of master-disciple relationship. In still other situations, where it is impossible to bring enough people into the Bible schools to provide adequate leadership, missions have taken the schools out into the villages for short-term intensive courses, with a constant emphasis upon putting every lesson into practice within the framework of the local church.

PART FOUR

Administrational Issues

XI

DIRECTED CONSERVATION

ROBERT CALVIN GUY

Several levels of administration engage in purposeful conservation of the results of mission. Since these results are multitudinous and include many outcomes other than the growth and multiplication of churches, all administration faces at the very beginning the need for establishing priorities. For *what* shall we conserve results? Among many good outcomes, which is *best?* All agree that church growth is important; but so are many other activities of Christian mission. Is any one of supreme importance?

Dr. Otto Piper, speaking at Southwestern Baptist Theological Seminary, recently made a pronouncement which casts light on precisely this question. He said that the Church does not witness as a wealthy man throws crumbs to a beggar but as a farmer sows precious seed, fully aware that his very life depends on the harvest. Christian mission is not an optional activity of the Church. It is not giving away something we can spare. It is doing something essential to our very churchhood, something without which our life withers away.

It is our belief that all levels of administration should act with clear realization that church growth is not only desirable but absolutely necessary. It is not one of many equally desirable outcomes; it is that outcome without which the Church will die. Without it the Church cannot be the Church of Jesus Christ the Savior. If a Church manifests no passion to save others, it may be an ecclesiastical organization, but it is not the Body of Christ. This clear recognition lays particular burdens on administration. Those whose task is to conserve the results of mission march under the necessity of intending the maximum planting of churches. They may be defeated. Some populations may be indifferent to God's call in Christ and look at the Cross with cynicism and unbelief. Administration cannot compel church growth; but it can patiently conserve all the results of mission that favor or achieve it. This we believe is its high privilege.

Conservation at the Board Level

At this level, church growth depends on the careful direction and redirection by board executives of every facet of a mission program toward planting churches and then more churches.

This must be done within the real situation, which may usually be defined in these terms: severely limited means must be used on unlimited opportunities. The choices would not be nearly so difficult for the administrator if he possessed unlimited means to use on limited opportunities. His task is painful. He receives many appeals and finds at his disposal resources to answer only a few of them. If he defines opportunities in New Testament terms and allows himself New Testament expectations, he will increase the pain of his decision. Yet he dare not diminish his burden by whittling down his expectations to human levels.

John R. Mott used the slogan, "The evangelization of the world in this generation." Some leaders today evaluate such an expectation as reflecting the security of a time now long past. They say that World Wars I and II destroyed any such wild optimism and that we must now be satisfied with a more realistic outlook. Perhaps Mott's tremendous expectation was a reflection not of the human possibilities of his day but of a magnitude of faith in and fellowship with Christ which we should strive to emulate. Mission administrators, while attempting great things for God, must expect great things from God. With men it may be impossible, but with God all things are possible. The magnitude of thinking required today will come only from Christ dwelling by faith in the hearts of men.

Evaluating and Conserving

The chapter on underbrush elimination (Chap. VIII) suggested surveys of church and mission program to measure theory against performance. Since budgets are always stretched to the limit, evaluation by skilled personnel often seems to the board an unwarranted expenditure; but in actuality it is an economical procedure. Industry is finding that cost surveys are rapidly repaid. If the objection be raised that mission is not commerce, one may reply that it is so much more important that every possible way of getting maximum mileage from Christian days and dollars must be sought. It is the King's business. In that, we must measure theory against performance.

Evaluation should be made realizing that mission has obligations to the program already operating. Fear that worthy men will be hurt and helpful projects rejected often causes administrators to hesitate in inaugurating surveys and revising present procedures. But it should not. Adequate knowledge of every aspect of the current operation is essential to every administrator. It enables him to determine whether to enlarge the operation, hold it at present level, diminish it, or—while discharging obligations toward it—discontinue it.

The creative administrator, bearing in mind the resources he has, tailors the cloth of the program to fit the opportunity. This is his major responsibility. Such tailoring is so important that the men of the younger Church and their assisting missions whose participation alone can make it effective should share in it to the fullest possible degree. If the administrator believes the cost/result ratio should be considered in determining a church or mission program, nationals and missionaries will benefit by thinking with him along this line. They should also share additional ideas and convictions with him. If a program-result inquiry is contemplated, the men who conduct it and must be judged by it should share in the thinking that precedes its implementation.

National ministers and missionaries often are hungry for help in defining their goals. Instead of rebelling against guidance they express deep desire for adequate definition of the primary task. My conversations with many missionaries show that few of them were given such guidance before being thrust into their work. They were obliged to evolve a plan of action as they went forward. In preparing themes for English classes in college some students write first and then construct the outline from the finished theme. This is hardly a desirable technique, and it is much less desirable in the vast program of mission. There the goals and methods of the program must be defined before projects are begun.

In defining goals for future work and conserving the results of past labors, the freest exchange of ideas between secretaries, nationals, and missionaries ought to be encouraged. Yet frequently there is not enough joint thinking. Despite efforts to share thought, a wide gap often develops between the mental processes of the men on the field and those of the board executive. This is even truer for nationals than for missionaries.

Still greater is the gap between the evaluation that nationals and missionaries may make of portions of the field program and their willingness to express it. In some cases such silence is sin. Paul suggested in Ephesians that we should "walk . . . forbearing one another in love." We should criticize and listen to criticism so long as the ends of love are served, understanding that the wounds inflicted by a friend are to be preferred to the kiss of an enemy. Conservation of results will be difficult so long as nationals or missionaries hesitate to make or hear honest appraisal of the work.

Pruning and Placing

If evaluation demands change in operation or policy, administration will face difficult decisions about pruning and placing. Adequate conservation certainly does not consist simply of continuing everything that has ever been started. Part of the existing work must be pruned and part redirected. Plans long cherished will often have to be limited. Occasionally a missionary will talk of resigning if certain projects are not approved, or a national leader balk at moves clearly good for the Church. Wise administration often requires steadfastness in the face of deep-seated disagreement. The choice between giving in to resistance and implementing wholesome changes for the sake of conservation and expansion faces all adminstrators.

If church growth possibilities are to be fostered, the administrator must direct his resources to the places of greatest harvest. This basic principle underlies all mission activity. Money is given to missions because Christians are convinced that God has prepared a harvest. Men are appointed as missionaries because God leads them into the fields that are white. Searching for responsive fields and committing maximum resources to them is perhaps the most significant act of the administrator.

Search for the ripe harvest will of necessity proceed in stages. For example, in evangelizing Japan the goal of a major Japanese Church and its assisting mission board in 1948 was to locate a minister and a missionary in every prefectural capital. This was the exploratory stage of mission. The next and more difficult stage in 1963 is that of evaluating discoveries in each of the fields entered. Evaluation in Japan requires modification of the initial process. The policy guiding administration might be phrased as follows: Plant a minister-missionary team in every prefecture, and then, discovering the cities that promise the greatest fruit, replant teams in them. Adhering to this policy will involve loss of some residences or church buildings. Such losses are implicit in the nature of evangelization and church establishment. Money is expendable. God-given opportunities ought not be.

The administrator must decide not only which fields to serve, but which ones not to. An illustration of this is found in the armed forces. Men in the medical corps are given these explicit instructions: In critical situations give major attention to victims most likely to recover, but only sedatives to victims unlikely to recover.

Which to serve and which not to is a difficult decision; it is one of the heaviest burdens of administration. In missionary terms we might say to the administrator: Give priority to programs having the fewest obstacles and the greatest promise of successful church growth.

The seriousness of the responsibility that rests upon missionary administration at all levels, but particularly at the level where top policy is made, is revealed in the following appraisals. Dr. Henry P. Van Dusen speaks of "the omnipresence and relative inconsequence of the Christian Church" in the Caribbean.[1]

Dr. R. Pierce Beaver, writing on Willingen, after review of the situation of the Church around the world today, says, "The missionary enterprise is in great measure a colossal system of interchurch aid, with relatively little pioneer evangelistic advance."[2]

Dr. E. L. Cattell says of the Church in India,

> This numerically large but highly nominal Christian Church must be immediately revitalized. There is no other comparable challenge to missionary effort in India to-day. These nominal Christians must be turned into vital, soul-winning Christians. This sets our strategy for the moment. During the present stalemate on the Hindu evangelistic front and while we aggressively hold the line there, the major evangelistic thrust must be made inside the Christian Church. This is our ripest field. Revival movements have begun. God has raised up Indian evangelists of real stature. The Spirit is beginning a work of renewal. This is not a time for missionaries to be general managers of mission and church enterprises. Indians can do that. The chief contribution of the missionary should be a quiet, spiritual one made from the background where he undergirds every work which the Spirit is doing and which brings new life to the Church. Then when the great day of harvest comes, the reapers will be plentiful.[3]

Administration over the years has either drafted or allowed the policies that have helped to create this "colossal system of inter-

[1] From a report by Frank K. Means to Foreign Mission Board of Southern Baptist Convention.

[2] D. A. McGavran, *How Churches Grow* (London: World Dominion Press, 1959), p. 11. Also New York: Friendship Press, 1959.

[3] Everett L. Cattell, "The Christian Impact on India," *International Review of Missions* (April, 1962), p. 162.

church aid." In missions we have been slow to place or accept responsibility for unhealthy conditions. Repentance and reappraisal should replace the "no discussion of failure" atmosphere. Creative leadership can then lead toward conservation of the most vital spiritual impulses and opportunities.

Conservation at the Church Level

Leaders of younger Churches are most influential administrators. We hope they will read what we have written about executive secretaries of boards and what we shall write about missionaries, knowing that it all applies even more truly to them. They face a responsibility for conserving every effort toward church growth. Many a mission secretary knows that the church-mission organization is achieving only minor church growth, but since the mission has transferred authority to the Church he feels helpless to do anything about it. If a suggestion comes from him or the missionaries, may not church leaders resent it as unwarranted interference?

It cannot be said too strongly, therefore, that the top leadership of the Churches of Africa, Asia and Latin America should engage in directed conservation so that their witness will, under God, lead to maximum church growth. Survival for many of them depends on achieving, while they are still receiving substantial aid from world mission, a mode of Spirit-filled growth which will turn their congregations into effectively redemptive societies.

It is one thing for Western board executives to back the humanitarian enterprises of Christian mission. It is good for England and America to be known as the source of philanthropic assistance. The promotional value to a missionary society of a hundred missionaries engaged in humanitarian enterprises may be as great as a hundred engaged in multiplying churches. But the leaders of the younger Churches will be shortsighted indeed if they do not press forward to realize all the church growth God intends to give them. No humanitarian enterprise is as good *for them* as the multiplication of their churches.

Conservation at the Missionary Level

The program of the Church and its affiliated mission in any field has been hammered out in broad outline. Although programs are in constant flux, already-established activities are likely to be regarded as more worthy than new proposals. The old has a higher priority than the new. Yet changes must be made. Missionaries often play an important part in making them; in some places they are still chiefly responsible for making changes in the direction of church growth. Board executives usually cannot know the details of local church growth situations. Church leaders may be too close to see them clearly. But the missionary brings to the situation both the devotion and the objectivity required to see the changes needed.

To be sure, in suggesting changes missionaries may well consider Paul's counsel: "In humility count others better than yourselves. Let each of you look not only to his own interests, but to the interests of others" (Phil. 2:3, 4). Change should be made looking to the interests—the needs—of others. Missionary administration should place the need of men for redemption ahead of the expansion of any personal project or auxiliary activity. Administration can do so only if it keeps the goal of the greatest possible church growth clearly in view.

Missionaries should also define conservation in New Testament terms. This does not mean such high standards and such effectiveness among such small numbers that no Christian ever defects. It means keeping the main thrust of the Church and mission in the direction of maximum discipling. It means involving as many members of the congregation as possible in spreading the Gospel.

Conserving Converts for Church Membership

The Demanding Message. Conserving the convert for fellowship and service begins with a message which makes adequate demands on the hearer. The kindhearted proclaimer who waters down the commission given him as ambassador of the King is no humanitarian if the total effects are taken into account. Persuading men to attach themselves to a pleasant and profitable enterprise is vastly different from proclaiming a message which God can use to bring them to conviction. Repentance is basic. The New Testament terms for salvation are dramatic: new birth, adoption, new creatures in Jesus Christ, and becoming sons of God.

We need to make effective use of the sociological factors that encourage response, but these must not be substituted for that demanding message from God which makes the response valid. For example, an invitation can be extended in such a fashion that a person reared in a culture which takes great care never to offend may answer yes out of courtesy. The offer of benefits to those who respond may lead to the patron-peon relationship so cherished in feudal societies. In other instances men may accept the invitation to profess faith in Christ, not because they love Christ but because they hate something else. The first evangelical preaching in Rome after Victor Emmanuel II came to the Italian throne found spectacular response. But the church organized on this anticlerical reaction had to be reorganized within four years. All this is to say that the message should offer what God offers, and make the demands He makes: repentance, confession, and total allegiance.

Handle with Care in Transit. The period from conversion to baptism and church membership is of vast importance. Differences of opinion exist about its length and the measures for teaching and testing that ought to be followed. It is the most strategic time in the life of the new believer. Sound guidance should be given immediately after profession of faith. Sometimes the question is raised about how the convert feels about becoming a Christian. Usually an emotional response is involved, but emotional response does not guarantee salvation, nor the lack of it negate the profession. The question the new disciple needs to face is not how he feels but whether he has committed his life to Christ. We must ask him: Have you met Jesus? Do you love Jesus? Are you willing for Him to be in control of your life, to help you make and remake decisions every day?

The convert should be warned that the devil will assault him and that doubts will arise. He should be given some idea of what the Christian life is like. At this point many current procedures leave a terribly false impression. In many fields his closest friends prior to his confession of faith become his inquisitors as they help to "prepare" him for church membership. This process is often as legalistic as Pharisaism. Does proof of salvation come in knowledge, in feeling, in ethics or doctrine? Does the new believer become a supersaint at once? Is he expected to work *for* Christ and the Church to work *with* Jesus in day-by-day fellowship and growth?

Is it possible that in many younger Churches screening is more for the purpose of protecting the Church than of helping the new believer? The very nature of the Church demands that imperfection in her members be an acceptable risk, often an obvious fact. The human material which is the Church's opportunity guarantees a measure of failure and defection. This should not be surprising. No other institution on earth expects the vast difference between the man for whom it searches and the man who becomes part of the fellowship. Jesus said He did not come to call the righteous but sinners to repentance. Part of the vocation of the Church is to trust that fellowship with Christ and the presence of the Holy Spirit will enable the babe just born into the Kingdom to grow and develop until he walks in maturity. Remarkable progress is often made at once; but the very terms "growth" and "discipleship" indicate that some progress should occur at once and some through the years.

Long Pre-baptismal Courses. Sometimes church leaders—nationals and missionaries—think that conservation requires long-continued teaching until stability is guaranteed. Miss Bertha Smith, lifetime missionary to China prior to Communist days, described the teaching process as needing to be continuous because there was always a "leaning side" to be propped up. But when revival fires began to burn in North China and the presence of the Holy Spirit became discernible, the people were stabilized effectively by "beyond-human" resources as they gathered for prayer and praise and witness.

The question about the amount of time that ought to elapse between profession and baptism can never find one answer. Conditions differ in different fields. Long-continued instruction—sometimes for three years—seems to have at least one unbiblical element in it: the expectation that time will do what the experience with Christ has not done. Men are not taught to be Christian; they are born into the Kingdom of God by faith in Jesus Christ. Once born anew, as a part of being His disciple the new convert goes on to perfect his techniques, understanding, and participation in Christian life.

Long-delayed baptism often loses converts rather than conserving and perfecting them. Roland Allen points out the New Testament practice of baptizing people as they trusted Christ, and negates the idea that the rich experience in the Jewish synagogue accounted for this "unseemly haste." Sometimes extreme care in screening converts before baptism is defended on the grounds that a church which has no stumbling members in it will have a greater testimony before the community. Purity of church life is important, but conversion of the community comes from spiritual power which God alone can give. In producing purity, revival in the church has always been much more potent than screening converts by human standards before baptism.

Conserving the Newly Baptized. The person who has confessed Christ should not be left dangling—neither of this community nor of that, neither Christian nor pagan. Some denominations enroll all such at once in a catechumen class. Others give them an identity card to provide a sense of belonging. All should encourage attendance at the worship of the church and regular instruction. In the event of long-delayed baptism, maintaining his sense of identity is vitally important to the person shifting his religious allegiance. Warm Christian love, lifting the stumbling convert, will be more effective than the scourge of harsh discipline. The back doors of some churches see as much traffic as the front. Some discipline is wise, but indiscriminate use of it is a far cry from New Testament forgiveness, encouragement, and restoration.

The new convert can be strengthened by being given a church responsibility suited to his ability. The Assemblies of God in parts of Central America use a step-by-step process of giving responsibility which leads to capacity for still larger responsibility. In this fashion the church itself becomes the proving and training ground for further workers.

Conserving converts for church life requires definition of the kind of church life for which they will be prepared. Here again detrimental cultural carry-over is apt to operate at full force. We naturally desire for them the best kind of church life. This is excellent—provided what we want is best for them. The "best" for a city-bred, educated, third-generation congregation in Texas is not best for a church made up of first-generation illiterate Christians in the African bush. Converts are most readily kept by a warm church life which fits their level of culture. Melvin Hodges presents many valuable suggestions in his books about this kind of conservation.

Precious New Impulses. When church growth is occurring and people of the world are finding Christ, an important part of conservation lies in welcoming the spontaneous expressions of new Christians. The new impulses of the redeemed soul are often unusual. If repressed in favor of "mature statements" which come only after "adequate training," they may never again see free expression. How refreshing to hear a new Chinese convert conclude her prayer, "Lord, I have enjoyed talking to you"!

Those familiar with churches in established areas are aware of the tendency to advise converts to sit by and watch while older Christians carry the burden. New Testament example does not support this procedure. The Samaritan woman seemed an unlikely witness, but she proved effective. A convert with modest theological equipment can fulfill Jesus' command—"Be my witness"—if he has had a genuine experience of salvation; but he should do it in his own way.

If the impulses brought into being by the experience of salvation are to be conserved, they should be honored and put to use at once. Roland Allen tells how the creative but untrained leader is apt to be set aside.[4] His first attempts are treated as inadequate. He

[4] Roland Allen, *The Spontaneous Expansion of the Church* (London: World Dominion Press, 1960), pp. 32–33.

withdraws from leadershp, and the next man, seeing how the first was regarded, is slow to venture.

Merle Davis suggests that conversion releases the convert from the cost of indulgence in immoral habits and burdens connected with the ancient worship.[5] If energies thus released are guided into Christian stewardship, the convert becomes a responsible member of the Christian fellowship. If, on the other hand, he habitually receives rather than gives, his usefulness in bearing part of the burden of the church is likely to be permanently impaired. Conservation of converts means enlarging their pre-Christian habits of giving and developing new ones.

Indigenous natural experiences of worship should be preserved. At a village in Thailand a spontaneous movement to Christian faith began. The people were gathering every night for discussion about Christ, prayer, and spontaneous worship. Missionaries considering how best to conserve this natural interest decided not to mention the "Christian" custom (common in both America and Bangkok) of assembling only on Sunday for worship. Weekly worship, they felt, would limit the life God had granted to this new group. They encouraged them to continue daily worship.

An African convert once told a missionary, "We meet for worship regularly from ten until twelve o'clock because you want us to. If you left us on our own, we would gather sometime Sunday morning, begin to sing when enough were there, and probably spend most of the day in worship." It seems likely that in the time-bound Western style of Sunday service some vital impulses have been lost.

How church and mission leaders meet the precious spontaneous expressions and vital impulses of new Christians elicited by their experience of God is important. Leaders should certainly avoid methods that put obstacles in the way of natural responses of new disciples and new churches. This principle summarizes the first half of Roland Allen's contribution. He is against the traditional, topheavy methods of missions, not because of their cost, but be-

[5] Merle J. Davis, *New Buildings on Old Foundations* (New York: International Missionary Council, 1947).

cause of the obstacles they erect. For example, subsidizing pastors creates spiritual, financial, and psychological difficulties which prevent natural growth processes in young churches. The missionary should be aware, therefore, of the pitfalls and difficulties in the subsidy system.

If obstacles are not erected artificially, the Spirit is free to work. Natural impulses toward growth will appear. Church leaders and missionaries may confidently depend on supernatural guidance and power for the realization of spiritual ends. This is the second half of Allen's contribution, which he never tires of emphasizing.

Planters of new churches should exercise great care not to erect obstacles. They should be just as careful to put ultimate reliance on the power of Jesus rather than on the mechanics or materials of mission operation.

Such a course will give primary emphasis to proclaiming the Gospel, persuading men to become His disciples, sharing with them the word of God, and "teaching them to observe all things" He commanded. Anything and everything else will be kept subservient. These primary aspects of New Testament advance are open to the newest Christian community. Until artificial or foreign standards are erected, the new community, receiving gifts from the Holy Spirit, can provide all that is necessary for fulfilling the essential functions of church life. Ephesians 4:11 says that Christ gave apostles, prophets, evangelists, pastors, and teachers. He gave them for the maturing of the saints (church members) that *they* might do the work of ministering, to the building up of the Body of Christ. It is still the function of the Holy Spirit to give leaders to the churches from among the ordinary members. We should plan our work expecting Him to do so.

Training Programs

Directed conservation demands that mission programs be defined in the simplest terms possible, *directed toward the largest number of believers possible, and based on the expectation of the greatest possible fruit.*

Are training programs designed to meet these demands? Are men prepared to lead in church growth or rather to minister to a few show-place congregations? When the New Testament says that the believers went everywhere preaching the word it suggests widespread growth, not static mission-fed churches.

Training the maximum number in the essentials of the Christian faith is a theological part of conservation for church growth. Train many because *God* expects it. This teaching should be given to every believer. Something like the training schools in Korea, where hundreds of village Christians studied the Bible for a solid month each year, could supply adequate knowledge and give inspiration for the work. Training must not be confined to the few paid pastors.

In future years, Evangelicals, rethinking the factors that influenced their movement, may discover that we have walked in almost blind faith in higher education. This has been true in the United States in almost direct relation to the age of the denomination. In the United States, Presbyterians and Congregationalists led in strength in the early years; but when the opportunity for expansion came to the entire Christian community, these two Churches chose to go only as far and as fast as the processes of education would allow.[6] They insisted on well-trained leaders. The result was that the frontier simply grew beyond the supply of ministers, and also grew away from men of that degree of education and culture. Baptists and Methodists grew greatly, not by the labors of highly trained leaders (Francis Asbury and others furnish important exceptions), but by the work of scantily trained preachers and lay people. Dependence upon God does not necessarily decrease as education increases, but there seems to be a constant temptation for us to let it do so.

Our day witnesses a call for more leadership on the part of the laymen in the church. Recently a new thought has been circulating: the pastor should be an assistant layman, rather than the layman an assistant pastor. This idea might help to heal the ancient

[6] Jerald C. Brauer, *Protestantism in America* (Philadelphia: Westminster Press, 1953).

breach between the clergy and the laity. Its significance for missions is not merely in the matter of identity, but also in the opportunity of enlisting all God's people in all of God's work.

Institutes for training lay preachers and ordinary church members have been held with great success in mission fields where churches are multiplying. Indeed, such lay training is usually partly responsible for great growth. One missionary from Brazil deliberately held institutes where severe problems developed. After several weeks in a training program, problems decreased or were solved. It was his practice to ask pastors to be the teachers, making use of their spiritual development and knowledge. It helped them to be part of the leadership training processes, and they gave help to their students. His churches were characterized by unusual growth.

Lay training in local institutes demands a high degree of mobility on the part of the training staff. By getting out where the people are, it is possible to train many without separating them from their environment. Fellowship between the national leader and missionary who live under institute conditions is a vital factor in producing harmonious working relationships. In lessening the gap between missionaries and national preachers, and national preachers and their congregations, institutes scattered over the country provide a practical answer.

A good many things work against such a plan. The usual tendency of a pastor with extensive theological training is to aim too high for his people. A pressure, the strength of which he does not recognize, drives him to minister in a "settled place." I suggested to a young missionary establishing a training program on a new field that the training be widespread, carried to the local churches, and consist in the simple essentials. He replied that he would try to do this. Yet this same pressure is driving him to develop a central institution where he stays most of the year, venturing out for a week's institute in the churches once in a while.

Adequate conservation of growth possibilities demands a mobility which most church and mission programs do not now possess. The call for maximum outreach conflicts with the tendency to stay at the mission compound or American-style house. Missionaries today will seldom need to be away from their families as Livingstone was, but a large degree of life out among the churches and the people is essential.

Training full-time paid ministers is also vitally important and demands a Bible school or seminary. Here again conservation demands the utmost wisdom in relating Bible-school students and seminarians to the Christians they will serve, both in standard of living and in the content of their training.

One vital element in conserving the spiritual resources of seminarians, rather than converting them into professional students, lies in giving them adequate outlet for ministering while they are still training. If young men being trained for pastoral leadership are too immature to place alone in pastoral and preaching responsibility, they may be too young to receive the training with maximum benefit. Seminary teachers would do well to spend part of their time training their men by personal example. The faculty can help students by creating opportunities for them to follow their example. A recent development in Mexico is a "caravan for Christ" led by teachers in the seminary, which engages seminary students and laymen from churches nearby in village preaching. Worshiping groups are being established in almost every place where the caravan has gone.

Realistic Evaluation of Church Size

Conservation by planning for a size of church possible to people of a given social background is important. Some worshiping units are too small, too long neglected, and too poorly led. Others go to the other extreme. Some missionaries try to recreate the large metropolitan church known so well in the United States. The average church in many lands of Africa, Asia, and Latin America is a small congregation, which usually increases to 40–60 in attendance and then either stagnates or splits. One cause of this is the limited ability of the pastors, which can be increased by training but not so much as is often supposed. Another cause is the face-to-face leadership that prevails in most of these lands, where men in government and business are almost unable to delegate authority or trust their subordinates. This influence affects church growth and church size.

Conserving the Spiritual Momentum of All Projects

Many tools may be used to spread the Christian news. Media of mass communication are coming into prominence in strategy considerations. They offer startling prospects if church planting is their clear goal.

Much Gospel information can be scattered abroad by the use of radio and newspaper. This is good if we make contact with and gather into churches those who are thus reached. Newspaper evangelism should include a form to be filled out and mailed for further instruction. Radio broadcasts should call for inquiries and commitments by mail. The Christian community should be prepared to contact each person responding. In addition, church-planting campaigns in sections of the city being prepared by radio should surely be planned. Churches should be established as rapidly as possible in areas which are receiving the benefit of the mass communication media.

This suggests that church expansion will probably come in concentric circles. We should place a church for fellowship and worship within reach of those who respond. To use these media without planting churches is to waste effort as did the men who planned the Tucker automobile; it was widely advertised immediately following World War II, and great interest was generated, but the car was never made available.

Literature can be an instrument for church growth in opening doors and following up contacts. Conservation of opportunity through a literacy program especially for the believer at an early stage of intellectual and spiritual development is long overdue. Optimum extension of the Christian community requires that we place in churches books and pamphlets written for many levels of intellectual and spiritual development and train many men and women to use them.

Conservation of best effects from institutions surely demands that specialists in church growth should be situated thickly around institutions and given a mandate to multiply churches. What a fallacy to build an expensive institution, staff it with men who can serve its purposes, and then decide that this particular place has too many missionaries in it to warrant stationing others there to follow up whatever openings are created by these institutions!

In summary, conservation for church growth demands planning. No missionary, no church, no institution will be automatically effective in church growth. Constant devising of ways and means to multiply churches is the hallmark of missions which are skilled in carrying out the Great Commission and reconciling men to God.

XII

ADMINISTERING FOR CHURCH GROWTH

MELVIN L. HODGES

The Scope and Purpose of Administration

Whenever there is church work, there is administration. The native pastor who guides a group of ten converts in church activity is an administrator, as is the missionary on the field. Each must lead those working with him to the achievement of goals. Certainly the field superintendent and the area secretary work largely in the realm of administration.

The purpose of mission administration is not merely to maintain the smooth functioning of the organization. It is more: it is *leadership directed toward the accomplishing of a biblical mission.* Administration is not simply a business concept; it is a scriptural principle needing the wisdom of the Holy Spirit as much as does any other ministry, such as evangelism. The Apostle Paul recognized this fact when he gave special admonition to one "that ruleth."

Someone has made the statement that 95 per cent of modern mission activities could be carried on just as well if there were no Holy Spirit! This may be nearer the truth than we would care to admit. If we would correct this condition we must remember that the nearer we can keep to the New Testament pattern in our missionary work, the more success we shall have. However, I must admit that our situation today is infinitely more complex than that faced by the Apostle Paul. We find in the early Church neither foreign mission boards and departments nor the many institutions today considered a normal part of missionary enterprise, such as printing plants, clinics, orphanages, day schools, and seminaries. All these require administration on a scale not described in the Scriptures.

I see no practical way to return to the simplicity of the New Testament Church. The situation is further complicated by the fact that the methods used by various denominations differ widely one from another. Many modern practices are essential in view of current circumstances, and although they lack a scriptural precedent they are not necessarily unbiblical.

The important guidelines are the principles underlying New Testament methods. We must be *flexible* in our approach to contemporary problems, endeavoring to understand the purpose and design of the Holy Spirit for our advance. This flexibility is in itself a New Testament principle clearly demonstrated by the apostles. We must, however, be careful that in our flexibility as to methods and approach we do not violate indispensable principles. Our *message* should be of the New Testament in content and emphasis. The spiritual life of the Church should be New Testament in experience. The churches we raise up should be expanding, indigenous New Testament churches.

Administration can reach the goals it sets through leadership. The U.S. Air Force Manual defines leadership as "the art of influencing and directing personnel to an assigned goal, in such a way as to obtain their obedience, confidence, respect, and loyal cooperation." The quality of leadership is a determining factor in the success of any enterprise, and missions are no exception. Mission leadership has the added responsibility of bringing New Testament *life* to our churches.

The Goal of Administration

In missions we are workers together with God. The goal for missions is not what we choose, but what God desires. The secret of successful administration in missions lies in the ability to recognize God's purpose and work with Him toward the realization of it. This will be the essential goal of Christian mission.

In missions it can happen that there are announced, printed, long-range goals, and then the "real" ones. These latter are unannounced but lie back of actual budget distributions, minister and missionary assignments, and building programs. These "unconscious" goals control much missionary administration. About them we seldom ask: *"Do these goals advance or retard the growth of the Church?"*

For example, we of the Assemblies of God are premillennialists. Our doctrinal position influences our goals and methods. We do not look for the world to grow continually better because of the influence of the Christian Church. We expect, rather, that evil men and seducers will wax worse and worse and that perilous times will continue and increase, climaxing in an Armageddon after which the Lord Jesus will return and establish a new social and spiritual order in the earth. We conceive the mission of the Church to be the evangelization and separation of a people from the present world order who will form the core of this new society. In the meantime, we are to give the Gospel as a witness to every creature, emphasizing the personal experience of salvation and the witness of each convert in a basically unfriendly world. In the Assemblies of God, administration naturally emphasizes reaching the individual and bringing him to a personal experience of Christ. We have placed little emphasis on the Church's participation in civic processes or on influencing legislation for social progress. We have seen a minimal value in institutions having for their goal the implementation of social change or sometimes mere physical rehabilitation.

On the other hand, postmillennialists believe that the Church is the good leaven of society and that Christian influence will gradually permeate the world until the reign of Christ is brought about in a spiritual sense, and thus the will of God will be done. It would be out of place here to discuss the correctness of these respective views; it is sufficient to point out that those who hold this second view often enagage in social reform as a major goal. Administration naturally emphasizes institutional and social work. In doing so it may unconsciously become so concerned with reforming society that it ceases to emphasize the regeneration of individuals.

The only safe ground here is to return to our original premise: that the goal for Christian mission should harmonize with and implement the goal of God. This goal is revealed in the Scriptures. It must be both our announced and our real goal. We are to preach the Gospel to all nations and to every creature. We are to follow the example of the apostles and establish churches. Putting these two biblical goals together, I formulate the essential goal for Christian mission thus: *We are to preach the message of God to every creature in such a way that regenerated converts will result. These will form local churches, established according to the New Testament pattern and operating as self-sustaining and self-propagating units, to the end that vital churches will multiply in every area of the world.*

The goals of missions are concerned with quality and quantity of converts. We will only have quantity when we establish the right kind of churches. Work that is inferior in quality will die out, for it lacks the essential vitality and stability. Work that emphasizes quality with no interest in increase in numbers will be weak, since it fails to reproduce. Mission administration must necessarily be interested both in the character of the churches and in their number.

The Task of Administration

Having established the goals of mission, the task of administration is to provide vision, inspiration, methods, and leadership to enable Christians, churches, and missions to reach their goals. This applies to the administration of the national pastor, of the missionary, and of the board office.

The task of administration in missions is infinitely more complex than in business or industry, where the goal is profit, the incentive the wage one earns, and there is a direct chain of command from the president down to the janitor. Work is assigned to an individual, and he must produce profits for the company or lose his employment. The mission administrator, on the other hand, cannot appeal to the profit motive. Nor can he control those who are working under him strictly on the basis of his own authority.

A spiritual tie may be the only relationship a missionary has to a national pastor. He can neither order him to do his bidding (a missionary is a foreigner—what right does he have to order a national to do anything?) nor can he invoke the authority of wages (the pastor's salary is paid by his church and not by the mission). The missionary's only claim on the allegiance of his co-workers arises from his spiritual stature, life, and ministry. Some have failed to recognize this distinction and have brought heartache to themselves and failure to their work. Fortunately, in many other cases the influence of the national worker with his converts, the missionary with the national pastors, and the mission administrator with the missionaries has been most positive and effective. The administrator of whatever rank inspires rather than drives. He leads by example and counsel. He is often *the* determining factor as between success and failure in the matter of church planning and growth.

Organize from Grass Roots Up

Probably the most common mistake in mission administration today is to organize the work from the top down, rather than from the grass roots up. We usually start in a field with a missionary organization. We place missionaries in key places of responsibility. We hope that in some way our principles and administration will seep down to the pastors and then to the converts, and that everyone will eventually find his proper place in the organization. What we really do by this procedure is to stifle the initiative of native converts. What chance of expressing his power of individual action does a convert or native pastor have with capable, energetic Americans in charge? They have a thousand promotional plans for the work, which they carry out according to American methods rather along lines that nationals can follow. How can a national hope to fill a position of importance and responsibility? Men with better training are already occupying the principal places. This is especially true if there is a large number of missionaries in proportion to national workers.

What usually happens when the field is organized on the basis of missionary personnel is that there is formed what I call—for lack of a better word—a missionary "crust" through which a convert or worker finds it almost impossible to emerge! His growth is stunted. Some national workers come to the conclusion that the only way they can fulfill a vital function is to get training of the American type and learn American ways. Missionaries invariably praise such men for understanding the missionary. They say, "He sees things from our point of view." I wonder whether by this process we can ever provide the Church with true indigenous leadership? What we have really done is make over nationals in our own image and perpetuate our methods through them. The workers in turn lose effectiveness as leaders among their own people, who see them as "missionary's men."

A serious, and not too uncommon, result of this is the idea among nationals that under mission control they cannot get anywhere. National workers may go along for years, patiently following the administration of the missionaries. There may be vague, unanalyzed desires in their hearts and a feeling that there should be more freedom and more opportunity for self-direction. Eventually a strong-minded leader will make himself the champion of the national Church, and suddenly the missionaries will find the beautiful work that has gone on so long disrupted, and division imminent and perhaps inevitable.

Maybe administration will awaken before this has gone too far and decide it is time to turn authority over to nationals. However, when work has been developed under complete mission control, the decision to turn over to national leadership may result in a major crisis. If people trained in dependence have suddenly to assume responsibility for decisions and are confronted with the need to support their own work, crisis can amount to catastrophe.

When we start building from the ground up instead of from top down, these dangers are avoided to a large degree.

A Right Beginning

The New Testament way was to start with converts who formed themselves into local churches. The local church became the vital unit, both for maintaining believers and evangelizing unbelievers. This, then, is our pattern. To achieve it is a task of tremendous importance. Merely having indigenous churches is not the key. Some indigenous churches are not really expanding churches. In fact, some churches grow more rapidly under control of the mission than after control is turned over to nationals. It is rather a matter of establishing a true pattern of growth.

Here we return again to the question of good seed. It is improper procedure to start a church with the hope that it will become indigenous later on. All churches should be *started* as indigenous, self-developing, self-expanding, self-supporting, self-governing units. The power of expansion, the power of growth, is normally built into the church by the Holy Spirit. It is not something that depends exclusively on the missionary.

How does administration go about establishing a church pattern which will produce rapidly expanding, responsible, self-supporting, self-governing units? The question of a right beginning takes us back again to the matter of *responsibility*. Each enlisted man must feel his personal responsibility to his Commander-in-chief. Every convert must feel that his salvation is a prized personal possession, granted to him by the grace of God, which he has the responsibility of sharing with others. The responsibility for witnessing must be his own. The church will be his church, the pastor his pastor, and expansion his problem, responsibility, and joy. He must feel *he* is sharing in spreading the Gospel.

If the missionaries tell the converts who is or is not to become a member of the church, and make all other decisions related to it, how can converts feel responsible for it? If the missionary rents the hall, pays the light bill, and carries the financial load, when and how will the converts ever feel that this is their work? If the missionary makes decisions related to a member who has fallen in sin, when will the church, as such, take the unpleasant responsibility of maintaining discipline among its own members? It seems to me that the only way to teach this responsibility, which will pay off in church growth and expansion later on, is to have converts exercise it from the very beginning.

In beginning a new church where there are no mature believers I suggest that new converts themselves have a voice in approving those who, after a period of preparation, are to be accepted into membership. This adds to the meaning of church membership. I would ask new converts to choose a small committee which would work with the missionary in examining converts for baptism and church membership. Then I would encourage them to help select their governing committee—even though, because mature men to serve as deacons are lacking, it is a temporary committee. Congregational government would give this local church the opportunity to approve the choice of a pastor during the first year, and after that he would be chosen by the congregation itself. The new members would be taught to bring their tithes and offerings to the church for the support of the work of God. Eventually, this would mean that the pastor would receive his support from the church rather than working in other employment—provided, of course, that the church attains sufficient strength to assume this responsibility.

Organize to Exercise Responsibility

Right from its inception, also, the church should organize its membership for evangelistic effort, assigning outposts or stations to local workers who will carry the Gospel to the regions beyond. Some, objecting that this is too much responsibility to put in the hands of new converts, may say that they could never carry the financial load. This would be true for an American church with American standards. It does not need to be true if we establish an indigenous church. Have you ever observed that when some group decides to work independently of the mission—perhaps having split off in anger—they can do all the things both they and the missionaries claimed they could not do? Why is it that they will sacrifice and take responsibility for evangelism when they are on their own as they will not do with the help of the missionary? Does not this reaction prove that they can assume responsibility, and that if the missionary carries on the work in such a way as to block their initiative, he is really hindering their progress?

After several local churches are organized, it is only a step to bind these churches together in some kind of general conference or convention. The churches send their representatives—pastors and lay delegates—to lay plans for further advance in the area. They will choose their own committees for evangelism and other activities. In the form of church government practiced by the Assemblies of God, we encourage them also to draw up a constitution and name permanent officers who give counsel and general supervision to the work. Right from the beginning these officers derive their authority from the churches they are serving, not from the missionary. Indigenous leaders are developed in this way under the guidance of missionaries without feeling subject to them as employers. Churches do not depend upon foreign support or administration for their maintenance. The obstacle of having "Westernized" nationals carry on in the format of an American organization is lessened. Truly indigenous leaders are developed by each church in its own area.

Administration and Missionaries

One of the duties of any mission administrator is to see that missionaries in a given area are welded into a working team which understands the goals and policies of the mission. This may not be easy. Missionaries are often individualistic. Further, many have begun work when policies and objectives were not as clearly defined as they are today. In some areas missionaries may still be making institutional work and the mission the center rather than emphasizing the church program. Younger missionaries have gone to the field inspired by indigenous church principles and anxious to put them into practice, only to find that older missionaries are not in favor of these methods. This inevitably makes for tension. In such circumstances missionaries may find themselves working at cross-purposes.

One of the duties of the mission administrator, then, is to orient missionaries to church-centered goals and policies. Our tool for accomplishing this is the Missionary Field Fellowship composed of all our missionaries who work in a given area. The purpose of this fellowship is not to legislate for the Church, but to let missionaries solve their own problems in relation to their missionary life, to clarify objectives, to establish good relations with each other and with the Church, and to become acquainted with policies and reach agreements which will permit them to work together as a team.

It is quite impossible to move forward in planting churches if there is no agreement among missionaries as to methods and policies to be followed. For example, if one missionary insists in paying workers from his own funds and maintaining an employer-employee relationship, this will make infinitely more difficult the task of another missionary working in the same area who endeavors to follow a policy of self-support for the churches. If missionaries can present a united front in regard to methods, the task will be made much easier.

Adjust Practice to Basic Policy

Another task of the administrator is to *bring practice into harmony with policy*. In too many cases policy is one thing and practice another, not simply because the mission society decides one thing and missionaries on the field do another, but because sometimes administration not only permits but encourages practices diametrically opposed to accepted policy. As an illustration, administration may announce the policy that self-sustaining, self-multiplying churches are to be established, yet in its publications make financial appeals for projects which are out of harmony with this goal.

Sometimes we administrators excuse ourselves by saying that the missionaries on the field know the needs and are closer to the situation than we are. Some failure to adjust practice to policy may be simply an oversight on our part. We fail to call to the attention of the missionaries involved that their projects are not in line with the Church's goal.

These failings are not easily remedied. To overcome them requires a long period of education, both of missionary personnel and home staff and constituency. The board secretary must have courage to initiate necessary changes, and patience while these changes are being worked out. If the changes are radical, he must be prepared for a period of disruption, even of loss. The latter may be more apparent than real, but will nevertheless be disturbing. An administrator comes to the field with a general understanding of missionary work and of the goals which the mission hopes to attain. He has the advantage of looking at a situation objectively. He is not involved in sentimental attachments, as the local missionary may be, nor will problems which seem insurmountable to the local missionary always impress him in the same way. He may recommend changes in location of missionaries as well as in the type of work they are doing; his task is not to avoid hurting someone's feelings, but to see that the mission of the Church is accomplished —that churches are multiplied. He must not think of how changes will affect his own prestige and security, but whether or not they will help attain the essential goal of Christian mission.

Recently, in one of our fields, the missionaries presented our board with a request for additional personnel to care for church planting in the provinces. All the missionaries were situated in the capital city. They felt they had their work cut out for them there and that to advance the work in the provinces it would be necessary to send additional personnel. The provinces had been slow in developing churches; response was very limited. Then, quite suddenly, through the ministry of a national brother from a neighboring country, revival came. The great need was to aid this brother and plant churches in the area where the revival was in progress. I called the missionaries together to study the situation and told them I could recommend sending additional personnel to their country only when I knew that every missionary there was occupied to his maximum capacity and greatest usefulness. As a result, two missionaries transferred from the capital to the provinces, with greatly increased usefulness to God, resulting in the establishment of many churches. Administration can and must help Churches and missions to reallocate missionaries so that the best opportunities for church growth can be met.

How Many Missionaries and What Kind?

Another point which mission administrators must keep in mind is the proper relationship of the number of missionaries in a given field to the need and development of the Church. Planting churches does not usually require flooding an area with missionaries. Missionary personnel should be spread out. The presence of too many missionaries in relation to the number of national workers cripples the intitiative of the national Church rather than developing it. Some Churches suffer from "too much missionary." Missionaries are needed in areas where there is no one to plant the Church but we should be slow in multiplying them where the Church is already planted. To achieve a good balance, the function of the national Church and the over-all need of the work must both be held in view. When missionaries are doing work a national could or should do, it is better for the missionary to move on. The missionary must plant the seed and then refrain from smothering the plant by too much attention and too close supervision. Nationals, rather than missionary personnel, should be encouraged to fill the vacancies.

The mission administrator will influence the foreign field in the selection of missionary candidates. Since our work is not likely to be better than the men who establish and inspire it, the type of candidate we send to the mission field is of utmost importance. Certain questions come to mind in this regard. Is the candidate rich in spiritual experience? Has he a definite call to this work? Does he depend on spiritual resources? Does he maintain a proper balance in his intellectual, social, and spiritual life? Is he a soul-winner? Does he know the meaning of teamwork? Is he a dedicated man, unreservedly committed to his call and ministry?

It is usually a mistake to send recruits to the mission field fresh from college or theological seminary. It is essential for them to gain experience in Christian work in their homeland. Missionary work is expensive. It costs about $25,000 to place a couple on the foreign field and maintain them for a four-year period. In the Assemblies of God we require a missionary candidate to qualify for ordination as a minister in the homeland before we will consider his application for foreign service. Why spend large sums of missionary money to send a man to a foreign land to learn by experience the basic principles of the ministry? We think there is no substitute for experience as a pastor. Two years in a church dealing with the different types of people who make up the average church, and working with an official board, will teach any missionary candidate valuable lessons in human relations and at the same time develop his spiritual maturity!

When Christ chose His candidates for apostleship, He spent the preceding night in prayer. Christ's example shows the absolute necessity of spiritual qualities in the administrator. Who among us would have chosen the men He picked? Would we not all have said we could not build the Church through uncouth fishermen—"ignorant and unlearned men"? He saw them, not as they were but as they could become through God's grace. The Lord of the Harvest has instructed us that the way to find laborers for the harvest field is to pray! Better than psychological and aptitude tests in determining candidates is the ability to hear the voice of the Spirit. We would have better candidates, and consequently more church growth, if we ourselves were more accustomed to being guided by the Spirit. This in turn comes from a life of communion with God.

SINGLEMINDED TO THE ESSENTIAL TASK

The administrator must ever beware lest he allow his work to degenerate into simply continuing existing work or keeping the wheels of the organization turning. This is an ever-present danger to all engaged in administration—in church, mission station, church headquarters, or board office. In whatever area his responsibility lies, the administrator must think first of the goals he is attempting to reach for the glory of God. Let me repeat the essential goal for Christian mission I stated earlier: *We are to preach the message of God to every creature in such a way that regenerated converts will result. These will form local churches, established according to the New Testament pattern and operating as self-sustaining and self-propagating units, to the end that vital churches will multiply in every area of the world.*

The administrator must exercise vision and courage, and be willing to give himself—to take up his cross and follow Christ. If this means he sometimes displeases those under his direction because he recommends the discontinuance of an unfruitful missionary effort in exchange for a course of action which he believes will produce church growth, he must be prepared to accept criticism and misunderstanding. He sees himself crucified with Christ and dead to the call of popularity and security. The kingdom takes priority over his person.

In spite of the details every administrator must handle, few will deny that the real importance of his work lies in the decisions he makes. In making these decisions he must rely on the guidance of God. In this sense, his work is primarily spiritual. We are workers together with God, and as we work with Him we can achieve our goals by His grace, so that we can say with the early Church, as recorded in the fifteenth chapter of Acts after the brethren had made a difficult decision: "It seemed good to the Holy Ghost and to us."

XIII

CONCLUSION

DONALD ANDERSON McGAVRAN

NOT SERIOUSLY ENOUGH

One of the principal questions reflected in all the preceding chapters is: How can the Household of God take church growth more seriously? We ask because it seems to us that in the last few decades, while Christian mission has known of church growth, it has not taken it seriously enough.

Church growth is eclipsed by other emphases. Little is known about it. What is, is locked up in denominational, geographical, and linguistic pockets. Many missionaries are trained for the specialized positions in which their boards and Churches will use them. Or it is assumed that training in a seminary in the West will fit them to plant churches in any foreign land. They are seldom trained in the many patterns of church growth and how best to communicate the Gospel in each. Many missions find themselves helping static younger Churches, engaging in "dialogues" of various sorts with various people, and getting involved in "all of life." No board is spending 1 per cent of its annual budget on research in church growth to discover better and more effective means to "disciple the nations." Few people have been trained as specialists in church growth.

It must be remembered that hundreds of missionary organizations are carrying on mission in hundreds of different populations. The degree of neglect of church growth principles and practices varies with each mission and in each piece of the mosaic. Indeed, some pieces are marked by ardent, intelligent concern for growth. It would be ridiculous to charge the Assemblies of God in Brazil, which have built up a Church of 700,000 communicants in the last forty-seven years, with neglect of church growth! Nevertheless, across the continents and the denominations, and even in communities which have shown unusual responsiveness to the Gospel, as we scan budgets, allocations of missionaries, and church and mission histories, neglect of church growth is often discernible.

Abundant evidence documents this bypassing of church growth. For just one example, take theological education in Africa south of the Sahara. This enormous section of the world contains probably 150,000,000 adherents of the so-called primitive religions. Bearing in mind the impact of education, technology, literacy, and the missionary efforts of Protestanism, Roman Catholicism, Islam, and Communism, it can be safely said that the vast majority of these animists will espouse some other religion in the coming decades. In this part of Africa 150,000,000 souls are looking for a spiritual home. Yet a recent learned article on theological education in Africa, which proposes training theological candidates in theology, Hebrew, Greek, the Bible, church history, worship, and counseling, never mentions training them in discipling men and multiplying churches. If church growth were being taken seriously across the world, an article with such a glaring (and probably unconscious) omission could be neither written nor published.

Neglect of church growth is not caused by external obstacles. Consider the ease of transportation today compared with the difficulties a century ago. Today's missionaries enjoy very good health when you consider the death rate among first-termers a hundred years ago. No missionaries are currently being eaten by cannibals! Practically all Western Churches and most nonoccidental Churches, too, have missions built into their budgets, so that altogether enormous sums are raised annually to carry on Christian missions. In short, it cannot be argued that we are so busy overcoming external obstacles that we have no time or energy left to multiply churches.

Neglect is caused, almost unconsciously one may believe, by internal obstacles. The Christian mission intends to be serious about church growth, but internal obstacles divert her. Let us look at some of them.

Bewilderment in the face of tremendous changes marks the present day. This diverts attention from church growth. One major change in the last forty years is the great increase in the religious relativism of the West. The tendency grows in a pluralistic society to equate all religions as roads to God. Although no Christian Church endorses religious relativism, all breathe its atmosphere; and consciously or unconsciously, thinking about the mission of the Church is affected.

Another change, the end of Western empires—the end of the political system under which modern missions started and grew strong—has necessitated radical rethinking of mission procedures and aims. And the continuing ferment of this century, manifesting itself in education, technology, economics, politics, and religion, must surely raise questions among earnest Christians as to what mission *should* be in these new times.

Certain sections of the Church, facing their own changed internal problems and a desperate need for recapturing Christian vitality, wonder if expansion is really what is needed. One international Christian proclaims that evangelism, far from increasing membership, ought to purge the rolls of nominal Christians. Such persons often fail to see the millions who would welcome Jesus Christ as Lord and Savior if becoming a disciple of His were only a real option to them. The pronouncements of these sections then impede the discipling of the nations. They touch the leaders of large Churches—full of nominal Christians—at a tender spot when they ask, "Must we not have something much deeper, more Christlike, and more spiritual than church growth?"

Church growth is often not taken seriously enough because, facing today's changes, many Christians believe there are more important things to do. "The church growth emphasis," said a friend of mine, "fails to take account of church mergers, the ecumenical tide, and conversations between Protestants and Roman Catholics which may heal the schisms of the Church and thus produce a much more powerful and Christlike Church. Church growth is such a narrow emphasis. There are so many more important things to do. It pays no attention to the tremendous revolutions of our day, the economic upsurge, the disinherited billion, the explosion of populations, and the issues of war and peace. Thus when forces like Communism and organizations like the United Nations, the Alliance for Progress, and the Peace Corps are seeking to meet the economic conditions of our time, emphasis on discipling and group conversion makes the Church seem less relevant and more marginal than ever."

Bewilderment is heightened by the theological justifications hammered out by vast vested interests in the missionary movement. The various divisions of Christian mission are not only departments doing good work but also highly self-conscious units, separately organized, with budgets that run into the millions. They have worked out theological justification of their existence, each proving that *it* is mission. When every activity becomes mission, making disciples often fades out of sight.

Further confusion arises in the attachment of new meanings to old words. Classically, evangelism has meant proclaiming Christ and persuading men to become His disciples and responsible members of His Church. But today we read about "industrial evangelism" and "inner city evangelism," whose primary aim seems to be neither to win men to Christian discipleship nor to multiply self-propagating churches, but rather to have existing Christians "enter into dialogue on important ethical and moral issues with the key leaders of industrial society." The Church becomes a means for achieving (it is hoped) a greater degree of justice, brotherhood, and decency. The goal is that "Christ's will become actual in modern situations." All this is good, of course, but should it be called evangelism?

Certain widespread assumptions undergird this contemporary

bewilderment as to what mission really is. Some hold that if we but work vigorously at the programs of the Church, members will increase as much as they should. Others say that if we but love God as we ought, mere harvesting will take care of itself. It is sufficient, according to some, "to be present in the world with a presence willed as a witness to the love of God." One wishes these assumptions were true, but suspects that they rest more on wishful thinking than on the objective measurement of beneficial results.

All this brings it about that church growth emphasis comes to many as a surprise. Books about it are held to be provocative. This emphasis seems to say that the task is simple—when "everyone knows" it is highly complex. It seems to assert that every Christian should be communicating the Gospel—whereas "everyone knows" that most Christians are properly engaged in something else. It actually proposes that the Church and its branches carefully measure their growth and make administrative decisions partly on the basis of what church growth is found—but "everyone can see" that this would upset the machine of missions.

The present volume has been written against this background. As the reader comes, presently, to the summary of what we have been saying, he should take into account *the situation to which we have been speaking.*

An eminent minister, author, and son of this century, reading the book in manuscript form, exclaimed, "This is Hocking's *Rethinking Missions* in reverse!" He was so immersed in the current background just described that the message of the book startled him. It will startle other readers also; perhaps the measure of their amazement will be the measure of their need.

Rising Interest in Church Growth

Fortunately the tide has begun to turn. An increasing number of leaders are feeling that a chief purpose of the Christian mission is to win men to Christ and multiply churches. They suspect that in responsive populations slight growth should not be accepted as normal or inevitable. Many church leaders have come to believe that major functions of mission boards, in addition to raising resources and carrying on "the work," are: constant measurement of membership increases, training church leaders (national and missionary) in church growth procedures, and so administering mission that churches actually multiply.

The Evangelical Foreign Missions Association (of America), whose member boards send out thousands of missionaries, devoted seven long sessions of a recent annual meeting to a careful consideration of church growth. The Division of Foreign Missions of the National Council of the Churches of Christ (USA) is emphasizing anew what, though recently somewhat neglected, its constituent boards have long proclaimed as their purpose. They have put out a statement agreeing that "church growth ought to be *one* important factor in determining mission policy and probably should receive higher priority than in most cases it now does." The impressive statement issued by the Iberville Consultation on Church Growth, mentioned in the Introduction and included as an appendix, indicates mounting concern of the Commission on World Mission and Evangelism of the World Council of Churches. Several boards have made church growth the topic of the annual school for their missionaries on furlough and candidates under appointment. All told, 526 missionaries on furlough concerning whom I have information studied church growth in the summer of 1963. A large conference has just been held in Lima, Peru, to consider the multiplication of churches.

Mission executive Louis L. King—whose board, the Christian and Missionary Alliance, sends out 800 missionaries—on visiting his seven Africa missions requested the missionary staff in each station to prepare accurate graphs of church growth in advance of his arrival. Then Dr. King discussed with the church leaders and missionaries of each station why the Church there had or had not grown and what it and its assisting mission could do to reconcile men more effectively to Christ. Dr. King in a letter to me writes, "These studies and the probing self-analyses they provoked proved to be the most significant and important business of this trip—or of any trip I have taken. A similar study will be made during my forthcoming trip to South America."

The founding of the Institute of Church Growth, a graduate school of Northwest Christian College, for missionaries on furlough and nationals—devoted exclusively to finding out more about church growth, teaching what is known, and publishing research in church growth—gives further evidence of a mounting concern that the Church be the Church *in its passion to reconcile men to God.*

The Message of This Book

The four authors of this book have written against a dark background shot through with a number of rays of light. Among the many aspects of church growth we have discussed, choosing our illustrations from Asia, Africa, and Latin America, eight major emphases may be discerned.

1. The church growth we advocate is sound and Christian. We emphasize spiritual reality and vitality in churches. We believe Christians should be Christ's people. Our clear conviction is that the Holy Spirit is active in any real Church. No one can read Melvin Hodges' discussion of church growth and imagine that he is speaking about a superficial, ephemeral ingathering or merely human activity. The kind of believers he is talking about should be multiplied in, not purged from, the Church. Calvin Guy, too, insists that spoon-fed groups should not be mistaken for churches. For him, real churches have spiritual power and grow precisely because God is in them.

Some people fear that emphasizing church growth will lead to "baptized heathen" and roll-padding. We reply that if anyone seeks church growth he should avoid these dishonest practices as he would poison. These are the surest ways to put an end to it. The only church growth worth striving for is sound growth which remains decade after decade.

Evidence from many lands proves that growing churches have

spiritual vitality. Look at the churches Wesley started—how they multiplied, and how deeply Christian they were! Look at the amazing church growth in the northwest provinces of Korea from 1895 to 1935, and how thoroughly it was based on study of the Bible purified by the flames of revival. To be sure, some fast-growing Churches have been scandalously neglected. The practical problem of how to assure adequate Christian nurture for inflooding multitudes is always keen. Nurture must be provided. Genuine Christianity is essential to church growth.

2. The authors take church growth seriously. We like the official statement of the United Presbyterian Church which reads:

> The supreme and controlling aim of the Christian Mission to the world is to make the Lord Jesus Christ known to all men as their Divine and only Savior and to persuade them to become His disciples and responsible members of His Church in which Christians of all lands share in evangelizing the world and permeating all of life with the spirit and truth of Christ.

Churches do many good things. We hope that they will contiue doing them. We hope even more that these good things will not obscure "the supreme and controlling aim" of the Christian mission. No one can take everything seriously; but every Christian should take communicating the Gospel seriously, for it is not an activity simply of theologians or missionaries—it is the privilege and obligation of every Christian.

The general secretary of a well-known board of missions said recently, "The time has come for me to devote special attention among my missions to church growth. We have been doing other necessary things. Now we must emphasize the essential function of all aspects of Christian mission—planting churches." We commend his decision.

Like every other enterprise, Christian mission from time to time discerns lacks and opportunities and moves to meet them. When they are met, it properly turns to other needs. But the communication of the Gospel is a continuing responsibility. It will not look after itself. Unless conscious effort is made to disciple, Christian mission tends to devote itself to serving or perfecting. Serving, perfecting, and discipling are all part of mission, but unless special attention is paid to discipling, ample evidence from many lands proves that it is consistently neglected. Unless it is taken seriously, it tends to become a small part of the picture—one of many "good things" to do.

Small or even moderate church growth, in ripe fields, should be no cause for complacency. The reader will recall Melvin Hodges' account of the ten-day prayer meeting in El Salvador, which was followed by great spiritual well-being and membership increase. It is important to remember that the Church to which Mr. Hodges refers had grown moderately before the prayer meeting. It had increased from nothing to about 2,600 in eighteen years, but in the receptive El Salvador society this degree of growth showed spiritual flabbiness. That Church had not been radically serious about communicating the Good News and had not grown as much as God wanted it to grow.

Missionaries go to the field under clear instructions from the board as to their main purpose, which usually takes church growth very seriously indeed. They are then often put to work where that purpose is choked by lush undergrowth. At this point Dr. Guy's impassioned chapter on underbrush elimination (Chap. VIII) makes a potent contribution. Lush growth, he declares, must be rooted out so that valuable timber can grow. What Calvin Guy says explicitly is to some extent implicit in other chapters. We all agree that priorities must be devised which effectively emphasize true growth. Only so will performance be brought into line with promise. Only so will theologically correct policy statements about church growth (very common) be paralleled by *theologically corret* budget distributions (conspicuously less common).

Realistic thinking about Christian mission today must make a sharp distinction between the receptivity of populations. All populations are not the same, and hence mission cannot be measured by a common foot rule. All the writers of this book have pointed out that in some places the Church can expect little or no growth. There are highly resistant populations where younger Churches and their assisting missions do well merely to hang on. When God sends men to these populations He measures devotion not by the numerical increase of Christians but by the intent of the missionary. In such populations genuine concern for evangelism may be great, while the amount of church growth may be very small. *In such populations* expectation of church growth may legitimately be small.

These unquestioned truths must not, however, be applied to missions in general. Small expectations need not and must not characterize Christian mission. *In receptive populations* concern for evangelism correlates closely with church growth. The long shadow of populations which solidly reject the Good News must not fall on those in which some branches of the Church are growing rapidy. Missionaries should not become accustomed to coming empty-handed out of ripe fields.

In responsive populations—and the number of these is larger than commonly imagined—our plea is that church growth be taken seriously. We have all urged that where the Church can grow, it ought to do so. How growth can occur, how it has occurred, and how it has been needlessly prevented, these things form one main strand in our message.

If I may add a personal note, I have keen sympathy for my fellow missionary whom God has sent to witness where the Church has little chance of growth. Yet, having worked for years in what appeared to be such a field, I counsel extreme caution in believing that any Church in fact cannot grow. All too often growth is prevented by remediable errors and omissions on our part. We shall discern more of these when we take church growth more seriously and learn more about it.

We trust that our brothers who do not need the message of renewed devotion to church growth will not imagine we have been addressing them. We hope that those who do need it will welcome it, graciously forgiving any stricture which, in their circumstances, seems an overstatement. We have spoken out of wide experience of many Churches and missions and know well that what fits one situation cannot exactly fit some others.

3. For the most part we are optimistic about Christian mission. To be sure, we recognize the sovereignty and power of God. His ways are not our ways. He may on occasion lead us through the valley of the shadow. We labor under no humanistic illusion that an automatic escalator carries us up to progress, Christianization, and a happy world! And between us there are differences in degree of optimism. For example, Dr. Nida is much more conservative in his views of future church growth than I am.

Yet none of us is overwhelmed by the massive pessimism, so prevalent in postwar Continental thinking and in some Christian missions facing today's enormous readjustments. We are full of hope. Men and multitudes are becoming disciples of Christ. A healthy self-criticism pervades the Church. A rich profusion of national Churches, each bringing its riches to the King of Kings, is arising. The era of church planting has only just begun. Many more churches would be planted if existing Churches would lift their eyes to the ripened fields and pray the Lord of the Harvest to thrust out more laborers.

The differential in receptivity, pointed out in the preceding section, is ample grounds for optimism. Christians should not be dismayed by resistant populations. They are not limited to them; many other populations are receptive. In these church growth can occur and often does. Causes of nongrowth can often be minimized or sometimes even eliminated, since so many of these obstacles are internal and their removal so often lies within the competence of the Church.

4. We seek to be honest. We fear self-deceit. Missions are necessarily promotional enterprises, but there is a place for plain speaking and the diagnostic approach. Nongrowth should be called nongrowth. Meeting it by disclaiming interest in growth can serve no useful purpose, and in any case it is theologically wrong. In the face of little or no growth we do not therefore say, "Something else just as good is being done," or, "Thank God we are not so earthy and success-minded as to desire numbers of Christians and churches!" In the face of nongrowth, we ask, "How can sound and rapid Christian growth be instituted?"

In thinking about the expansion of the Church, nothing takes the place of the truth. Especially those who administer the Church and its assisting missions must have the truth about how much church growth has occurred, what it consists of, its age groupings, where it came from and where it goes to, how large its losses are from reversions, excommunications, and removals, and what units of the general population are obeying the Gospel. Rationalizations are not helpful. This book is from beginning to end a plea for factuality and honesty.

5. A fifth major emphasis of this volume is use of the principles of sociology and anthropology. Eugene Nida makes a most valuable contribution here. He brings a wealth of evidence to bear on the planting of ongoing multiplying churches. The more we know about how men organize their lives, make innovations, shift to new cultures, and graft new ideas into their intellectual rootstock, the better we can help them to make the transition to the Christian faith. By themselves these sciences are neutral. They neither favor nor oppose the expansion of the Christian religion. They are bodies of knowledge about how men behave. We believe this knowledge can be used to the glory of God and the expansion of His Church. We yoke these sciences to the missionary passion and use them in the service of the Great Commission.

The dissatisfaction with the status quo felt by some minority groups is a sociological fact. Dr. Nida's penetrating analysis shows the part this dissatisfaction plays in their willingness to hear the Gospel. We see how the fact can be harnessed to the purposes of mission.

One of the principles of anthropology is that the way in which a particular change contrasts with existing patterns of life is often diagnostic of its potential acceptance. Dr. Nida shows clearly and cogently how this principle bears on the spread of the Gospel.

The existence of relatively homogeneous units within large national social structures is an anthropological fact relevant to all lands. These homogeneous units are often called subcultures. In Chapter V, I showed how recognizing them can accelerate the growth of sound Christian churches.

6. A sixth major emphasis urges extensive cross-denominational and cross-continental comparisons in church growth.

While it is true that no homogeneous unit is exactly like another, it is also true that most units fall into general classes and the units in each class can be fruitfully compared. Tribal populations, for example, have great similarities the world over. So do the advanced, cultured elite of the new nations. So do the masses in all Latin American countries. Consequently church growth among the masses in Brazil has meaning for church growth among the masses in other Latin American lands, and that among the Papuans of West Irian has a fair margin of value for churchmen at work among the Fali, Higi, and Bura in northeast Nigeria.

Throughout this volume we assume that if one Church is getting good growth in, let us say, Guatemala, this is a trumpet call to other Churches in Guatemala and all Guatemala-like populations. We four authors, coming from different denominations, believe that "concern that men know Christ" ought to be a common bond among all Christian Churches. If God is granting the Episcopalians healthy church growth in Kenya, other Churches at work in Africa ought to pay close attention to the way in which He is doing it. Similarly, the great growth of the Presbyterians in Taiwan, the Assemblies of God in Brazil, and the Christian Churches (Disciples of Christ) in Congo has comparative meaning to other Churches in like situations.

A greatly neglected aspect of the ecumenical movement is just this comparative study of church growth. With the rise of a spirit of co-operation and good will between Churches, every bit of growth granted to any Church should be studied by other Churches to draw from it the maximum instruction concerning the way in which churches grow.

Graphs of growth to be most useful should be of several different Churches at work in one population. As each denomination compares its lines of growth with others, realistic appreciation of the possibility of church extension increases. If there is any complacency, it will give way to sober self-appraisal. The 180,000-member Southern Baptist Church in Brazil, for example, might with profit look long and hard at the 360,000 Congregação Cristã and the 700,000 Assemblia de Deus, whose growth has been achieved with a very small fraction of the missionary resources long available to the Baptists.

7. Administration for church growth is another major emphasis which runs through several chapters and leaves traces in all. Administration in missions exists at four levels. Most ministers of the younger Churches are local administrators of one or more congregations. Many missionaries are administrators of a block of work at the same local level. Mission secretaries on the field are administering at the second level. Church secretaries, moderators, and bishops of the younger Churches administer mission on the third level. Executives of mission boards manage missions at the fourth level dealing with recruitment, training, and maintenance of missionaries, assistance of the younger Churches, or the direction of pioneer work in new fields. All these many persons can administer mission for church growth.

Alternatively, they can direct mission toward other ends—keeping the whole organization functioning smoothly, carrying on a seed-sowing ministry to Gospel rejectors; helping backward peoples to a greater degree of education, health, and production; building bridges of brotherhood across the chasms of race and national pride; or furthering equality, democracy, and economic and political justice. These are admirable ends, yet in this book we stress none of them. Here we are saying that administrators can manage their responsibilities *so that the Church grows.* That is one of their main functions. We agree for example that good organization is needed. It is even more necessary, we believe, to have an organization which intelligently and purposefully multiplies churches to the limits of its ability.

Mr. Hodges' wisdom and experience in church planting, set forth in the chapter titled "Creating Basic Units of Indigenous Churches," should become common knowledge throughout the Church. The steps he outlines are administrative in nature. Dr. H. A. Mayer, Executive Secretary of the Board of Missions in Foreign Countries of the Lutheran Church–Missouri Synod, thought so highly of this chapter that he asked the Institute of Church Growth for permission to mimeograph and send it to Missouri Synod missionaries. In helping his missionaries further to understand church growth, he was taking an administrative step.

Administrative issues were considered so important by the authors that two chapters deal with them. It is no accident that Mr. Hodges, Executive Secretary for the Assemblies of God in Latin America, where the Assemblies are growing very rapidly, contributes a chapter on "Administering for Church Growth." Or that Professor Guy, through whose classes have passed at least four hundred missionaries now on the field, should write a whole chapter on "Directed Conservation." Many of the issues discussed by Dr. Nida and myself are administrative in nature. All of us hope that churchmen at all four levels will read this book, asking themselves: "What bearing have these issues on our policies? How can we manage the affairs God has entrusted to us so that His holy will concerning the extension of His churches may be carried out?"

8. Finally, we believe in constant measurement of church growth and intelligent use of the facts discovered.

Because facts of church growth have in the past sometimes not been carefully recorded or wisely used, it has become popular among some to attach very little importance to church statistics. Men do not lightly dismiss scientific statistics nor scoff at the lines which portray the output of steel or the sale of stocks and bonds. Educators take the normal curve of distribution of students according to mental ability very seriously. City planners project the lines of population to predict that a given city now having a population of 540,792 will in 1975 have 747,438. But for church statistics there is often little real respect.

Scorn is justified for carelessness in gathering data of any kind or for presenting data in ways easily misunderstood. The cause of truth is not advanced, for example, when the *Year Book of American Churches* published by the National Council of Churches of Christ in the United States of America says on page 251 that in 1960 "There were reports from 226 Protestant bodies with 62,-543,502 members. . . . The Roman Catholic total figure is 40,-

871,302 this year." That in 1960 there were 62,000,000 Protestants and 41,000,000 Roman Catholics in the United States is the totally erroneous implication commonly drawn from these two true sentences. The 62 million were (mostly) communicants: the 41 million were community. Communicant and community figures are strictly noncomparable. The many true facts compiled in the *Year Book of American Churches*—a valuable publication—are damaged by the policy of presenting year after year its most quoted figure in a way that is consistently misunderstood.

Well aware of all this, and warning our readers about mishandled statistics, we four believe that church growth data carefully gathered and meaningfully used merit respectful attention. They reveal in brief compass important aspects of church expansion. All twelve preceding chapters assume that church growth should be measured, trends discerned, weaknesses spotted, difficulties anticipated, and future developments foreseen. We trust valid data on church growth. We have used statistical facts throughout the book. We believe that the facts of church growth are an indispensable aid to Christian mission.

Careful measurement of church growth implies research. Past researches have aided us in forming our judgments and convictions about church growth. Unless the missionary enterprise makes continuous scientific studies of the increase and decrease of Christians and churches, it operates in the dark. With sure light on what has happened and is happening, an entirely new dimension of growth becomes possible. We agree with Bishop J. W. Pickett, who writes, "A vast amount of useful information about church growth is yet to be uncovered and made available to those who direct missionary effort. A really informed missionary program should produce incomparably greater results than are now being achieved."

We shall not be surprised if missions soon embark on continuous serious study of church growth. The vast increase of the world's population today outpaces the growth of the Church. It would benefit Christian mission to spend 1 per cent of its income on research in the ways in which God is in fact increasing His churches. Indeed, research is an important way in which the

Church can take its saving task more seriously. It can with the light of truth dispel the fog that now surrounds growth.

What Does God Desire?

We believe God desires to reconcile men to Himself through Jesus Christ in the Church of Jesus Christ. We advocate church growth not for reasons of self-aggrandizement, but because God desires it. The nature of God revealed in Christ demands it. The Church must therefore seek to be ever growing in numbers as well as in the grace and knowledge of her Lord.

God wants lost men found. He sends shepherds to find and bring home the lost. He is not pleased with token search. The issue is not whether His shepherds search out of gratitude for their own salvation, obedience to His command, or some other motive. He wants His children back in their Father's house.

When ninety-nine were safe and one was lost, our Lord commended the man who went out to search for it. How much more will He commend the man with one safe who searches for ninety-nine lost! And what will He think of him who returns home after a token beating of the bushes to spend his days feeding and watering the one?

God is God-Who-Finds. He is interested in the number of lost sheep found or ripe sheaves brought to the threshing floor. The Churches and their assisting missions please God when they keep careful track of their growth. If one measure is not accurate and meaningful, another must be made. The Christian should not be unaware of whether ninety have been found—or two. On biblical grounds we make bold to affirm that God will take a dim view of shepherds who have no idea in which part of the jungle findable sheep are likely to be. He wants a real finding of countable persons. In responsive populations at least, it is theologically wrong to say that God sends men out to labor fruitlessly. On the contrary, three Gospels strongly suggest that He sends men into ripe fields *to bring in sheaves.*

The nature of God Himself, we believe, requires the Church to take church growth with utmost seriousness. If God were Atman, the impersonal Ultimate according to Hindu thought, He would not care about church growth; but God our loving heavenly Father, revealed in Jesus Christ His only begotten Son, of one substance with the Father, and present in His Church as God the Holy Spirit, cares enormously. This is one main meaning of the Cross. Because God cares, His Church must care, too.

APPENDIX: The Iberville Statement on the Growth of the Church

(Drawn up at a Consultation on Church Growth convened at Iberville, Quebec, July 31–August 2, 1963, by the World Council of Churches Department of Missionary Studies. At this Consultation all six continents were represented, as were fifteen Churches ranging from Anglican to Pentecostal. The Iberville Statement arises from a particular concern and makes no attempt to cover other special situations, such as those in America or Germany today.)

THE GROWTH OF THE CHURCH

1. *The Church's Mandate*

The Church of Jesus Christ has been commanded by her Lord to proclaim the Gospel to men and women in every human situation. Her mandate is nothing less than the making of all nations His disciples. In her inner life, the Church offers herself daily to God; in the world she is to live for those who have not yet heard or received the Gospel. It is her very nature to be an outward-looking fellowship of witness. "That which we have seen and heard we proclaim also to you, so that you may have fellowship with us" (1 John 1:3). The Church must therefore seek to be ever growing in numbers, as well as in the grace and knowledge of her Lord and Saviour—not for reasons of self-aggrandizement, but in pursuance of God's desire that all men should be saved. So great a commission requires a total dedication of the Church's resources, a working recognition of the unity of God's People and of the unity of the task, and above all, complete dependence upon and obedience to the Holy Spirit. It calls for a constant, self-forgetful concern for the world for which Christ died.

2. *Her Sin Is Introversion*

The vast increase of the world's population today outpaces the growth of the Christian Church. In spite of this tremendous challenge, we have to confess that churches are often introverted, and missions frequently unfruitful. There are notable exceptions, but in far too many places Christians seem to have lost all expectation that the multitudes can be converted or that churches will significantly increase in size. Such introversion has its roots in the egocentricity of the natural man, still unchanged into the likeness of Christ's selfless care for others. Its lack of expectancy not only betrays weakness of faith, it is also evidence of a profound misunderstanding of the measure of God's redemptive purpose. For the Church is called into being not merely as a saved community, but as a saving community. It is more even than a manifestation of Christ's gathering into one all the scattered children of God. It lives as a witness to, and a servant of, God's plan to reconcile, and to sum up, in Christ all things in heaven and on earth. Thus a church without a dynamic missionary purpose belies its own true nature.

3. *A Call to Renewal*

Only constant reformation and renewal, through the power of God's Spirit, can save the churches from self-centered piety, and from this tendency to live as beneficiaries of the Gospel only, instead of as benefactors through a loving sharing of its blessings with others. Static and introverted churches are to be found in every continent. Why are the questions raised by absence of church growth so seldom squarely faced? We appeal for self-examination, in a spirit of penitence and hope. It was when churches in Chile asked themselves whether they could not reproduce the life of the New Testament Church that they won New Testament experiences, and started a remarkable movement which has persisted for half a century.

4. *"Now Is the Acceptable Time"*

There are many indications that there will be abundant opportunities for winning men and women to faith in Christ in the years immediately ahead. There remain, as there have always been, difficult and unresponsive areas in the world. Missionary endeavor from the West, moreover, is likely to experience increasing handicaps in other lands. But the home base of the Church's mission is everywhere, and every church must answer for its use or neglect of the special opportunities which are given to it.

5. *Study Each Situation*

In surveying the world missionary situation, generalities are of little help. Each population presents its own distinctive problems regarding church growth, and solutions from one area must not be naïvely projected, without examination, into another. Analytical techniques can help immensely toward recognition and understanding of the facts, and at this point careful statistics are of great use. If we are willing to replace defensive prejudices by comparative study of situations in which the churches have or have not grown, we shall find much to learn.

6. *God Gives the Increase*

We fully recognize that it is God who "gives the increase." It is the Holy Spirit who converts men to Christ, not we. But not only are a planting and a watering committed to us, so also is reaping in the times of harvest which God gives. Often, however, when there has been a movement of the Spirit, churches have been slow to perceive it, and fearful to co-operate. Instances have been known of whole communities turning toward God, yet of churches being unwilling to baptize, or, having baptized, of failing to provide resources for a proper shepherding of the ingathered flock. Opportunities have thus been tragically lost.

7. *A Discerning Strategy*

Emphasis upon care for the times and places of special opportunity for church growth does not imply the abandoning of unfruitful fields. It does imply a waiting and watching for such movements among people, and an obedient readiness to deploy, in a properly ecumenical spirit and strategy, the resources of personnel and funds required for true co-operation with the Spirit's work. What God asks of us is creative expectancy and faithful obedience in His service. When both have been forthcoming, wonderful events have taken place among responsive populations.

8. *Expectancy Creates Expectancy*

We have to confess that we have often failed in both expectancy and obedience. One reason for this is that, though churches which are not themselves dynamically engaged in evangelism may send missionaries to other lands, such missionaries are liable to reproduce the same contentment with static church life. It is truly missionary churches which are most likely to plant missionary churches. On the other hand, churches which are not winning fresh converts are by that very fact on the way to becoming yet more introverted. When people are won to Christ, they should immediately be led to realize that they are themselves called to participate in the Church's task of witness and service. If the creation of a special class of paid evangelists shows itself as weakening the sense of evangelistic responsibility that all church members should feel, the cause of church growth is in fact retarded, however faithfully such evangelists may serve. Every Christian needs to be trained for missionary service, each according to his own gifts and opportunities.

9. *The Crucial Question*

Is the church growing, or not; and if not, why not? This is the fundamental question which ought to be asked in every situation. Numerical expansion and quality of Christian life are not alternatives, but correlatives, inasmuch as each is vitally related with the other. Again and again, it has been shown that the spontaneous expansion of a church quickens its own spiritual life; on the other hand, a church which is truly growing in grace thereby grows in concern for its missionary outreach. It is through seeking to share his knowledge of Christ with someone else that each Christian grows most surely in his own apprehension of the faith.

10. *Past Mistakes*

Experience has demonstrated that many missionary methods used in the past are wrong, yet these continue to be repeated and defended, because they are not honestly examined in the light of their results. Sometimes, for example, the strategy adopted has been primarily to approach the most influential members of the community, although these may actually have good reason to be ardent defenders of the status quo. Again, the convert has often been isolated from his natural community; what has been intended as a protection has thus frequently itself become an additional ground for hostility, and anyway has had the devastating result of preventing the new Christian from witnessing in daily life to his own people. Missions have bought land and built houses before any church has been gathered; in consequence the missionary has felt unable to respond to the opportunities created by the Spirit in unforeseen localities. Although teaching, healing, and other ways of meeting basic human needs have always been an integral and vital part of witness to God's Kingdom, yet an overemphasis upon institutions has often retarded rather than forwarded the missionary cause. Especially has this been so when teaching and healing have become divorced from preaching—though it is equally important that proclamation of the Gospel should make clear its relationship to the whole world in which men live. Institutions tend to absorb a disproportionate amount of the Churches' resources for their missions, and to be regarded as created for the benefit of Christians rather than for the service of others in Christ's name. A more personalized care for the sick and the uneducated would be more truly Christian. Much of what is being undertaken by missions, with foreign resources, would be immeasurably more effective as a witness to the Gospel if spontaneously undertaken, according to their own means, by members of the local church.

11. *Discipling and Nurturing Are Two Stages*

In situations where whole communities have been ready to turn to Christ, the mistake has often been made of implying that qualifications other than repentance and faith are required for entry into the Christian community. The New Testament shows that discipling, the winning of an understanding allegiance to Christ, comes first, and that this must be followed by careful nurture in personal faith and in personal Christian life. Churches need to place fuller reliance upon the power and wisdom of the Holy Spirit. To demand evidence of Christian growth before a convert is brought into the fellowship of the church is a denial of the meaning of the Gospel, and one of many reasons why churches fail to grow as they should. What is required is far greater emphasis upon post-baptismal training, in which help in making immediate and sustained witness to Christ is extremely important.

12. *A Need for Research*

At our Consultation here, we have considered many illustrations of factors which favor or retard church growth, of the complexities which require examination before situations can be adequately understood, and of the prevalence of mistaken ideas on this subject which call for radical correction. These have left us more than ever convinced of the need for scientific research into many different matters, some related to sociology, anthropology and similar disciplines, others to church administration and structures, all to the strategy of the Church's mission. What, for example, is the effect of financial aid upon the churches' capacity and willingness to witness? How is pastoral training related to church growth? What are the reasons for taking great heed of the different strata within any unit of a population? Have marriages between Christians and non-Christians in fact served more to spread the Gospel than to hinder it? These and many other questions call for study, area by area, study which could most fruitfully be undertaken by the churches in co-operation with one another.

We welcome the pioneering work of the Institute of Church Growth in Eugene, Oregon (USA), and desire to see similar centers established in time in Asia, Africa and Latin America. Reliable information concerning areas of special need and opportunity as regards church growth ought to be constantly collated and circulated. We urge earnest consideration of these matters by the WCC Division of World Mission and Evangelism, and by such bodies as the East Asia Christian Conference and the All Africa Conference of Churches. The object of this is that churches and mission boards in every part of the world may be stimulated to give to study of questions of church growth the importance which belongs to a subject so essential for fulfilment of the Church's mission in the world.

La Serpiente y la Paloma (La Iglesia Apostolica de la Fe en Jesucristo de Mexico) by Manuel J. Gaxiola, $2.95 paper, 194 pp.

People Movements in the Punjab by Margaret and Frederick Stock, $8.95 paper, 388 pp.

Profile for Victory: New Proposals for Missions in Zambia by $3.95 cloth, 224 pp.

The Protestant Movement in Bolivia by C. Peter Wagner, $3.95 paper, 264 pp.

The Protestant Movement in Italy: Its Progress, Problems, and Prospects by Roger E. Hedlund, $3.95 paper, 266 pp.

Protestants in Modern Spain: The Struggle for Religious Pluralism by Dale G. Vought, $3.45 paper, 168 pp.

The Religious Dimension in Hispanic Los Angeles by Clifton L. Holland, $9.95 paper, 550 pp.

The Role of the Faith Mission: A Brazilian Case Study by Fred Edwards, $3.45 paper, 176 pp.

Solomon Islands Christianity: A Study in Growth and Obstruction by Alan R. Tippett, $5.95x paper, 432 pp.

Taiwan: Mainline Versus Independent Church Growth by Allen J. Swanson, $3.95 paper, 300 pp.

Tonga Christianity by Stanford Shewmaker, $3.45 paper, 164 pp.

Understanding Latin Americans by Eugene A. Nida, $3.95 paper, 176 pp.

A Yankee Reformer in Chile: The Life and Works of David Trumbull by Irven Paul, $3.95 paper, 172 pp.

THEOLOGICAL EDUCATION BY EXTENSION

An Extension Seminary Primer by Ralph R. Covell and C. Peter Wagner, $2.45 paper, 160 pp.

Principios del Crecimiento de la Iglesia by Wayne C. Weld and Donald A. McGavran, $3.95 paper, 448 pp.

Principles of Church Growth by Wayne C. Weld and Donald A. McGavran, $4.95x paper, 400 pp.

Theological Education by Extension (revised edition) edited by Ralph D. Winter, $9.95 paper, 656 pp.

The World Directory of Theological Education by Extension by Wayne C. Weld, $5.95x paper, 416 pp. *1976 Supplement only,* $1.95x, 64 pp.

Writing for Theological Education by Extension by Lois McKinney, $1.45x, 64 pp.

APPLIED ANTHROPOLOGY

Becoming Bilingual: A Guide to Language Learning by Donald Larson and William A. Smalley, $5.95x paper, 426 pp.

Christopaganism or Indigenous Christianity? edited by Tetsunao Yamamori and Charles R. Taber, $5.95 paper, 242 pp.

The Church and Cultures: Applied Anthropology for the Religious Worker by Louis J. Luzbetak, $5.95x paper, 448 pp.

Culture and Human Values: Christian Intervention in Anthropological Perspective (writings of Jacob Loewen) edited by William A. Smalley, $5.95 paper, 466 pp.

Customs and Cultures: Anthropology for Christian Missions by Eugene A. Nida, $3.95x paper, 322 pp.

Manual of Articulatory Phonetics by William A. Smalley, $4.95x paper, 522 pp.

Message and Mission: The Communication of the Christian Faith by Eugene A. Nida, $3.95x, 254 pp.

Readings in Missionary Anthropology edited by William A. Smalley, $4.95x, 384 pp.

POPULARIZING MISSION

Defeat of the Bird God by C. Peter Wagner, $4.95 paper, 256 pp.

God's Word in Man's Language by Eugene A. Nida, $2.95 paper, 192 pp.

The Task Before Us (audiovisual) by the Navigators, $29.95, 137 slides

The 25 Unbelievable Years: 1945-1969 by Ralph D. Winter, $2.95 paper, 128 pp.

REFERENCE

An American Directory of Schools and Colleges Offering Missionary Courses edited by Glenn Schwartz, $5.95x paper, 266 pp.

Bibliography for Cross-Cultural Workers edited by Alan R. Tippett, $4.95 paper, 256 pp.

Church Growth Bulletin Vols. I-V edited by Donald A. McGavran, $4.95 paper, $6.96 cloth, 404 pp.

Evangelical Missions Quarterly Vols. 7-9, $8.95 cloth, 330 pp.

The Means of World Evangelization: Missiological Education at the Fuller School of World Mission edited by Alvin Martin, $9.95 paper, 544 pp.

The World Directory of Mission-Related Educational Institutions edited by Ted Ward and Raymond Buker, Sr., $19.95x cloth, 906 pp.